The Intersecting Realities and Fictions
of Virginia Woolf and Colette

THE INTERSECTING
Realities and Fictions
OF
Virginia Woolf and Colette

HELEN SOUTHWORTH

THE OHIO STATE UNIVERSITY PRESS • Columbus

56449

Library of Congress Cataloging-in-Publication Data

Southworth, Helen.
The intersecting realities and fictions of Virginia Woolf and Colette / Helen Southworth.
    p. cm.
Includes bibliographical references and index.
ISBN 0–8142–0964–5 (cloth : alk. paper)—ISBN 0–8142–5136–6 (pbk. : alk. paper)—ISBN 0–8142–9041–8 (CD) 1. Woolf, Virginia, 1882–1941—Criticism and interpretation. 2. Women and literature—England—History—20th century. 3. Colette, 1873–1954—Criticism and interpretation. 4. Women and literature—France—History—20th century. 5. Literature, Comparative—English and French. 6. Literature, Comparative—French and English. I. Title.
    PR6045.072Z8769 2004
        823'.912—dc22
            2004013077

Cover design by Dan O'Dair.
Text design by Jennifer Forsythe.
Type set in Galliard.
Printed by Thomson-Shore, Inc.

The paper used in this publication meets the minimum requirements of the American National Standard for Information Sciences—Permanence of Paper for Printed Library Materials. ANSI Z39.48-1992.

9   8   7   6   5   4   3   2   1

For Caleb

Contents

List of Figures

Acknowledgments

I CANNOT BEGIN to thank all those who have contributed to this project in all kinds of different ways or to express the great pleasure that the appearance of this book brings me.

Thanks to the Colette community, including Claude Pichois, Alain Brunet, Jacques Dupont, Julia Kristeva, and the Société des Amis de Colette, for their prompt responses to my requests for information. Also, warm thanks go to the Woolf community for suggestions, encouragement, and discussion, both at the annual Virginia Woolf conferences, where I presented some of the material for the book, and via e-mail, including Vara Neverow, Janet Winston, Beth Rigel-Daugherty, Etel Adnan, Ian Blyth, Michael Whitworth, and all of those on the Virginia Woolf listserv.

I am grateful to all those who have helped me track down photographs and paintings for the book, including Rose McMahon, Curator and Research Officer, Denbighshire Heritage Service; Melody Ennis at Rhode Island School of Design; Tara Wenger and Linda Ashton at the Harry Ransom Humanities Research Center at the University of Texas at Austin; Miranda Seymour, Philip Goodman, Matthew Bailey, and Terence Pepper of the National Portrait Gallery in London; Samia Bordji of the Centre d'études Colette; and Nina Beskow and Sally Cline. I would also like to thank the Oregon Humanities Center at the University of Oregon for their contribution to the cost of photographic permissions.

The faculty, office staff, and students at the Robert D. Clark Honors College at the University of Oregon have been unfailing in their encouragement, support (financial and moral), and good company. Special thanks go to former director David Frank, to current director

Richard Kraus, and to my colleagues fellow Woolfian Henry Alley, Louise Bishop, and Francie Cogan. I would like to thank my dissertation advisors, Peggy Kamuf, Peter Starr, and James Kincaid, who saw this project through its very early stages. For their intellectual and moral support, I would also like to thank Lawrence Driscoll, Danielle Muller, Stacey Shimizu, Cindy Benton, Diana Riesman, Jolisa Gracewood, Heidi Kaufman, André Lambelet, Sophia Murphy, Kristen McCleary, Hannah Fearnley, Catherine Brindley, Emma Fenton, Paul Southworth, Mira Geffner, Leah Pickup, Joanne Poole, Samantha Vaughan, and Daniel García. And for their encouragement and intellectual example early on, I am grateful to Margaret Beddard, formerly of Hitchin Girls' School, and Terence Allott, formerly of Westfield College, London University. Very special thanks go to Ellen Mulligan for proofreading, encouragement, and many years of friendship. Also thanks go to Jean Eudes Biem for further proofreading.

I would like to thank my parents, John and Susan Franks, as well as other family members and old friends in England, Holland, and Los Angeles, including Caroline Franks, Chris Miller, Nicholas Franks, Angelien van Putte, and Oliver Franks, for their help and support and their attention to things Bloomsbury-related. Thanks also to my parents-in-law, Darlene and William Southworth, for encouragement and support, for Friday afternoon martinis and other assorted misadventures, and for Darlene's careful proofreading and suggestions, undertaken on top of her own packed research agenda.

Very special thanks go to my editor, Heather Lee Miller, who gave this book its first chance, and to Maggie Diehl and the production staff at The Ohio State University Press. I am also extremely grateful to the reviewers, Shari Benstock and Bethany Ladimer, for their astute comments and support of the project.

I dedicate this book to my husband, Caleb Southworth, whose involvement in the writing of this book was indispensable. His talents are many and various, but here I thank him for sharing the adventure that is his life with me, for believing in this project, and for his unconditional love and support.

A version of chapter 3 was originally published as "Rooms of Their Own: How Colette Uses Physical and Textual Space to Question a Gendered Literary Tradition" in *Tulsa Studies in Women's Literature*, Fall 2001, and a version of chapter 1 was previously published as "Correspondence in Two Cultures: The Social Ties Linking Colette and Virginia Woolf" in the *Journal of Modern Literature* 26, 2, Winter 2003.

Introduction

The Bluestocking and the Schoolgirl

THE FRENCH WRITER and portrait painter Jacques-Émile Blanche, a renowned Anglophile, painted portraits of both Colette and Virginia Woolf. His 1905 portrait of Colette at twenty, entitled *La Bourguignonne au sein bruni* (figure 1), painted at his Paris studio, portrays her in a classical full-length pose, in the style of nineteenth-century portraiture, reclining on a chaise longue, vulnerable, her eyes cast down, her shoulders bare. The dark interior, weighed down by the browns of the painting, oppresses the painting's subject, the author, most recently, of the *Claudine* series, who, according to Blanche, spent much of the sitting in tears over the most recent indiscretions of her first husband, Henry Gauthier-Villars, better known as Willy.[1]

Blanche's 1927 portrait of Woolf offers just head and shoulders of his model (figure 2). The portrait, it appears, was painted either from a sketch made in Normandy where Woolf and Blanche met briefly at Château d'Auppegard, the home of American artist Nan Hudson, just subsequent to the publication of *To the Lighthouse,* or from a photograph exchanged by mail at a later date (Collet 73). The light pinks and blues and the soft brushstrokes of this less traditional portrait, the more forthright pose of the subject, who looks forward, into the eyes of the artist and viewer, and the informal jacket—her pose leads the viewer to imagine she has her hands in her pockets—suggest progress and modernity. Blanche's portraits capture both authors at pivotal moments in their writing careers; and we detect in his work an effort to transfer a sense of each writer's work to the canvas.

I begin this book with Blanche and with these two portraits for several reasons. First, Blanche's encounters with Colette and Woolf, and

1

Figure 1
La Bourguignonne au sein bruni, *Jacques-Émile Blanche's portrait of Colette.*
© *2004 Artists Rights Society (ARS), New York/ADAGP, Paris.*

the very different work that was produced as a result, are informative in terms of conventional conceptions of these two writers. Colette has never completely escaped her association with the saucy schoolgirl Claudine, heroine of her first (coauthored) novels; Woolf is still largely conceived of even today in her role of plain, pale bluestocking.[2] Just as the paintings appear initially to have nothing in common, so Colette and Woolf are considered to be diametrically opposed the one to the other. What could the two writers have possibly had in common?

While they set the two writers apart, these two paintings and Blanche's involvement with both writers remind us that these two

Figure 2
Jacques-Émile Blanche's portrait of Woolf. Museum of Art,
Rhode Island School of Design; Museum Works of Art Fund.

women were contemporaries. Woolf (1882–1941) and Colette (1873–1954) lived and wrote at approximately the same time: Colette's first novel, *Claudine à l'école,* was published under her first husband's name, Willy, in 1900, and her last, *Le fanal bleu,* appeared in 1949; Woolf's first novel, *The Voyage Out,* appeared in 1915, and her last, *Between the Acts,* was published posthumously by her husband, Leonard Woolf, in 1941. These portraits also remind us that the two writers were connected via a complex network of mutual friends both in England and in France. Indeed, Blanche was just one of a number of artists/photographers who captured images of both women.[3]

Woolf met Blanche via Hudson, who was a friend of her sister, the artist Vanessa Bell, and other Bloomsbury artists. Many of these figures lived in France, including painter Duncan Grant (the father of Vanessa's daughter Angelica Bell), who trained at one point under Blanche.[4] Blanche was the son of a highly educated and well-connected doctor with a taste for the company of artists and writers. As a child and, subsequently, of his own choice as an adult, Blanche divided his time between England and France. While he is known primarily for his portraits of writers and artists, ranging from Thomas Hardy to Walter Sickert, Marcel Proust, Henry James, André Gide, Woolf, and Colette, he was also a prolific writer of novels, memoirs, including *souvenirs littéraires,* and art criticism. Subsequent to their meeting, Woolf corresponded with and solicited a memoir from Blanche, whose talk of the many French and English artists and writers he had met and painted (most notably for Woolf, Marcel Proust) fascinated her.[5] Her plan to publish the memoir at the Hogarth Press never came to fruition and it appeared with J. M. Dent.

Blanche, for his part, did much to promote Woolf's work in France. Among his articles is a profile of Woolf that appeared in the French literary paper *Les nouvelles littéraires* in August 1927, concerning *To the Lighthouse.* The interview is accompanied by several passages from *To the Lighthouse* and Woolf's short story "Kew Gardens," both translated by Blanche.[6] A couple of years later, in February 1929, Blanche wrote an article on Woolf's *Orlando* for the same publication. Blanche also included tributes to Woolf in the second volume of his memoirs, *More Portraits of a Lifetime,* and in *La pêche aux souvenirs.*

Familial ties link Blanche and Colette: Blanche's wife was a cousin of Colette's first husband. He painted Colette, and Willy, several times; a painting of husband and wife made in 1898 was later destroyed (it is reproduced in Pichois and Brunet).[7] Both Blanche and Colette were part of a dense network of artists and writers living in Paris, many of whom Blanche painted, among them Proust, poet Anna de Noailles, Singer sewing machine heiress and promoter of the arts Winnie de Polignac, and writer André Gide, who confessed that he liked Colette's *Chéri* despite himself. Blanche includes a portrait of Colette in his *La pêche aux souvenirs.* He describes his first meeting with Willy's new wife and his intrigue as to who might be "la n-ième victime du bouffeur d'âmes et de chair féminines" (238) ("the umpteenth victim of the gobbler up of feminine souls and flesh"). Blanche's account of his subsequent encounters with Colette suggests the longevity of their acquaintance and at once reminds us of the scope of Colette's career: he remembers her as the shepherd girl in the fluted schoolgirl collar of their first meeting, naked, an animal skin flung over her arm, knelt before Willy in a top hat on the stage of the Folies Bergère, and as the woman of letters, in sandals, honored at the Académie royale belge de langue et de littérature françaises with the red ribbon and the commander's cross, which she received in 1936 (289). Colette refers to Blanche numerous times in her work: in *Mes apprentissages* (1025), in *De ma fenêtre/Looking Backwards* (199), in her portrait of Proust, and again in *Le pur et l'impur* (144). As my first chapter demonstrates, these represent only a few of the many links—familial, social, and literary—connecting Woolf and Colette.

One notes a faint smile lingering around Woolf's lips in Blanche's painting and a subtle coyness lifting the downcast eyes of Colette. What would Colette and Woolf have said to each other had they had an opportunity to meet? While no record exists of a meeting of the two writers, they did exchange several letters, none of which appear to have survived. In 1936, in a letter to Jane Bussy thanking her for sending on Colette's *Mes apprentissages,* Woolf refers to a cryptic note that she had received from Colette with a copy of one of her books (she is unclear when), and in another letter in the same year she tells Ethel Smyth that she has dispatched a response to Colette and sent it via a mutual friend, Winnie de Polignac. In characteristic fashion, Colette makes no mention of Woolf or Woolf's work in letters or diaries—she was famous for her reticence when asked to evaluate the work of her contemporaries; however, Woolf does describe her impressions of Colette's work. Woolf read at least three of Colette's works, *Mes apprentissages, Sido,* and *Duo* (a copy of the latter remains in the Woolfs' library housed at Washington State University, along with an early critical text, Jean Larnac's *Colette* [1927]). A great admirer of French language and literature, an admiration she explains in some detail in her essay "On Not Knowing French," Woolf is carried away by Colette's prose, finding in it "a new combination" and a "dexterity insight and beauty" of which she is envious (*Letters* 6: 301).[8]

Critics have connected Woolf and Colette in their work. Among the best-known treatments are Jane Marcus's all too brief exploration of the ties linking the two writers at the level of the sentence, in terms of biographical detail, and via an exploration of literary influences in the introduction to her *Virginia Woolf and the Languages of Patriarchy,* Nancy K. Miller's reading of Colette's *La vagabonde* via Woolf's *A Room of One's Own,* and Margaret Crosland's numerous references to Woolf in her groundbreaking work on Colette.[9] Several doctoral dissertations have addressed the question of ties between the two writers—in terms of "the female presence" in the works of Woolf and Colette (Bonne 1978), women and middle age (Booth 1996), spatial form (Franks [Southworth] 1999) and marriage (Tucker 1995). Minor references include Rachel Bowlby's linking of Colette's treatment of the mother-daughter relationship to that of Woolf and American writer Willa Cather (*Virginia Woolf,* 1992, 80). Anne Ottavi also addresses similarities in the treatment of the mother figure in a short essay focusing on Colette's *La maison de Claudine* and *Sido* and Woolf's *To the Lighthouse,* while adding, however, that everything else related to Woolf and Colette seems to be in opposition: "tradition nationale, milieu culturel, problématique personelle, projet esthétique" (181) ("national tradition, cultural milieu, personal problematics, aesthetic project"). In *Writing of Women: Essays in a Renaissance* (1985), Phyllis Rose describes how reading Woolf led her to Colette among other women writers: "Jean Rhys, Edith Wharton, Kate Chopin, Charlotte Perkins Gilman, Anaïs Nin" (9).[10] Discussing the grouping together of the trio of Woolf, Colette, and Djuna Barnes, proposed by Andrew Field, author of *Djuna: The Life and Times of Djuna Barnes,* Rose recognizes the compatibility of Woolf and Colette, but she throws out Barnes in favor of Gertrude Stein: "Field offers us another trio as incongruous as Eliot, Joyce, Barnes. 'Colette, Woolf, Barnes,' he tells us, 'might in time sit more comfortably on the Parnassus of their time with Proust, Eliot and Joyce, than many writers of the time whose work already shows clear signs of becoming period pieces.' For the resolution of a chord beginning with Colette and Woolf, my own choice would be Gertrude Stein" (29). Bethany Ladimer briefly compares the detachment of the older Eleanor Pargiter in Woolf's *The Years* and that of "the aged Colette, self-assured, writing with ease in her new name at the end of her life, [gazing] at others and at 'youth'" ("Colette: Rewriting the Script" 245). Hermione Lee makes just one reference to Colette in her Woolf biography—Colette shares a sentence with Vita Sackville-West. In 1936 "[Woolf] had read an essay by Colette, quite unknown to her, whose writing she at once liked enormously; and she read Vita's book on St Joan, which she did not like" (672).[11]

Despite this recognition of ties, parallels, and overlaps, a comprehensive study has yet to appear. The reasons for this omission are numerous and merit a brief review.

1. Literary inheritance, social class, and education have separated the two writers. Woolf is of literary stock, classically educated, extraor-

dinarily well read, and engaged in a vital intellectual culture both at home and abroad. By contrast, Colette is a writer by accident, by her own admission, without literary entitlement. Like the protagonist of her first novels, Claudine, she is somewhat haphazardly educated, her work is provincial, and she belongs to no single school of writing, as Jean Cocteau remarked. Nicole Houssa's careful cataloguing of literary allusions affirms the narrower focus of Colette's work: "Colette pays more attention to the present than the past, more attention to French literature than foreign literature; the man interests her as much as, if not more than, the work, or even the writer; she often made of the literary work a concrete vision, and she rarely takes the time to show off what she knows" ("Citations, références et allusions" 24).[12]

2. In terms of narrative style and content Woolf and Colette are judged by critics to have little in common. The literary theoretical establishment, even once it acquired more of an international bent, has always regarded the work of Woolf as more worthy of critical attention than that of her French contemporary. Malcolm Bradbury and James McFarlane do include Colette in the chronology of their book *Modernism*. However, they incorrectly attribute Georges Bernanos's 1926 *Sous le soleil de Satan* to her. As Bonnie Kime Scott suggests in *Refiguring Modernism*, "Woolf is the token woman [among Modernists], acceptable because most comparable in her experiments to the men" (xxii). The theoretically sophisticated Modernist style, "high aesthetic self-consciousness and non-representationalism" (Bradbury and McFarlane 25), of Woolf's prose is judged as at odds with what is seen as Colette's naturalist/realist fictional form—a form that Modernists, like Woolf, deemed an inadequate response to the chaos of the age of modernization.

3. While Woolf's *A Room of One's Own* is considered by many to mark the birth of the modern literary feminist movement (for Marcus, "our literary feminist bible" [1987:5]), the themes addressed by her contemporary appear light and trivial: actresses' love affairs (*La vagabonde* and *Chéri*) and schoolgirls' indiscretions (the *Claudine* series). In her study of its complexity, Mieke Bal labels Colette's *La chatte* "un roman populaire" ("a popular novel"). Like her female protagonists, Colette's work lacks the breeding and respectability of Woolf's. Colette's antifeminist comments did little to improve her ratings among feminist readers.[13]

4. Perhaps in an effort not to see Colette subordinated to Woolf, several Colette critics have underscored the differences between the two writers. Thus, in her book on Colette, Nicole Ward Jouve asserts: "The two women did not know each other: would they have seen the point of each other's book, and form?" (Jouve, *Colette* 168); and in her biography of Colette, Judith Thurman echoes Jouve:

It is not hard to see why Colette always felt more of an affinity with the courtesans, actresses and artistes she had frequented in her youth than she did with the bluestockings, the militants for women's rights, or the gentlewomen of letters living on their allowances. She respected those ambitious entrepreneurs of her own sex whose notion of a bottom line would never be Virginia Woolf's five hundred a year and a room of one's own, but fifty thousand a year and a villa of one's own, with a great chef, a big garden, and a pretty boy. (Thurman xiv)

And perhaps most emphatically, in her book on Colette, Elaine Marks argues that the heterogeneity of Colette's work prevents a comparative perspective:

One approach [to Colette's work] might be sought in such words as heterogeneity, hybrid, or mongrel. There is a crossing, a mixing in all Colette's texts of genders (male and female), of social classes (the demi-monde, the marginals, and the bourgeoisie), of cultures (learned and popular) and most importantly of genres (narrative and dramatic fiction, autobiography, biography). Attempts to situate Colette in relation to the women authors of the turn of the century whom she frequented (Renée Vivien, Natalie Clifford-Barney, Lucie Delarue-Mardrus, Anna de Noailles) or to women authors of other cultural traditions (Gertrude Stein, Virginia Woolf), or attempts to relate her to the "classical generation of 1870" (Marcel Proust, André Gide, Charles Péguy, Paul Valéry, Alain) fail and for the same reasons. *Neither sexual identity nor contemporaneity can cope with the difference between the texts of the best-known French woman writer of the first half of the twentieth century and those of other writers.* Their texts function within the protocol of a group and hers do not. Where then is she located, and how does this peripheral location account for the heterogeneity within her texts? (my emphasis; Marks, "Foreword: Celebrating Colette" x).

Reading at once with and against these assessments, I want to argue that these very objections in fact provide the ground for a comparative study. The apparent differences, social and educational, geographic and linguistic, that have separated these two writers are indeed concepts addressed, frequently in some detail, in the writing of both, and they provide the foundation for a study of the two writers and their work.

Difference is key to my analysis. Thus, Clarissa Dalloway's exclamation in Woolf's *Mrs Dalloway* as she watches her elderly female neighbor move about her house, from a window on the stairs in her own house, is instructive: "And the supreme mystery [. . .] was simply this: here was one room; there another" (127). It is at those moments where the two bodies of work, the two agendas, the two writing styles come momentarily together and then veer off in different directions that provide the most fruitful insights. It is in those places where the work of the one bridges the gaps in the work of the other that connections might be made. Such an approach enables a redrawing of the map on which the literary and biographical voyages of Woolf and Colette have been traced. Rather than locate each writer simply within her particular national, cultural, and geographical setting, this study resituates the writer and in so doing raises questions about style, themes, and influence that have yet to be explored.

Thus, in the first chapter, I establish a biographical connection between Woolf and Colette via an exploration of the social ties the two women shared. Here I set out to establish the likelihood of a shared set of concerns and ideas based on relationships formed by both women with a specific set of writers, artists, and intellectuals. In the second chapter, I demonstrate how biographical ties such as those explored in chapter 1 provide the basis for close textual analysis of the literary works of Woolf and Colette. Thus, Radclyffe Hall's involvement with both Woolf's *A Room of One's Own* and Colette's *Le pur et l'impur* suggests a significant connection that is borne out by a close reading of the two works, the latter of which I read as a response to, and an inversion of, the former.

In the third chapter I take stylistic and textual ties a step further, reading three of Colette's novels, *La vagabonde, Duo,* and *Le toutounier,* in terms of Woolf's projection of the shape of women's writing in *A Room of One's Own.* I tie Woolf's use of space in her novels to Colette's. In the fourth and fifth chapters, I explore diachronic connections, first textually with an exploration of fathers in the first fictions of both writers— Woolf's *The Voyage Out,* Colette's *Claudines*—and then biographically and anecdotally, looking at how women writers, English and French, have received the work of both.

In the concluding chapter, I examine the themes of food and sex in the works of both writers. Issues considered central and natural to Colette's work, these are items Woolf is conventionally thought to handle with difficulty. The juxtaposition of the treatment of food and sex in a range of texts by both writers serves to suggest the lighter side of Woolf's work and her enjoyment of these Colettian vices, and to emphasize the sophisticated way in which Colette deals with questions of food and sex. As in the earlier analyses, this last chapter complicates conceptions of the two writers as diametrically opposed one to the other, breaking down borders between the bluestocking and the schoolgirl, the literary elite and the music hall performer, "the worldly intellectual" and the "sensual,"[14] the entitled writer and the reluctant writer, the hot and the cold, the English and the French . . .

1

A Dense Network of Friends

WHILE IT APPEARS unlikely that Virginia Woolf and Colette ever met, they certainly communicated, albeit indirectly. Evidence suggests that they knew each other's work.[1] This mutual knowledge was facilitated in part by the network of friends that they shared, many of whom traveled frequently between England and France. These mutual acquaintances included Singer sewing machine heiress Winnaretta (Winnie) de Polignac, the composer, suffragist, and writer Ethel Smyth, writers Vita Sackville-West, Violet Trefusis, Radclyffe Hall and her lover Una Troubridge, the poetess Comtesse Anna de Noailles, bookstore owners, publishers, and translators Sylvia Beach and her lover Adrienne Monnier, and the photographer Gisèle Freund.[2]

A number of the women linking Woolf and Colette were themselves part English or American and part continental European (for example, Sackville-West, Polignac, and Trefusis), their itinerant lifestyles a result of their search for a place where their unconventional ways and ideas, for many their homosexuality or bisexuality, would not raise eyebrows. Some, such as Polignac, had close relationships with both Colette and Woolf; others, such as Trefusis and Freund, had firsthand experiences with one or both writers; and still others had contact with one and indirect contact with the other. Vita Sackville-West learned about Colette from Violet Trefusis; Troubridge and Hall, not part of the Bloomsbury set, had a professional rather than a personal relationship with Woolf. In retracing these relationships and encounters, both the long-lived and the fleeting, one finds a paper trail, in French and in English, that leads from Woolf to Colette and from Colette to Woolf (like the journal of Eleanor Butler, one of the two Ladies of Llangollen, described in

11

Colette's *Le pur et l'impur*). A number of these writers do write about
both Woolf and Colette, in some cases at length; however, none makes
explicit comparisons between the two women or their work. The purpose of this analysis is to make those connections.[3]

Woolf wrote often about France. On a number of occasions she
describes her relationship to the French in reference to Colette, each
time contrasting herself with her French contemporary. In a letter Woolf
tells Jane Bussy, daughter of French artist Simon Bussy and Dorothy
Strachey Bussy, Lytton Strachey's sister, that Colette's autobiographical
work *Mes apprentissages* (which Woolf read in the original) makes her
feel "dowdy." She extends her comparison of herself with her French
contemporary to the French in general.

> What a good friend you are my dear Janie, to remember that book.
> It has come at the very nick of time when I've nothing to read. And
> it looks—for I've only just cut the pages—full of the most entrancing,
> wicked, underworld Bohemian life, and just after my taste, though I
> still can't think how Colette being what she is, to look at, ever sent
> me her discourse with that cryptic message. She makes me feel so
> dowdy. The French always do. (July 29, 1936, *Letters* 6: 60)

On a second occasion, this time while in northern France in June 1939
with Leonard, in a letter to Ethel Smyth, Woolf makes another implicit
connection between France and Colette, whose novel *Duo* she is reading as she travels.[4]

> [B]ut Lord how rapturous and civilized and sensuous the French are
> compared with us, and how it liberates the soul to drink a bottle of
> good wine daily and sit in the sun, and even the white robed clergy
> under Palanquins dont [*sic*] offend, but even induce in me regrets for
> our stony and grim Protestantism. . . .

> [and a few lines on]

> And I'm reading Colette, "Duo" [1934]; all about love; and rather
> too slangy for my vocabulary, but what a born writer! How she walzes
> [*sic*] through the dictionary. (June 18, 1939, *Letters* 6: 341)

Again here, French sensuality highlights the "grim Protestantism" of
the British; Colette's fast-paced *patois* outsteps Woolf's grasp of the
French language. This difference, this other culture creates desire in

Woolf. On returning home from this same trip, in a letter to Elaine Robson, Woolf expresses a wish to be half French: "I wish I were French and English as you are, like an ice that is half strawberry and half lemon" (*Letters* 6: 339). This choice of metaphor describes the relationship the quintessentially English Woolf shared with her French contemporary, Colette, and sets the stage for a comparative analysis of their lives and works.[5] In terms of temperament, the two writers appear to stand in diametric opposition to one another. However, like Woolf's ice, the two flavors and colors of which bleed into each other, the line dividing the two women wavers. Woolf's confession that, although Colette's *Mes apprentissages* makes her feel dowdy, it is also "just after [her] taste," coupled with her desire to be half French, suggests the complexity of the relationship that exists between the two writers. Woolf at once "envies" Colette—she asks, "Is it the great French tradition that lifts her so serenely, and yet with such a flare down, down to what she's saying? I'm green with envy" (Woolf, *Letters* 6: 49)—but sees her as no threat since she is not writing in the same language.[6] Colette writes directly to Woolf but in a cryptic language that her English contemporary cannot decipher. Colette, notorious for her reticence with regard to the work of her contemporaries (Goudeket 146), leaves no concrete evidence as to whether or not she read Woolf's novels. Like the lines of correspondence via which I will trace the ties linking the two women, Woolf's relationship to Colette's work is qualified and mediated.[7]

Correspondence in Two Languages

All of the figures explored in this chapter have interesting stories of their own to tell. For my purposes, however, I read their novels, memoirs, and biographies only where they relate to the two writers on whom this chapter focuses. In figure 3 I offer a graphical representation of the network mediating relations between Woolf and Colette. The lines indicate face-to-face encounters; square boxes accompany the names of English and American women, circles the names of French women, or those who lived in France for substantial amounts of time, such as Freund, and diamonds those who were of mixed heritage and divided their time between France and England.

Gisèle Freund's photographs establish the contemporaneity of Colette and Woolf and provide a visual link between the two writers.[8] Her portraits show Woolf and Colette face to face, as did those of

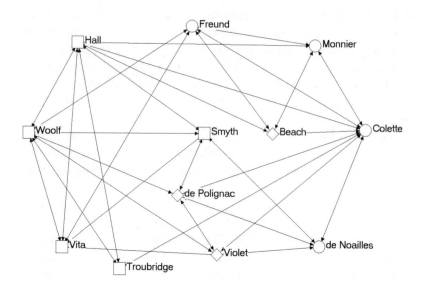

Figure 3
The network mediating relations between Woolf and Colette.

Jacques-Émile Blanche. Freund, a German Jew who simultaneously worked as a photographer and studied the history and sociology of the camera in Paris, photographed both women in 1939 as part of a larger series, which included some of the best-known European and South American writers. Freund met many writers as a student at the Bibliothèque nationale in Paris. A chance encounter with Adrienne Monnier, proprietor of the rue de l'Odéon bookstore La Maison des Amis des Livres, and through her with the American Sylvia Beach, whose Shakespeare and Company bookstore sat across the street from Monnier's store, gave her further access to Parisian literary circles.

In 1939 Woolf is at work on her biography of painter and fellow Bloomsburg group member Roger Fry, her novel *Pointz Hall,* which would later become *Between the Acts,* and her brief memoir "Sketch of the Past"; just two years later she will commit suicide in the River Ouse.[9] In the same year, Colette, recently inducted into the Académie royale belge de langue et de littérature françaises (1935), publishes *Le toutounier,* the sequel to her novel *Duo.* As Woolf comes to the end of her career, Colette begins to receive the recognition denied her in her early years of writing. A pivotal year historically, 1939 marks the end of a reprieve between the two wars, a moment both Woolf and Colette individually contemplated with horror and incredulity. On August 29,

1939, a month after her return from a holiday in northern France with Leonard, Woolf writes to Vita Sackville-West: "I cant [*sic*] help letting hope break in,—the other prospect is too mad" (*Letters* 6: 354). Colette writes to Hélène Picard: "I would never have believed that human kind would come to this a second time" (my translation: *Lettres à Annie de Pène* 201).[10] On September 3, 1939, Britain and France declared war on Germany.

In the two photographs I have chosen (see figures 4 and 5), Woolf (age 58) and Colette (age 66) hold a strikingly similar pose. Both photographs are close-ups; both represent the subject looking slightly sideways at the camera. Colette's fist is clenched, Woolf's hand open as she holds a cigarette. The strength and solidity of Colette's pose and the warm colors of the photograph (she wears a red scarf) contrast with the ambivalence suggested in Woolf's raised eyebrows, perhaps indicating her reluctance to be photographed evidenced by her reaction to the request for the sitting, and the lighter colors (the white lace blouse front) of her photograph. Freund's descriptions of her encounters with the two women, Colette within the context of a longer relationship and Woolf over a single couple of days, support this reading of her photographs.

Freund photographed Colette for the first time in color in the spring of 1939 at her Parisian apartment in Palais Royal. Colette, propped up in bed—her signature location as she became steadily more crippled with arthritis—was at ease with Freund: "Colette was not concerned about looking beautiful on film. What she wanted, above all, was to fascinate. With her penetrating eyes and her studied gestures, she was a born actress who loved the lens and understood its requirements" (*The World* 114).

Colette's aim was to capture her audience with her reality, but, as Freund suggests, hers was the reality of "a born actress." Her appearance is studied and staged. For Freund Colette's colors, her flame-red hair, her favorite blue paper, and her crimson scarf, define her.

"I always work lying down," she told me. "I have arranged a little table which slides over the bed." The lamp attached to the working table was covered with periwinkle-blue paper, like the sheets she used for writing. Even at that early hour her face was carefully made up. Her hair, thick and crisp, flaming red, was cut short and fell in bangs over her forehead. It framed her face, brightened by her dramatic eyes, like a crown of flames. A crimson scarf, tucked into her navy-blue dressing gown, created a symphony of color that was perfect for the photograph. (*The World* 114)

Figure 4
Colette by Gisèle Freund. Copyright Nina Beskow Agency.

In her description of her encounter with Woolf, Freund remarks on Woolf's absence of color. In sharp contrast to "the symphony of colors" evoked by Colette, Woolf is luminous. While Freund portrays Colette as round, fleshy, and warm, Woolf, although beautiful and sensuous also, is angular, fleshless, and cold.

> The impressions we form of writers' faces from their books are often inaccurate. To me H. G. Wells looked more like a country doctor than a novelist. But Virginia Woolf, frail and luminous, was the very embodiment of her prose. She was fifty-eight when I met her. Her hair was turning gray. She was tall and slender, and her features, at once sensual and ascetic, were astonishingly beautiful. Her protruding eyebrows jutted out over large serious eyes in deep sockets. Her full and tender mouth was touching in its sadness. Her very straight, delicate nose seemed fleshless. Her face, as if bathed in inner light, reflected both a visionary's sensibility and great sincerity. Indeed, that very reserved woman generated a captivating atmosphere. (*The World* 130–31)

Freund had approached Woolf on the suggestion of James Joyce, who

Figure 5
Woolf by Gisèle Freund. Copyright Nina Beskow Agency.

after an initial refusal in 1938 himself became the subject of a photo-essay by Freund.[11] Freund gained access to Woolf with the help of Victoria Ocampo, editor of the Argentinian review *Sur* and a friend and correspondent of Woolf's: "I met her during those unquiet months when the English were beginning to realize that another war was inevitable. She was shattered by the prospect" (*The World* 129).[12] Woolf agreed to the sitting, after an initial refusal, and asked that Freund photograph Leonard and her dog also. Woolf chain-smoked during the sitting, perhaps reflecting her discomfort. She later wrote in her diary how much she had disliked the sitting, calling it "detestable & upsetting," resulting in "a life sized life coloured animated photograph" (*Diary* 5: 220). While Freund realized Colette "loved the lens," she understood that "[Woolf] had a horror of anything that might expose her private life" (134). Woolf never saw Freund's photographs; she was in the countryside on Freund's subsequent visit to England. When Freund later went to Argentina in flight from the Nazis, she learned that Woolf had reproached Ocampo for having brought Freund to her house. Freund, initially surprised at Woolf's reaction, contends that "[Woolf] probably felt threatened by the idea that [the photographs] might be published without her having chosen the ones she preferred" (134).[13]

Freund reads both women as she would their work. She conceived of herself in literary terms, as a translator of sorts: "A photographer is asked, not to create forms, but to reproduce them. In the hierarchy of artists he is closest to the translator, and a good translator must himself know how to write" (*The World* 250). Woolf, evasive, "frail and luminous," is "the very embodiment of her prose." Colette, "a born actress," like many of her protagonists, is independent and unafraid, yet enigmatic and masked. When Freund photographed Colette in 1952, celebrating her eightieth birthday, it was at the Hôtel de Paris in Monte Carlo, a location that might have come, Freund suggests, "straight out of one of her novels" (115). Thus, Woolf's transparency and vulnerability stand in contrast to Colette's controlled confidence. However, the similarity of the pose struck by each writer, Colette's aim to fascinate and Woolf's ability to captivate, and the coincidence of the dates of the photographs suggest a commonality between these two contemporaries.

Freund's characterization of herself as a translator takes us back to Beach and Monnier, Freund's benefactors in a number of ways, and for whom Freund functioned, as Nicola Luckhurst has suggested, as an "official portraitist" of sorts—her photographs adorned the walls of both women's bookstores (Caws and Luckhurst 6).[14] Like Freund, Beach and Monnier acted as bridges, their bookstores, the one English and the other French, at the heart of what Monnier called Odéonia (the area surrounding the rue de l'Odéon on Paris's Left Bank where the two bookstores stood), becoming the site of a dialogue among contemporary writers and artists, the importance and proportions of which are today almost inconceivable. The wealth of names we find in Beach's memoir *Shakespeare and Company* and in Monnier's *The Very Rich Hours of Adrienne Monnier*—Joyce, Ernest Hemingway, H. D., the writer Bryher (Winifred Ellerman, whose work the two women translated), André Gide, André Malraux, Radclyffe Hall, and Rainer Maria Rilke, to name but a very few—suggests the centrality of these two lesser-known figures to the Modernist movement.

While it appears that Beach and Woolf did not meet, they shared a set of friends and acquaintances in common, including T. S. Eliot, Joyce, the poet Edith Sitwell, and Gertrude Stein. Beach sold Woolf's works at her Shakespeare and Company bookstore, and J. H. Willis estimates that Shakespeare and Company "stocked selected Hogarth Press books from at least 1925 on" (392). Among these was Theodora Bosanquet's *Henry James at Work,* purchased at Beach's bookstore by George Spater (coauthor of *A Marriage of True Minds: An Intimate Portrait of Leonard and Virginia Woolf*) in 1925 (Willis 426 n. 24).

Woolf purchased her copy of Joyce's *Ulysses* from Beach (Fitch 105), a purchase she references twice: first in her diary of August 1922—she cannot buy clothes because she is "horribly in debt for Joyce & Proust at this moment" (*Diary* 2: 187)—and again in a letter to Roger Fry in October of the same year—she has "[bound herself to Ulysses] like a martyr to a stake," having finished it "thank God," she hopes to sell it for £4.10 (*Letter* 2: 566. While Beach, in her capacity as self-described "midwife" to Joyce's *Ulysses*, would have found herself distanced from Woolf (and Bloomsbury in general), with whom Joyce had mixed relations, she certainly read Woolf's work, discussing Woolf and other contemporary women writers in letters she exchanged with Bryher (Fitch 86).[15] A copy of a photograph of T. S. Eliot and Virginia Woolf forms part of Sylvia Beach's collection at Princeton University (reproduced in Bonnie Kime Scott's *The Gender of Modernism*). Among the chapters of her 1956 memoir is one entitled "A Bookstore of My Own," perhaps a reference to Woolf's *A Room of One's Own*.

As Thurman suggests, Beach, and I would assume Monnier also, met Colette at fellow American expatriate Natalie Barney's salon (386).[16] Monnier also got to know Colette via mutual friends. In *The Very Rich Hours of Adrienne Monnier,* Monnier describes her "Lunch with Colette," the title of her piece about Colette, which first appeared in *Le figaro littéraire* in 1942. Initially apprehensive—"I cannot imagine how one can give pleasure to Colette when one is not a flower or an animal, a taste or a scent, a color or music" (197)—Monnier finds Colette warm and accessible. They eat and discuss food and rationing, haunted houses and fortune-telling—books are conspicuously absent from their conversation. Monnier reads Colette's palm, finding there, not unexpectedly, indications of a "rich sensuality," but one accompanied by a thumb that connotes violence in its possessor, "extraordinary," Monnier suggests, in a woman (199). Colette confirms her penchant for violence—"'I love knives, blades, not revolvers [. . .] a silent blade with a fine taper'"—and Monnier expresses relief that this violence has been channeled into Colette's work (199). Despite the fact that the two women moved in different circles, Colette on the Right Bank, Monnier the Left—although Colette, as Benstock reminds us, had herself once resided on the Left Bank also (*Women of the Left Bank* 204)—their paths crossed on several other occasions, Colette visiting Monnier at home (Monnier 481) and from time to time bringing books and coffee (Pichois and Brunet 430). The two women shared provincial ties and an acquaintance with contemporary French writer Rachilde (Benstock, *Women of the Left Bank* 204–5). Colette's association with a woman of "quality" such as Monnier, assert Pichois and Brunet, demonstrates Colette's ability to move outside, despite herself, they suggest, her close group of friends represented in *Lettres de la vagabonde* and *Aux Toutounet* (430).

Beach and Monnier function as surrogates mediating between Woolf and Colette in particular and between the anglophone and francophone communities of Paris, and more broadly Europe and the United States (specifically in terms of Joyce's *Ulysses*), in general.[17] The spatial proximity that determined the relationship of Beach and Monnier, one at odds with that shared by Woolf and Colette, their role as traffickers in books, both selling and lending, and as translators, publishers, and memoirists (Monnier also wrote poetry), highlights the possibilities for ties between the two contemporaries on whom this chapter focuses.

While Freund's photographs establish a linear, contemporaneous link between Woolf and Colette, similar in its multifacetedness to those of Woolf, Beach, Monnier, and Colette is the set of relations shared by Woolf, Vita Sackville-West, Violet Trefusis, and, more peripherally, Colette. These relationships underscore the depth of the connections linking Woolf and Colette and their social proximity. Woolf, Vita, and Violet variously had love affairs, met face to face, corresponded by letter, referenced each other in memoirs, and based characters in their novels on each other; Colette enters this set of relations in a secondary, but nonetheless important, role. Colette's involvement in this group emphasizes the role nationality plays in this cluster of relations.

Vita was a figure central to Woolf's life. She first met Woolf in 1922 and became Woolf's lover and the inspiration for the novel *Orlando*. Vita functions as a channel by which Woolf gains access to a different France from the one she sees with her husband.

France played a central role in another of Vita's extramarital affairs. Prior to her relationship with Woolf, Vita had had a love affair with Violet Trefusis (spanning the years 1918–20). Violet, an English expatriate, more at home in Paris than London, developed a close friendship with Colette in the later years of Colette's life. Writing in French and in English about the relationship between England and France, Violet brought France to the British and England to Colette and her French contemporaries (Jullian and Phillips 72–73).

The mixed nature of Vita's and Violet's heritage and their itinerant lifestyles contrast with the relative national homogeneity of those of Woolf and Colette (despite the possibility of Colette's Martiniquan heritage and Woolf's French ancestry). Vita was the granddaughter of an internationally renowned Spanish dancer, called Pepita (about whom she wrote a book); her mother was half-Spanish, her father English. Educated in France as a child, she returned often as an adult. Violet's Scottish paternal grandmother had been brought up in Greece; those on the other side of the family, the Keppels, were of Dutch descent (Jullian and Phillips 9–10). When Vita and Violet eloped in 1920, they ran to France. Once retrieved by their husbands, in order to avoid scandal Violet and her husband, Denys Trefusis, moved permanently to Paris, where Violet wrote and presided over a literary salon.

On the single trip to France that Woolf and Vita took alone, Vita, unwittingly perhaps, introduced Woolf to Colette's France. In 1928 Woolf traveled with Vita to Burgundy, Colette's *pays natal*. "It amuses me," wrote Vita to her husband, Harold Nicolson, "to be suddenly in the middle of Burgundy with Virginia" (*Vita to Harold* 204). "[Woolf] loved travelling," she later told Jean Russel Noble in an interview:

> She was as excited as a schoolgirl on arriving in Paris. We went out after dinner and found a bookseller's shop open, and she perched on a stool and talked to the old bookseller about Proust. Next day we went south to Burgundy. There she forgot all about Proust in the simple enjoyment of the things we found. A fair in a French village, roundabouts, shooting-galleries, lions and gipsies giving a performance together, stalls with things to buy; all was sheer fun. We bought knives and green corduroy coats with buttons representing hares, pheasants, partridges. They were said to be gamekeepers' coats, but Virginia preferred to think that they were poachers.' The poacher would naturally be dearer to her mind than the keeper. (Noble 135–36)

The two women went on to Avallon and Auxerre, where they visited the cathedral and curiosity shop, then to Vézelay where Virginia sat among the vines and wandered with Vita down "unfamiliar French lanes" (Noble 136). Colette's Burgundy thus becomes an important place in terms of Woolf's sexual history and her relationship with Vita.

Woolf met Vita's former lover, Violet, in 1932—a meeting, Woolf suggests in a letter, occasioned by Violet's desire to publish her novel *Tandem* (1933) at the Hogarth Press (*Letters* 5: 123). Violet recounts the meeting in her memoir and, I would argue, reimagines it for the purpose of her novel *Broderie anglaise*, while Woolf describes it in a letter to Vita. Common ties with Vita shape their encounter. Although Violet portrays herself as facilitator of a meeting between Woolf and her famous mother, Mrs. Keppel, the mistress of Edward VII, Woolf casts

Violet in a more central role. Violet describes her mother and Woolf as
anxious to meet each other but then unable to address their admiration
the one for the other, instead talking in a code of sorts.

> It would have been difficult to find two people more dissimilar than
> Virginia Woolf and my mother. Yet, strange as it may seem, they were
> deeply interested in one another, and longed to meet. [. . .] After
> about half an hour's spasmodic conversation, we were longing to see
> if the experiment had been a success—we unobtrusively moved
> nearer—they certainly seemed very animated. "Personally, I've always
> been in favour of six cylinders though I know some people think four
> are less trouble." "My dear Mrs Keppel, you wouldn't hesitate if you
> saw the *new Lanchester with the fluid fly-wheel!*" Neither knew a thing
> about motors; both thought they were on safe ground, discussing a
> topic on which they could both bluff to their heart's content. (*Don't
> Look Round* 107–8)

Woolf describes for Vita another somewhat awkward and cryptic
encounter, this time with Violet:

> Lord what fun! I quite see now why you were so enamoured—then:
> she's a little too full, now, overblown rather; but what seduction!
> What a voice—lisping, faltering, what warmth, suppleness, and in her
> way—and its not mine—I'm a good deal more refined—but thats not
> altogether an advantage—how lovely, like a squirrel among buck
> hares—a red squirrel among brown nuts. We glanced and winked
> through the leaves; and called each other punctiliously Mrs Trefusis
> and Mrs Woolf—and she asked me to give her the Common R.,
> which I did, and said smiling, By the way, are you an Honourable too?
> No, no, she smiled, taking my point, you, to wit. (*Letters* 5: 121)

The obtuse and formal nature of the communication described by
Woolf, the winking and glancing through the leaves, the use of last
names, and the mention of being an Honourable, a veiled reference to
Vita, parallels Violet's description of the coded nature of her mother's
exchange with Woolf. Both accounts reflect the mediated nature of the
relationship Violet and Woolf shared.

This series of real links is rewritten in the pages of their novels. Both
Violet and Woolf wrote fictional versions of their relationship with
Vita—both responses inspired by Vita's (and Violet's) fictional version
of their love affair, *Challenge* (1923). In Violet's novel, *Broderie anglaise*
(1935), Alexa, an unmarried quintessentially English novelist, is Woolf,

and her lover John Shorne, Vita.[18] Violet herself figures in the novel as the mysterious "almost foreign" Anne Lindell, John's former lover, now married and living in France (19). *Broderie anglaise* is a tale of revenge. Vita's character John visits and then takes leave of his lover, Woolf's Alexa, who is secretly preparing for a visit from her rival, Violet's Anne. After a frank talk with Anne, over éclairs, in which Anne reveals that John has lied to Alexa about how their relationship ended (it was John, dominated by his mother, who broke it off, not Anne), Alexa finds the strength to reject John: "Thanks to what Anne had told her she was going to be able to confound John and make him suffer for once. She and Anne were now colleagues, both on the same side" (95). Violet's descriptions of "tall, narrow, contemplative" (15) Alexa are rather unflattering: "The vagueness, or, rather, the limpness, of her clothes lent her movements the undulation of a sea-anemone. She was fluid and elusive; a piece of water weed, a puff of smoke. Her face, she discovered, was one of those that was untranslatable to foreigners, arousing in them only pity or scorn" (12). As does Freund, Violet paints Alexa/Woolf in pale colors. "'I've got a youthful eye, an elderly neck, and a finely chiseled mouth and chin. But the whole thing lacks colour. I'm a drawing, a dry-point etching, not a painting'" (11). Anne/Violet celebrates her own acquired foreignness and holds Alexa/Woolf's Englishness against her: "'What a bore it is,' sighed Alexa, 'that I can't lay claim to any misalliances! My family consists of nothing but respectable middle-class citizens, much too learned and rather sexless. Our only flirtations have been with theses, and all we've ever carried away is an audience'" (40).

Violet's novel can be understood as a response to Woolf's *Orlando*, where Woolf portrays Violet as Orlando's first love, Sasha, the Russian princess.

> She was like a fox, or an olive tree; like the waves of the sea when you look down upon them from a height; like an emerald; like the sun on a green hill which is clouded—like nothing he had seen or known in England. Ransack the language as he might, words failed him. He wanted another landscape, and another tongue. English was too frank, too candid, too honeyed a speech for Sasha. For in all she said, however open she seemed and voluptuous, there was something hidden; in all she did, however daring, there was something concealed [. . .] [S]he never shone with the steady beam of an Englishwoman. (47)

The portrayal by each one of the other as a foreigner suggests that nationality is central to this case of romantic literary rivalry. In *Orlando*

Violet/Sasha is "faithless, mutable, fickle" (64), lacking the refinement and reliability of an Englishwoman; English, writes Woolf, is too frank a language to describe her. In *Broderie anglaise,* Woolf is limp and colorless; her face "untranslatable" to a foreigner.[19]

Violet's conception of Woolf's uncompromising Englishness is challenged by Vita, who expresses regret in a letter to Violet that she has not had the opportunity to better get to know Woolf, whose un-English side, Vita contends, would have appealed to Violet:

> [Virginia] has a twist to her mind which I think would please you,— rather like the sudden scratch of a cat's claw. Very un-English.
>
> Virginia and I talked about you. She says she thinks of you as being all chestnut and green in colour (I fancy she described you something like that in "Orlando"? I must look it up.) If you had gone to live at Coke's House, which is not very far away from where she lives, I would have arranged to take you over to see her again. (1941; Jullian and Phillips 227)

Colette enters this set of relations via Violet. Paralleling Vita's suggestion that Violet could have profited from knowledge of Woolf, Violet suggests in a letter written to Vita in 1920 that she read Colette, hinting that the key to an understanding of her relationship with her husband is hidden in the pages of Colette's *Chéri:*

> I know there is going to be a row sometime today. Denys's idleness gets on my nerves and I could scream. In a book by Colette, I find the most wonderful description of what I feel . . . It has never been so well expressed. How well she writes, that woman. Have you read 'Cheri' by her? It is one of the cleverest books that ever came my way. (*Violet to Vita* 255)

A jealous Denys Trefusis burned Vita's letters to Violet. Thus, Violet's question regarding Colette's work is unanswered.

Violet met Colette in Paris several years later. Colette's directness at their first meeting contrasts sharply with the obtuseness Violet encountered in Woolf at their first meeting: "The first time I met Colette she asked me to repeat my name. 'Violet Trefusis,' I replied sheepishly. 'Moi,' came the bucolic Burgundian voice, 'je vous appellerai "Géranium"'" (*Don't Look Round* 90). In contrast to Woolf, the instinctive and intuitive Colette communicates with ease. Violet says of Colette: "She is one of the rare people who have given me the impression of being an *aliment complet,* both tender and brutal, experienced and incorruptible. I have no hesitation in setting her down as a genius, a genius in the art of loving, and in the art of living, and of describing those arts" (90). Despite being very different in terms of temperament, Violet "ethereal, seeing everything as if through a prism" and Colette "earthy, always in contact with everything" (Goudeket, quoted in *Violet to Vita* 255), the two women formed a close bond.[20]

Violet describes Colette's reluctance to "talk shop." She was particularly reticent about her own books, according to Violet, more at home in the kitchen than in the drawing room. Colette's quintessential provincial Frenchness defines who she is.

> [G]et her on the subjects of flowers, trees, animals, or food, and there
> was no limit to her knowledge. She had all the peasant's cult of *le
> labour,* his fatherly solicitude for the vine; she was a connoisseur of
> wine of the first category. That is to say, she could tell a *grand crû*
> from its aroma, and, approximately, the year of its *mise en bouteille,* by
> tasting it. She was not a native of Burgundy for nothing. (*Don't Look
> Round* 88–89)

While the cluster of relations formed around Vita and Violet involved Woolf more closely than her French contemporary, Colette had closer ties with English writer Radclyffe Hall and her lover Una Troubridge. Unlike Violet and Vita, both of whom were married and whose love affair was short-lived, Hall and Troubridge lived together for many years. They left England for Italy after a well-publicized divorce trial in which Troubridge's husband cited Hall as the reason for the failure of his marriage. While Hall and Troubridge certainly knew Woolf, their relationship was distant and formal, despite a family tie linking Woolf and Troubridge—Woolf had known Troubridge as a child, and her aunt, Julia Cameron, was a friend of Troubridge's family (Cline 259). Hall was not well received by the Bloomsbury set, who disliked the openness with which she dealt with her homosexuality. According to Richard Ormrod, Troubridge's biographer, Troubridge and Hall and Woolf, Vita, and Violet did not associate themselves with each other.[21] As Sally Cline suggests, Hall's realistic depiction of gender and sexual identification conflicted with the Bloomsbury group's approach to the subject (232). While Woolf's writing is "emotional, elusive, imaginary or symbolic," for Hall and, Cline suggests, for Vita, too, "realism is the core" (259).[22]

Hall's *The Well of Loneliness* received poor reviews in Britain. In a letter to Vita, Violet described the book as a "'loathsome example of homosexual literature'" (quoted in Cline 273); Woolf's responses were condescending. She proclaims the work "dull" and impossible to read (*Letters* 3: 556). Vita, too, admitted that she could not call the work "good," but she was outraged at the attempts made to suppress it. Woolf, and along with her Leonard Woolf, joined Vita in support of Hall "on principle," offering to testify at *The Well of Loneliness* trial (Ormrod 181–82).[23] At the defense, Hall and Woolf spoke briefly—the Woolfs offered to stand bail for Hall. Woolf's *Orlando*, a more elusive treatment of the very same subject, which appeared in 1928 only three months after *The Well of Loneliness* was banned under the Obscene Publications Act of 1857 in Britain, met with no opposition.

In contrast to her British contemporaries, Colette liked *The Well of Loneliness*, although she objected to Hall's portrayal of her protagonist's feeling of abnormality. Colette criticizes Hall for having Stephen, the heroine, *feel* abnormal. If she feels abnormal, according to Colette, she is not abnormal. An "abnormal" person, she explains, would not conceive of himself as abnormal:

> But there is a point at which I am anti-John, because, without doubt, I am quite an unrefined creature: it is Stephen's impression of abnormality. Now, what I mean to say is that if an "abnormal person" feels abnormal, he's not abnormal. Wait, I'll explain it better: an abnormal person, male or female, should never feel abnormal; on the contrary, a woman who loves another woman (or a man another man) thinks: "What is this world full of monstrous pigs who are different from me?" This is what I'd really like to say to you about the book. (My translation)[24]

Despite her criticism of *The Well of Loneliness*, Colette admired Hall's courage. In a letter to Troubridge, she describes Hall as a pioneer: "'She is a peaceful builder of great buildings, and I build only bungalows'" (my translation).[25] On Hall's death, Colette wrote: "'Her memory is alive to me, and very physical, the beautiful shape of her head, the gilded silver of her hair, and her lovely features, and this Spanish sombrero she liked to wear . . . Certain beings are not meant to die'" (my translation).[26]

Reception of Hall's *The Well of Loneliness*, then, enables the reader to trace Woolf's and Colette's divergent conceptions of sex and sexuality and their treatment in the literary work. Their reception of this particular work also highlights the difference in the environments occupied by both writers, contrasting the closed elitism of Bloomsbury with the openness of contemporary Paris—a cultural divide that Stephen of

Hall's *The Well of Loneliness* is forced to negotiate.

Hall and Troubridge were introduced to Colette in the early 1920s by American writer Natalie Barney, who presided over a literary salon at her home on the rue Jacob in Paris (Ormrod 147).[27] Both women were immediately taken with Colette and formed a friendship with her. In her memoir, *The Life and Death of Radclyffe Hall*, Troubridge, writing about friends in Paris, makes special mention of "the ever enchanting Colette, whose genius we revered while we reveled in her rare personality" (84).[28] In a letter to Evguenia Souline, a Russian nurse residing in France, with whom Hall fell in love and formed a relationship in the latter years of her relationship with Troubridge, Hall describes Colette as overindulgent and excessive, yet an impassioned and "masterly writer":[29]

> Colette, who loves good food and too much of it; Colette who loves the sexual act and too much of it; Colette who has a peasant's outlook on money the while she overindulges herself. Yes but Colette who adores the wind and the rain, the sea and the earth and the fruits of the earth . . . a great woman . . . and a masterly writer. (Quoted in Cline 214)

As with Vita, Violet, and Virginia, literary links exist—links that shed further light on both Woolf's and Colette's conception of homosexuality. Both Hall and Troubridge helped Colette research an English couple, Miss Sarah Ponsonby and Lady Eleanor Butler, known as the Ladies of Llangollen, for Colette's *Le pur et l'impur* (1932). A true story, the two young women, who in certain ways resemble Troubridge and Hall (and to whom, according to Pichois and Brunet, Colette likens them),[30] eloped together and lived in seclusion in late-eighteenth-century Wales. In 1931 Woolf contemplated writing a review of the journals of Lady Eleanor Butler, the *Hamwood Papers*, but later changed her mind, perhaps suggesting that she was reticent to address the nature of the relationship shared by the two women. They have done themselves too perfectly, she suggests to Ethel Smyth (*Letters* 4: 313). *Chase of the Wild Goose*, a fictional biography written by Mary Gordon, based on the story of the Ladies of Llangollen, was published by the Woolfs in 1936. In *Le pur et l'impur* Colette discusses at some length the journal of Lady Eleanor. The use of occasional French words in the journal suggests a gesture toward a culture less closed than her own. (For further discussion of the Ladies, see chapter 2.)

Troubridge herself translated a number of Colette's books, including *La maison de Claudine*, and, in 1930, organized an unsuccessful

Figure 6
Radclyffe Hall with her pet dog Colette. Copyright Corbis.

staging of a theatrical version of *Chéri* (Ormrod 202). She also sent
Colette novels in English. In 1932 in a letter to Troubridge, who had
sent her D. H. Lawrence's novel, Colette wrote, " . . . and what do you
think of this poor childish excited person, the author of *Lady What's-
her-name's Lover?* It's terribly high schoolish [. . .] what a narrow
province obscenity is, suffocating and boring" (quoted in Pichois and
Brunet 285). These were criticisms to which Colette's own work was
subject. Further, Troubridge suggests, Hall gathered much of the
material for *The Well of Loneliness* in France. In *Me and the Swan,* Naomi
Jacob contends that Hall, unable to use a typewriter, used Colette's
famous blue paper instead: "[writing] in clear legible handwriting on
thick pale blue paper, which she acquired by permission of the writer,
Colette, who used nothing else" (quoted in Brittain 43). In honor of
Colette, Hall named one of her dogs Colette and another Mitsou, the

title of Colette's 1919 novel (see figure 6).

Further emphasizing the density of the network mediating relations between Woolf and Colette, a third set of women, Singer sewing machine heiress Winnie de Polignac, French poet the Comtesse Anna de Noailles, and English suffragist, composer, and writer Ethel Smyth, were all linked socially to both Woolf and Colette. These women also knew each other, as well as Violet, Vita, Hall, and Troubridge. Hall met Polignac and Smyth in London, sharing with the former an interest in Greek culture, and forming with the latter an allegiance in support of the "Vote for women campaign" (Baker 48). In this way, their relationships form a dense network that informs the relationship between contemporary French and English literary cultures.

Polignac knew both Colette and Woolf and, as evidenced by Woolf's letters, she relayed messages from one writer to the other. A patron of the arts, a bridge of sorts between the artistic and literary cultures of France and Britain, Polignac was interested in the works of Woolf and Colette.[31] Like Violet, she communicated with Woolf in the language of literature, while with Colette she connected in terms of more earthly pursuits. Polignac encouraged Woolf's reading of Proust and Colette and financed Colette's foray into the commercial world. Polignac's mixed heritage, her movement back and forth between England and France, suggests the proximity of the two cultures.

Having asked Ethel Smyth, who had sent her Colette's work, for the French writer's address, Woolf hesitates and says instead she will send a message via Polignac: "Thanks for sending on Colette. Very good of you. Whats her real name—address? Never mind: I'll thank through Mm de P. [Polignac]" (*Letters* 6: 52). Polignac, the child of a French mother, Isabelle Eugénie Boyer, and an American father, Isaac Singer, founder of the Singer Sewing Machine Company, traveled between France and England. Polignac's own marriage, like Vita's, was open. Her husband was bisexual and gave her license to pursue love affairs with whomever she pleased. Among these relationships was one with Violet, on which a play entitled *La prisonnière* by Edouard Bourdet is said to have been based (Souhami 147; de Cossart 174). According to Souhami, Troubridge and Hall saw the play at the Théâtre Femina in Paris in 1926. "'Awful rot, but fun,' Una said of it" (147). In the 1930s, interested in the activities of the Bloomsbury group, Polignac sought out Woolf (de Cossart 201–2). After disappointment with *The Years,* the English writer enjoyed listening to Polignac's stories and news from the French literary scene (de Cossart 201–2). The two women wrote to each other. A favorite subject of theirs was Marcel Proust, whose work

Woolf admired greatly.[32] Polignac's mediation of Woolf's relationship
with Proust reflects Woolf's apprehension at attempting to take inspiration from Proust. In the same way that she marveled at Colette's command of the French language but kept her distance, she feels unable to
imitate Proust, precisely because he is writing in a different language: "I
wonder if this next lap will be influenced by Proust? I think his French
language, tradition, &c, prevents that: yet his command of every
resource is so extravagant that one can hardly fail to profit, & must not
flinch, through cowardice" (*Diary* 2: 234).

Polignac was also a close friend of Colette (see figure 7). While
Colette and her first husband, Willy, frequented Polignac's musical salon
in the 1920s (Francis and Gontier, *Colette* 107), it was only later,
according to de Cossart, on the death of Anna de Noailles, a mutual
friend, that the bond between the two women was cemented. Descriptions of Polignac's relationship with Colette echo Violet's. Rather than
engage each other on literary topics, Polignac and Colette indulge
themselves together in material things. At Colette's house, Polignac
enjoys the domestic comfort she cannot find at home ("the princess
would settle down comfortably at home in Colette's house, whereas in
her own she often had the appearance of a slightly embarrassed guest"
[de Cossart 198]). "Over a 'picnic' of hot wine and 'a debauch of
cheese'" (198), they share dreams of a simpler existence. Polignac's
anglicized French, suggests de Cossart, complemented Colette's Burgundy French: "Both naturally witty, clever and down to earth, in public they could keep up an entertaining repartee or a complementary dialogue, their distinctive accents contrasting delightfully with each other,
Colette's rich, rolling Burgundian and Winnaretta's dry anglicized
French" (de Cossart 197–98). Polignac showered Colette with gifts,
including a table that perched like a bridge over the bed where Colette,
crippled with arthritis in later years, liked to work (Francis and Gontier,
Colette 328–29).

Like Polignac, Noailles and Smyth mediated between Woolf and
Colette, but less directly. Each had a strong tie with one of the two writers and a weaker tie with the other, Noailles closer to Colette and Smyth
to Woolf.[33] Smyth sent Colette's work to Woolf, including her speech
honoring Noailles as she succeeded her at the Belgian Academy. Noailles
chaired a French committee that awarded Woolf a literary prize,
designed to honor English writers who informed the French about England. Noailles's frailty suggests a resemblance to Woolf, and Smyth's
directness recalls Colette.

Figure 7
Colette and Winnie de Polignac in the garden of Polignac's house in Paris, 1938.

Noailles, Romanian by birth, was married to a Frenchman. Among the best-known writers of their time, Noailles's renown has not survived abroad as has Colette's. Contemporaries describe the two women as opposites. Polignac, Trefusis writes, liked to contrast Colette's provincialness, she was the *percheron* (from La Perche), with Noailles's pedigree. The French writer Jean Cocteau describes Colette as the sun, Noailles as the moon (*Colette* 46–47).[34] Such characterizations suggest parallels between Noailles and Woolf: they respond to Colette's person and her prose in a similar fashion. According to Noailles, Colette appears "tired of dissimulation, provocative, enigmatic, sure of herself, she is as calm as a sibyl and as enigmatic as an African goddess, at once cat and tiger" (my translation).[35] Her writing, Noailles asserts, is similarly opulent and fertile.

I will not describe Colette's genius here; let her use an entire dictionary, she will hollow out a home for herself there; she will produce in
spurts and with labor, she says, a succulent, fiery, organic work, in
which all the terms will appear to have been rifled and distributed
without, however, any addition that might weigh down a story that
takes as its authority life and necessity. (My translation)[36]

Noailles's connection to Woolf is a literary one. She presided over the
Prix Femina Vie Heureuse–Bookman Prize. The purpose of the prize,
awarded in France and in England, was to reward a work that informed
one culture about the other.[37] Woolf's reaction to the prize reflects her
ambivalent relationship with reception abroad, as well as her own fal-
tering self-esteem.[38] Woolf coveted the prize but received it reluctantly
for *To the Lighthouse,* in 1928, calling it "the most insignificant and
ridiculous of prizes" (quoted in Caws and Wright 56). The Woolfs'
library also contains a copy of Noailles's *Les éblouissements* (1907), suggesting that Woolf was familiar with the work of her contemporary.
Woolf also comments in her diary on Noailles's death.[39]

Smyth is one of several friends who sent Colette's books to Woolf
(see figure 8). Hence, Smyth courts Woolf via Colette, as Violet courts
Vita. Further, just as Noailles in a sense doubles as Woolf for Colette, so
Smyth's flamboyance and directness make of her a Colette-like figure for
Woolf. Often in Paris, Smyth probably heard of Colette and of her work
via Polignac, whom she met and with whom she fell in love in 1903. De
Cossart calls Polignac's "collision" with Smyth, who arrived "meteor-
like," "unfortunate." He suggests that Smyth behaved in a brash, heavy-
handed way; and when rejected by Polignac, who preferred "young,
beautiful and submissive women," she set to turning Polignac's friends,
including Noailles, against her. After Smyth's passions had calmed a little, the two women became close friends, and Polignac did much to
promote Smyth's music (86–88). Collis cites a letter that Polignac wrote
to Smyth in 1940: "'My heart is full of gratitude for all you put in my
life, your music, your incomparable singing, even your bouts of anger.
It will be something I remember to the last. . . . I think of you so much,
my darling'" (87).

Woolf's relationship with Smyth is known for its problems. "We're
hopelessly and incorrigibly different," Woolf wrote of Smyth in a letter
(*Letters* 5: 237). Long an admirer of Woolf's work, especially taken by
those sentences in *A Room of One's Own* about women in her own field,
music, Smyth first contacted Woolf in 1930.[40] "'I want to see you, if you
do not detest the idea too much? You *might* (who knows?) quite like me

Figure 8
Woolf and Ethel Smyth in the garden of Monks House, Rodmell, Sussex.

if we were to meet'" (quoted in Collis 175). This hesitation set the tone for a relationship that was often difficult. Echoing Vita, Violet, and Freund, Smyth laments the difficulty of getting close to Woolf: "'[o]ne can't have relations with [Virginia] as with others. The fact is you have to take what you can get of Virginia . . .'" (quoted in St John 222). "'When she comes into the room it is as if one from another world entered. Her distinction? So exquisitely delicate, yet such sense of strength . . . The only thing she can't do well is . . . laugh. 'Le rire fidèle' is not her line, and that's odd for there is occasionally a very hilarious streak in her work, and as for her letters! Ah!!'" (quoted in St John 224). In response, Woolf portrays Smyth as brash and shabby, but a great talent. "'She has descended upon me like a wolf on the fold in purple and gold, terrifically strident and enthusiastic—I like her—she is as shabby as a washerwoman and shouts and sings'" (quoted in Collis 177).[41] Smyth's directness and frenetic enthusiasm recall Violet's description of Colette; her purple and gold, Freund's description of Colette's "symphony of color" (114).

Thus, while clear evidence of a strong individual tie between Colette and Woolf is not available—it is unlikely the two writers ever met face to face—the web of mutual acquaintances confirms their social proximity and suggests a plethora of other possible connections. The shared literary projects, such as Hall and Troubridge's collaboration with Colette, Woolf's, Violet's, and Vita's literary sparring, and Troubridge's translations of Colette's work; the exchanging of texts across national borders, such as Smyth's gift of Colette's work to Woolf, Violet's mention of Colette's work to Vita, Polignac's talk of Proust and Colette to Woolf, and Troubridge's offer of Lawrence's work to Colette; the personal support and professional interest, evidenced in letters and memoirs, exchanged by this network of women—these details support the contention that the relationship between Woolf and Colette had an impact on the lives and work of both writers. Further, the responses to the two writers of their contemporaries, for example, that of Freund, of Violet, and of Hall and Troubridge, allow us to locate not only Colette and Woolf, but also those other writers who form part of the network, in a contemporary international scene comprising two tightly interconnected cultures, French and English.

2

"Ces Deux Opiniâtres Amies": Reading Colette's *Le pur et l'impur* as a Response to Woolf's *A Room of One's Own*

> I have this moment, while having my bath, conceived an entire new book—a sequel to A Room of Ones Own—about the sexual life of women: to be called Professions for Women perhaps—Lord how exciting! (Virginia Woolf, 1931, *Diary* 4: 6)

IT IS GENERALLY agreed that Virginia Woolf's projection of a sequel to *A Room of One's Own* about "the sexual life of women" was never written. *Three Guineas*, a logical choice as sequel to *A Room*, treats war, not sex—a reflection, as Juliet Dusinberre has suggested, of where Woolf's concerns lay in 1938 with the specter of a second world war looming.[1] However, war was not the only thing that kept Woolf from her sequel. A certain reticence on the issue of sex seems to have held her back. In the essay "Professions of Women," the title considered for the sequel, based on a lecture delivered a day after the original diary entry, the topic—"telling the truth about my own experiences as a body"—is broached, only to be deemed too shocking (62).[2] Further, in her penultimate novel, *The Years*, another sequel candidate (identified by way of a later annotation to the first diary entry), the sexual life of the female characters is addressed in only a very marginal fashion—more often than not in negative rather than positive terms.[3]

Concurrent to Woolf's conception of a book about the sexual life of women, Colette was at work on just such a piece: *Le pur et l'impur*, the three elliptical dots of its original title, *Ces plaisirs . . . qu'on nomme à la légère physiques*, appearing to gesture toward and intersect with the ellipses of both *A Room* and *Three Guineas*.[4] Colette's text follows *A Room* in terms of style and structure, while it centers on issues of female sexuality. Woolf's projection and Colette's execution of this project draw these two writers together while simultaneously setting them apart. Colette's *Le pur* is at once sequel to and elaboration on *A Room,* and it is its undoing as it challenges and toys with the assertions of *A Room.*

While it is uncertain whether Colette read Woolf's *A Room,* which preceded *Le pur* by three years, or any of her other works—although we do know the former was available in Paris in, among other places, Sylvia Beach's Shakespeare and Company, where Victoria Ocampo found Woolf's *A Room* in 1929 (Lee 660; Meyer 102)[5]—there is sufficient evidence to suggest that *Le pur* might be read as a response of sorts to the earlier text. Overlaps, I show, exist not only in terms of the style, structure, and content of the works but also in terms of the circumstances of their respective composition.

Implicit in *Le pur* is a description of the relationship of Colette's work with Woolf's *A Room.* In one episode, Colette recounts the true story of the Ladies of Llangollen, two English women of wealthy families who eloped together and set up home in rural Wales in the eighteenth century. The diaries of the older of the two Ladies, Lady Eleanor, collected under the title *The Hamwood Papers* (1930), provide the foundation for Colette's version of the Ladies' lives.

Colette's choice of the story of the Ladies for *Le pur* suggests ties to Woolf and *A Room.* Woolf knew of the story of the Ladies of Llangollen and in fact in 1927 sketched a plan to use their story for the novel that later became *Orlando.*[6] The Ladies came up at many different points in Woolf's life: Woolf's father Leslie Stephen included a reference to the Ladies in his *Dictionary of Literary Biography;* Woolf would have also found references to the Ladies in *Wild Wales* by George Borrow, a writer on whom her father wrote a short article in 1880;[7] at fifteen, in 1897, Woolf read about the Ladies in John Lockhart's *Life of Sir Walter Scott,* a birthday present from her father; in 1907 Woolf's review of E. V. Lucas's *A Swan and Her Friends,* which contains a version of the Ladies' story, appeared in the *Times Literary Supplement;* in 1931, in a letter to Ethel Smyth, Woolf writes of her decision not to write a review of *The Hamwood Papers,* claiming that they had done themselves so perfectly; and in 1936 the Woolfs' Hogarth Press published a fictional biography based on the Ladies, *Chase of the Wild Goose* by Mary Gordon.

The Englishness of the Ladies, their literariness—they are "enivrées du roman" (127) ("drunk on novels"), especially French novels—their self-sufficiency despite material difficulties, the discreet nature of their relationship, and their creation of a room of their own—the Ladies are furnished with "a well-stocked library, a delightful site and view . . . A calm and peaceful life, a perfect friendship" (116)—also ties them to Woolf herself and to *A Room* and its focus on material things.[8] Like the Ladies, Woolf's lesbianism was discreet; like them, she was a great admirer of French literature. A specific correlation exists between the Ladies of Llangollen and the two working women of *A Room*, Chloe and Olivia, the imaginary protagonists of the novel of Woolf's fictional contemporary Mary Carmichael.

As several critics have suggested, Woolf's Chloe and Olivia episode reads as an implicit reference to the controversy surrounding Radclyffe Hall's novel, *The Well of Loneliness*, banned on obscenity charges for its explicit treatment of homosexuality only months prior to the publication of *A Room* (see Marcus, *Languages* 163–87; Cline 282–84).[9] In the lines preceding her discussion of Chloe and Olivia in *A Room*, Woolf asks that audience members check that Sir Chartres Biron, the magistrate presiding at the *Well* trial, is not among their number. At the very end of *A Room*, Woolf also mentions Sir Archibald Bodkin, who was the Director of Public Prosecutions (111). According to Marcus and Cline, Judith Shakespeare, Woolf's fictional sister for William, also constitutes another possible *Room* reference to Hall, who was renowned for her claim to have descended from Shakespeare's daughter Susannah Shakespeare. Hall's "coded appearance," to borrow Cline's term, in Woolf's *A Room* ties it to Colette's *Le pur*. Hall and her lover Una Troubridge befriended Colette in Paris in the early 1920s and in fact helped Colette gain access to a copy of *The Hamwood Papers*. In part, perhaps, as a result of this collaboration, as well as similarities in the status (and the style; see figures 9 and 10) of the Ladies' lives and those of Hall and Troubridge, Colette identified Hall and Troubridge with Lady Eleanor and Lady Sarah.[10] This identification provides a parallel to the Chloe and Olivia–Hall and Troubridge tie. Hall and Troubridge thus function as mediators between Woolf and Colette, *A Room* and *Le pur*, on a number of levels. The story of their lives and works appears in both *Le pur* and *A Room* (when Colette asks us to imagine the Ladies of Llangollen in 1930, one hundred years after Sarah Ponsonby's death, does she invite us to see Hall and Troubridge, or Hall's Stephen and Mary in *The Well?*). Their involvement with both writers suggests that they provided Colette with access to *A Room*, a copy of the text, or word of the text, as they provided her with access to *The Hamwood Papers*.

Indeed, Colette reads Lady Eleanor's diary as she would have had to read Woolf's *A Room* in 1930 (and Hall's *The Well*): in the original, although, she admits, slowly and with some difficulty. *A Room* was not

Figure 9
*The Ladies of Llangollen. Lithograph by J. H. Lynch pirated from a portrait
of the Ladies (after 1831).*

translated into French until 1951, twenty-two years after its original
publication date in Britain and the United States.[11] Her reconstruction
of the story of the Ladies, like her revision of, or provision of a sequel
to, *A Room,* is undertaken without protocol, illicitly. As Elizabeth
Mavor suggests, in reference specifically to the passage from *Le pur*
where Colette imagines the Ladies a hundred years on in 1930, not
1830, Colette's interpretation of the Ladies, though sympathetic, is
"very much in terms of her own times" (206). Colette "translates" Lady
Eleanor's diaries quite liberally into her native language as she translates

Figure 10
Hall, Una Troubridge, and the dachshunds. Alpha Photographic Press Agency Limited.

Woolf's *A Room*. She changes things around and does not apologize for having done so; she pays no attention to chronology. "Je traduis ça et là, j'intervertis et ne m'en excuse point" (134) ("I translate here and there, I reverse the order, and I do not excuse myself at all" [114 n.]); "je néglige, à dessein, toutes les dates de ce 'journal'" (136) ("intentionally, I neglect all the dates of this journal" [124]). What intrigues Colette about the story of the Ladies is what is missing from the work: first, specific references to the sexual life of "ces deux opiniâtres amies" (125) ("these two opinionated ladies" [115])—only one mention of a shared bed or bedroom ("je ne découvre, sauf erreur, qu'une seule fois les mots 'la chambre,' et 'notre lit'" (136) ("and if I mistake not, the words 'the bedroom' and 'our bed' occur but once" [124])—and second, the voice of the younger Lady, Sarah, "la proie" (the victim): "What I would have liked to have is the diary that would reveal the victim, the diary that the younger of this couple, Sarah Ponsonby, might have kept [. . .] The secret here is Sarah, who says nothing, and embroiders. What a light would be shed by a diary she kept" (125–26).[12] Similarly, I want to argue that what draws Colette to *A Room* is the unsaid, the gaps, ellipses, and prohibitions in the text, the references to the body not made, in the words of Woolf: "something about the body, about the passions which it was unfitting for her as a woman to say" ("Professions" 61).

    However, Colette's interest in these omissions in both cases, she asserts, is not a lascivious one—she aims to respect the Ladies' story as she aims to respect Woolf's: "je ne suis pas un lecteur ordinaire" (138) ("I am not an ordinary reader" [127]), she asserts. Colette's subject is not eroticism (for the male reader) but rather kinship (for the female reader). The gaps in Lady Eleanor's diaries mark the efforts of the Ladies not to be "la parodie d'un couple" (138–39) ("the parody of a couple" [127]); the gaps in Woolf's *A Room* result from her efforts not to engage with the male critic, historian, or writer on his own terms, not to *replace* his history with hers, but rather to provide a supplement to it, as she suggests in *A Room* (45).[13] Thus, when Colette fills the gaps in Lady Eleanor's diaries, she imagines Lady Sarah and Lady Eleanor in a comforting embrace, "sleeping together, lying awake together, experiencing together nocturnal terrors," and in a relationship that involves everyday life, material things (127).[14]

A Shared Structure and Style

Woolf's *A Room* began its life as a lecture, conceived in part while at Thomas Hardy's funeral in January of 1928, delivered twice at the women's colleges Newnham and Girton in Cambridge in October of the same year (*Diary* 3: 173). The lecture, the originals of which do not exist, was subsequently divided, rewritten as six pieces, and published a year later in 1929. On completing *A Room*, Woolf writes in her diary that she felt constrained by facts and the proximity of her audience in this case. She suggests that the work, although important, is "watery and flimsy and pitched in too high a voice," and that it has "an uneasy life in it; you feel the creature arching its back and galloping on" (*A*

Writer's Diary 141–42). She anticipates that her friends will not like the work, that it will elicit little criticism "except of the evasive jocular kind, from Lytton [Strachey], Roger [Fry] and Morgan [E. M. Forster]," and that she will "be attacked as a feminist and hinted at for a Sapphist" (*A Writer's Diary* 145). Woolf downplays the significance of her lectures, describing them as for an audience of young people (those "who have not yet come of age" [*A Room* 104]) in need of some encouragement: "But my 'book' isn't a book—its [*sic*] only talks to girls" (*Letters* 4: 102).

Colette's *Le pur,* nine loosely connected portraits, also originated as a series of separate pieces, among them a supplement to Don Juan written as part of a series of supplements to great works (*Œuvres* 3: x). Biographer Michèle Sarde suggests that Colette came up with the idea for *Le pur* while sailing on the North Sea (in British territories?) aboard the yacht of Henri de Rothschild, *Eros,* a name appropriate to Colette's topic (400). *Le pur* was published under the title *Ces plaisirs . . . qu'on nomme à la légère physiques* in 1932, following the abrupt interruption of its serialization in the French magazine *Gringoire* in 1931, due to poor reviews from readers.[15] Among other titles Colette considered for *Le pur* were *Écumes* (*Foam*), *Remous* (*Eddy, Eddies*), and *La fourbe* (*Treachery*). In a letter to Hélène Picard, Colette says that while "Remous fits the subject matter (or absence of subject matter) better," *Écumes* is "the prettier word" (*Letters from Colette* 116). Nicole Ward Jouve has suggested that the first of these titles (*Écumes*) ties Colette's work to Woolf's *The Waves,* published the year before *Le pur* (*Colette* 168). Colette, like Woolf, defines *Le pur* in terms of what it is not—it "isn't a novel" (*Letters from Colette* 128). Maurice Goudeket describes it as "le plus difficile de ses livres, et le plus nouveau" (84) ("the most difficult and the newest of her books"). Like Woolf, Colette downplays the importance of her work, which she nonetheless predicts will one day be considered her best book: "It's about old love related things, deals with unisexual loves—in short, it does what it can";[16] and to Polaire, "this book that is only a gallery of sins" (my translation).[17] Celebrated by a few, *Le pur* disconcerted most readers, according to Goudeket (85). Sarde notes that Colette's friends must have had some difficulty recognizing their Colette in *Le pur* and an earlier novel, *La naissance du jour:* "After turning fifty," Sarde explains, "after her second divorce and the unpleasantness it entailed, her books changed. They began to turn slowly back to the past, to a journey back in time, away from the present, in a kind of renunciation" (408).

Both writers experiment with the form of the work.[18] In *Le pur* Colette, as Marcus has suggested of Woolf in *A Room,* "[invents] a female language to subvert the languages of the patriarchy" (*Languages* 187). Both texts couch their inquiry in terms of a voyage or city tour— Woolf on the campus of a fictional Oxbridge college and at Fernham, and then in London; Colette in Paris and in the French provinces. Woolf and Colette perhaps find common ground in Jean-Jacques Rousseau's *Les rêveries du promeneur solitaire* or his *Confessions,* in Montaigne's *Essais* (all favorites of Woolf's), or in the work of their British contemporary, Rebecca West, such as her essay "The Strange Necessity," which mixes literary criticism with a walk around Paris. In each case, the mobility of the flâneur-narrator matches the meandering, "stream-of-consciousness"-like prose and the grammatical volubility of the sentence, broken frequently by dashes, ellipses, semicolons, and code names, usually initials (examples include von X. and Mr A in *A Room* and X and D in *Le pur*). A series of loosely related encounters, conversations with real people, and engagements with authors via their texts shape the development of ideas in the work. "A game of reverberations, echoes, relations" ("tout un jeu de rappels, d'échos, de relations") ties these disparate episodes together in Woolf's *A Room,* as they do in Colette's *Le pur* (*Œuvres* 3: 1509).[19]

The tone of both works is satirical, a matter of some seriousness wrapped in a light veil of humor. Fact masquerades as fiction and fiction as fact. The mock anonymity and objectivity of the narrator (in *A Room,* Woolf's narrator asserts: "Here then was I (call me Mary Beton, Mary Seton, Mary Carmichael or by any name you please—it is not a matter of any importance)" [5]; in *Le pur,* among her homosexual male colleagues "Absent yet present, a translucent witness, [Colette's narrator] enjoyed an indefinable peace, accompanied by a kind of conspiratorial pride" [139])[20] and the subject (frequently coded with initials) in both works raises questions about the relation of subject and object, subjectivity and objectivity—offering only an uncertain foothold in each case. Teased and led on by the narrator, the subject is invited to condemn himself or herself in both of these works.

"Two pictures disjointed and disconnected"

In the opening pages of the first chapter of *A Room,* Woolf's narrator introduces the subject of her polemic. She has been asked to address the question of women and fiction. This topic will dictate the shape of her text, which, she suggests, will be a sort of fiction: "Lies," she writes, "will flow from my lips, but there may perhaps be some truth mixed up with them" (4). What follows is a series of investigatory trips, onto the lawn, into the chapel, and into the library of the Oxbridge college she invents for the purpose of her writing, and to the fiction and history shelves of the British Museum in pursuit of the elusive solution to the question on which the text opened.

Le pur opens in a similar way, as Colette's narrator, like Woolf's, engaged in a "professional assignment" of sorts, fashions her topic first in fictional terms. Her subject, unlike Woolf's, is not suggested to her, but comes to her at the end of the second chapter of *Le pur:* "The veiled face of a woman, refined, disillusioned, [skilled in deception and delicacy; my addition] is a suitable preface to this book, which will sadly treat of sensual pleasure" (25).[21] Thus, Colette, as she focuses on sensual pleasure, also, like Woolf, treats women and fiction, women and "l'art de feindre" ("the art of pretending"). Again what follows is a series of trespasses in search of an answer. In Colette's *Le pur,* however, an inversion of sorts takes place: the vaulted roofs of the British Museum of Woolf's *A Room* become the high ceilings of the atelier/opium den in Paris.

Woolf considers four possible ways to approach her topic—"women and fiction"—"women and what they are like [. . .] women and the fiction that they write [. . .] women and the fiction that is written about them," or a combination of the three (3). She dismisses the easier option—which would include "a few remarks about Fanny Burney; a few more about Jane Austen; a tribute to the Brontës"—and embarks on a more complex journey, one she doubts she will ever complete: "I should never be able to come to a conclusion" (3). To do her duty as a lecturer, that is, to hand her audience "a nugget of pure truth," might prove an impossibility (4). Personalizing her quest, she offers instead to give her "opinion upon one minor point"—the crux of the essay—that is, that "a woman must have money and a room of her own if she is to write fiction" (4). She begins with an account, a story of the two days preceding her arrival, of how she "made [the question] work in and out of my daily life" (4).

Having been ushered off the Oxbridge lawn, a place off-limits to the uninitiated, by a beadle, "a curious-looking object," she is drawn to the library in pursuit of several manuscripts (6). Her interest in these (significantly for my focus here) is revision, rewriting. Woolf's narrator, remembering Charles Lamb's assertion that Milton's decision to change the words in his poem "Lycidas" (the manuscript of which is held in the British Museum library) was "a sort of sacrilege" (7), wonders which words those were. A study of revisions, she feels, might be useful: she believes that a look at alterations in the manuscript of Thackeray's

Esmond, held in the same library, will reveal whether the eighteenth-century style of the text was natural to Thackeray or not. However, she comes up against another obstacle: she is again denied access based on her sex (9). Arriving next at the chapel, she elects to remain on the outside and to examine the edifice and its contents from a distance, rather than to attempt to gain admission: "But the outside of these magnificent buildings is often as beautiful as the inside" (8). The theme of inclusion and exclusion introduced here runs through to the end of the chapter; it sets the stage for Woolf's focus on difference, highlighted by the juxtaposition of two related but disjointed scenes.

The latter part of this first chapter includes the description of two meals attended by the narrator: the first, lavish and sumptuous on the fictional Oxbridge campus; the second, meager and bland, at a fictional women's college called Fernham. Woolf's narrator juggles here questions of fact and fiction, truth and illusion, laughter and anguish: "two pictures disjointed and disconnected" (19). At the first of these meals, in spite of the "profound, subtle and subterranean glow" lit "halfway down one's spine" by the sumptuous sauces and salads and the free-flowing wines, Woolf's narrator detects a lack or a gap (embodied by the tail-less Manx cat she sees from the window) (11), a difference between this party and a similar one that took place before the war, between the prewar illusion that produced the poetry of Tennyson and Christina Rossetti (Woolf has the one poet harmoniously responding to the other) and the postwar truth, the latter being the preferable state of affairs, Woolf suggests uncertainly. At this point in the text, woven in with Woolf's cogitations are both the poetry of Rossetti and Woolf's own poetic prose: "purples and golds burn in window-panes like the beat of an excitable heart" (16); "[t]he windows of the building, curved like ships' windows among the generous waves of red brick, changed from lemon to silver under the flight of the quick spring clouds" (17).

In contrast to the imposing buildings of Oxbridge, an institution founded solidly on the gold and silver of England's leaders (10), the unendowed Fernham, the setting for Woolf's second meal, is set apart and fronted with wild, open gardens. The narrator's mother and the mother of Mary Seton, a science professor with whom Woolf's narrator sits and talks after a meal with the Fernham students, raised children, not money (which would anyway until forty-eight years previous have fallen into the hands of their husbands). Woolf's narrator marks the discrepancy between Oxbridge and Fernham in terms of the sensual. Water takes the place of wine at Fernham; prunes and custard and a plain gravy soup the place of the Oxbridge partridges "with all their retinue of sauces and salads [. . .]; their potatoes, thin as coins but not so hard; their sprouts, foliated as rosebuds but more succulent" (10–11). This chapter comes to a close as the narrator returns to her inn, contemplating as she goes the impact of poverty and tradition, and of inclusion and exclusion, on the mind of a writer.

The first two sections of *Le pur,* like the opening chapter of *A Room,* juxtapose two (disconnected) episodes, two disjointed ideas (truth and illusion): in *A Room,* lunch at Oxbridge and dinner at Fernham; in *Le pur,* two meetings with Charlotte, both of which take place at the same opium den. The overlap of Charlotte's name with that of Colette suggests that Charlotte functions as a double of sorts. The first of these opening sections finds Colette's narrator as a visitor, a trespasser, like Woolf's narrator in *A Room,* one not attuned to her surroundings, which here consist of a vast studio (like a market, "comme une halle") with faux oriental decoration. The second finds her more at ease in conversation, again like Woolf, with a single female interlocutor.

In the opening scene, the aroma of the opium smoke hanging listlessly in the air relaxes the narrator, stimulates her appetite, and endows her with a general sense of well-being (parallel to the optimism with which Woolf begins her inquiry). The narrator enjoys the glow of the veiled lights and the white almond-shaped flames of the opium lamps. The narrator sees a head (with "hair slicked down like the hair of a drowned person" (4), reminiscent of Woolf's tail-less Manx) leaning over a balustrade but is unable to discern if it belongs to a man or a woman. Colette's narrator's contemplation is interrupted by an unnamed colleague, encountered by chance, whose questioning of the purpose of her visit, like that of Woolf's beadle, is accusatory—she is there to watch, not to participate, he suggests; she is incapable of indulging in this base pleasure—an accusation, however, that Colette's narrator confesses is not misdirected.

At this point in the text, the narrator is interrupted by the voice of a woman: "a furry, sweet, yet husky voice that had the qualities of a hard and thick skinned velvety peach" (6).[22] This first intrusion of a woman's voice, Charlotte's, into the text (paralleling Woolf's efforts to enter the library, although whereas Woolf attempts to break in, Charlotte's voice breaks out) is cut short by the voice of the male lover, first with a "non [. . .] elle n'est pas ici pour ça" (10) ("no [. . .] she didn't come here to sing [for that]" [7]) and then, the smashing of a cup and "oui, elle est là. Elle est ici avec moi " (11) ("Yes, she's here. She's with me" [7]). Her third interruption comes a page later in the form of a cry of rhythmic orgasmic pleasure, this time permitted because in the service of her partner:

> But from the depths of this very silence a sound imperceptibly began in a woman's throat, at first husky, then clear, asserting its firmness and amplitude as it was repeated, becoming clear and full like the notes the nightingale repeats and accumulates until they pour out in a flood of arpeggios . . . (8)[23]

On leaving the opium den, Colette's narrator encounters Charlotte, now wrapped in a coat, veiled, and they agree to share a cab home. Stepping outside with her companion, Colette's narrator revels in the fresh air, a moment reminiscent of Woolf's celebration of the exterior of the chapel in the first section of *A Room*—"L'air libre, frais, encore obscur, me désaltéra" (14) ("It was still dark outside, and the cool night revived me" [10]). The figure cut by Charlotte takes the narrator by surprise: a woman of forty-five with a short nose and a fleshy face, she looks, according to the narrator, like the favorite models of Renoir, beauties of 1875 (14/10). Something about her is out of place and out of fashion, *démodé*. While the conversation begins with banalities, Colette's narrator once again focuses on Charlotte's voice: "What seduction was in her voice, how delightful the way it rasped out certain syllables and the suave and defeated way it had of letting the ends of phrases fall into the lower register . . ." (11).[24] Reflecting the subdued tenor of her voice, Charlotte cautiously urges Colette on arriving home to get out of the taxi a slight distance from her door, so as not to compromise her reputation: the hour is late. When Colette refuses, Charlotte responds: "C'est beau, la liberté. Moi . . . moi, je ne suis pas libre" (17) ("Freedom is a wonderful thing. But as for me . . . I'm not free" [13]), echoing Woolf's focus on access in the opening chapter of *A Room*.

Time passes between Colette's narrator's first and second encounters with Charlotte. Colette's narrator does not look for Charlotte. Instead, she prefers to imagine Charlotte, to keep her in the realm of fiction, for fear of destroying "the mystery we attach to people whom we know only casually" (15).[25] However, an encounter does occur at a book signing, leading to the second meeting at the same opium den. This bridging encounter serves to remind the reader of the status of the narrator—she is the author, Colette—and of the (possibly) fictional status of the text. Colette's second visit to the opium den contrasts with the first, as does Woolf's first meal at Oxbridge and her second at Fernham. This time, she finds Charlotte alone, without façade or pretense:

"[b]are-headed, very neat, and looking rather plump in her black dress, she had not donned the ritual kimono" (16).[26] Their location affords a sense of anonymity—the opium den is "as accessible and inhospitable as a railway station," according to the narrator, and neither woman knows whose place it is (16). Indeed, Colette's narrator wishes that this anonymity extended to her own identity. As strangers, Colette's narrator and Charlotte can confide in each other and are able to understand one another in a way good friends cannot. With Charlotte's lover out of town, she is enjoying, she says, a respite from lying—a comment that bemuses Colette's narrator. Why lie, she asks? And the narrator recognizes of what Charlotte's lie consists, "mélodieux et miséricordieux" (23) ("melodious and merciful" [18]), of what a woman's fiction must consist. Her lies are a "romanesque recompense," which give the lover the illusion of superiority, a strength he does not possess in reality: "those full notes reiterated again and again, precipitated until their trembling equilibrium broke in a climax of torrential sobbing . . ." (18).[27] Colette recognizes Charlotte as a "woman who knew how to reassure men":

> This substantial Charlotte was a female genius, indulging in tender subterfuge, consideration, and self-denial. And here she was, this woman who knew how to reassure men, sitting beside me, limbs relaxed, idly waiting to take up again the duty of one who loves best: the daily imposture [. . .] (18)[28]

Instead of the debauched confession Colette's narrator had hoped for from Charlotte, the woman turns, as does Mary Seton in *A Room,* to the material, to the economics of pleasure—an explanation of how business is transacted in the opium den. "Une aussi claire ordonnance" (25) ("so straightforward an accounting") of debauchery, says the narrator, would have troubled any listener other than herself. Charlotte does not conform to the stereotype of woman, those who "guetter [et] convoiter les maladies de l'homme [pour qu'elles puissent] tendre les mains à tout vase souillé, tout linge moite . . ." (26) ("hope and pray for their man to fall ill so they can handle dirty basins and clammy rags" [21]); rather, like Mary Seton, she is, the narrator surmises, wise and controlled.

Like Woolf, Colette ends this first section with a consideration of the senses. At this point Charlotte puts up her guard, distancing her heart and her body from that of the narrator. Charlotte remains a mystery to the narrator, her sex "inexorable." The word inexorable, the narrator suggests, describes the bundle of forces to which we have been able to give only one name—her book's subject, the senses. Why not, she asks, refer to it in the singular—one sense of which the other five are sub-parts, sense (pleasure?) dominating all of them—in this way suggesting a single, unifying theme for her work. Who, asks Colette's narrator, posing the central question around which the work turns, has the ability or the power to fix the unstable limits of the empire of the senses?

The narrator's second interview with Charlotte comes to a close with a return to order—"protocolairement" (30) ("punctiliously" [25]). Charlotte utters a banality—one that significantly ties *Le pur* to *A Room* with its reference to keys, locks, and access: "'The only really masterful sound a man makes in a house is when, on the entrance landing, he fumbles with his key in the lock of the door . . . '" (25).[29] What remains of Charlotte for the narrator—the basis on which the rest of *Le pur* will be built—are "ténèbres," shadows (the enigmatic figure of a veiled woman), which the narrator has no plans to dissipate, echoing Woolf's assertion that her inquiry precludes a coming to a conclusion: "When I think of Charlotte, I embark upon a drifting souvenir of nights graced neither by sleep nor certitude" (25).[30]

"Give nothing—take nothing"

From the Oxbridge campus, *A Room* shifts to London. In the second section of *A Room*, Woolf's narrator makes her way to the British Museum in pursuit of "the pure fluid, the essential oil of truth" (25), recalling the later title of Colette's work. She pursues questions suggested to her during her trip to Oxbridge: "Why did men drink wine and women water? Why was one sex so prosperous and the other so poor? What effect has poverty on fiction? What conditions are necessary for the creation of works of art?" (25). Material things concern Woolf's narrator at this point. As she enters the museum from the bustling London street, she blurs the line dividing the two, the high from the low, anticipating her request that the contents of the museum shelves address fundamental questions about material things: "London was like a workshop. London was like a machine. We were all being shot backwards and forwards on this plain foundation to make some pattern. The British Museum was another department of the factory" (26). The domed head of the British Museum buzzes with responses; however, all are proffered by men and all are different. While the narrator scribbles "contradictory jottings" erratically in her notebook ("[i]t was distressing, it was bewildering, it was humiliating," writes Woolf, "[t]ruth had run through my fingers. Every drop had escaped" [30]), a picture emerges from the chaos: "It was the face and figure of Professor von X. engaged in writing his monumental work entitled *The Mental, Moral and Physical Inferiority of the Female Sex*" (31). An unattractive man, "heavily built," with "a great jowl" and "small eyes," and "very red in the face," Professor von X.'s motives for an attack on women bemuse Woolf's narrator (31). Was he rejected by his wife in favor of a younger, more handsome man, or— and here Woolf turns his own discipline on him—was he laughed at as a baby by a pretty child? She concludes that it is anger that motivates the professor and all of those others who write so profusely about women, but anger "disguised and complex, not anger simple and open" (32).

Later, seeking out lunch in a restaurant near the British Museum, Woolf's narrator's search continues. A paper abandoned by a previous diner confirms her findings in the museum. A visitor from another planet could not fail to notice, suggests Woolf's narrator, that "England is under the rule of patriarchy," and she returns to the professor:

> Nobody in their senses could fail to detect the dominance of the professor. His was the power and the money and the influence. He was the proprietor of the paper and its editor and its sub-editor. He was the Foreign Secretary and the Judge. He was the cricketer; he owned the race-horses and the yachts. He was the director of the company that pays two hundred per cent to its shareholders [. . .] With the exception of the fog he seemed to control everything. Yet he was angry. (33–34)

Woolf's narrator attributes this anger to a concern regarding his own superiority and the potential loss thereof. She affirms this idea with a foray into "daily life," remembering when Z (another anon), "most humane, most modest of men," his vanity wounded, condemned her contemporary Rebecca West—a real name among all the anons—as an "arrant feminist" for having labeled men snobs: "[I]t was a protest against some infringement of his power to believe in himself. Women have served all these centuries as looking-glasses possessing *the magic and delicious power* of reflecting the figure of man at twice its natural size" (my emphasis; 35). Echoing Colette's Charlotte, Woolf's narrator asserts that woman is bound to lying, to fictions. For, if she begins to tell the truth, "the figure in the looking-glass [the image of him that she maintains] shrinks" (36).

Woolf rapidly curtails her "contributions to the dangerous and fascinating subject of the psychology of the other sex," and returns once again to material things (36). She pays her bill and tells the story of her own inheritance, the news of which arrived almost at the same time as the news that she could vote. Endowed with a fixed income of £500 per year for life, Woolf's narrator feels the bitterness and hatred that had been born of her lack of independence subside. She is free at last "to think of things in themselves" (this is a phrase she picks up in the concluding pages of *A Room*), to have an opinion about a building, a picture, a book (39). In the last pages of the second chapter, Woolf's narrator returns home, pondering woman's future as she goes. As she steps indoors she returns to the central question of the lectures: "but what bearing has all this upon the subject of my paper, Women and Fiction?" (40).

In chapter 3 of *A Room*, Woolf's narrator's resolves to narrow her inquiry and look to the historian for facts, specifically about how women lived, in England, "in the time of Elizabeth" (41). Here, she feels, lies the answer to why women did not write, for fiction depends, she asserts, on the material:

> [F]iction is like a spider's web, attached ever so lightly perhaps, but still attached to life at all four corners. Often the attachment is scarcely perceptible; Shakespeare's plays, for instance, seem to hang there complete by themselves. But when the web is pulled askew, hooked up at the edge, torn in the middle, one remembers that these webs are not spun in mid-air by incorporeal creatures, but are the work of suffering human beings, and are attached to grossly material things, like health and money and the houses we live in. (41–42)

Here Woolf's narrator introduces a second figure, Professor G. M. Trevelyan, author of a history of England (42). According to the narrator, what emerges from Trevelyan's history, which was first published in 1926, is a picture of woman as "a very queer, composite being" (43), "an odd monster," "a worm winged like an eagle" (44), one who in reality had little or no power, but in fiction (and memoirs) had both character and intellect. "Imaginatively she is of the highest importance," Woolf's narrator concludes; "practically she is completely insignificant" (43). What Woolf's narrator wants to know, returning again to the material, and what history is unable to tell her, is how the Elizabethan woman lived: "at what age did she marry; how many children had she as a rule; what was her house like; had she a room to herself; did she do the cooking; would she be likely to have a servant?" (45).

From here Woolf's narrator spins her story of Judith, a fictional sister to Shakespeare, her writer's talent buried at home, bound to marry a man she has not chosen, while her brother builds a family and a career in the theatre at the "hub of the universe." A runaway, unmarried and with child, Judith Shakespeare is pushed to suicide (47–48). Women, Woolf's narrator concludes, could not have written in the sixteenth century, a feat that was masked by women even as late as the nineteenth century under a masculine name (and she mentions Currer Bell, George Eliot, and George Sand). And even today, she adds, "[t]he desire to be veiled still possesses them" (50). Discouragement, Woolf contends, citing Mr. Oscar Browning's confident assertion that the most intelligent woman is no match for the intellectually weakest man, must have taken its toll on women. How, asks Woolf, could she have overcome

> that very interesting and obscure masculine complex which has had so much influence upon the woman's movement; that deep-seated desire, not so much that *she* shall be inferior as that *he* shall be superior, which plants him wherever one looks, not only in front of the arts, but barring the way to politics too, even when the risk to himself seems infinitesimal and the suppliant humble and devoted[?] (55)

In the third section of *Le pur*, Colette, like Woolf, broadens the scope of her inquiry. Like Woolf's narrator, Colette's seeks answers about women first from men: "je ne suis pas allée bien loin chercher des confidences masculines" (32) ("I never had to go out of my way to be let in on masculine secrets" [26]). The neutral eye of Woolf's narrator perusing the shelves at the British Museum is matched by that of Colette's narrator, whose frigidity or vice puts her interlocutor (a celebrated lover ["[un] célèbre amant" (33)] as opposed to an author of a "monumental work" about women [31]; a Don Juan rather than an Oxbridge don) at ease. Colette's narrator is conscious of her role as listener throughout the book. Colette's anonymous interlocutor, "Mon ami X . . . ," like Woolf's, is a comical caricature of sorts, here animated by rivalry and resentment rather than anger. Like Woolf's von X., Colette's X is hostile, in this case to mistresses who have exploited him sexually (he desires a woman who will refuse him, but when she does, so gripped is he by lust that he throws her to the floor and takes her anyway). Colette's narrator contrasts this hostility with the lack thereof felt by women for men—a woman, she suggests, knows she is an inexhaustible store of plenty for a man—and asks herself, perhaps indicating the central thrust of this section of the work, one that matches Woolf's narrator's bemusement at how little men know about women: "Am I, then, going to find myself, in the first pages of a book, declaring that men are of less use to women than women are to men? We shall see" (27).[31]

The setting of Colette's narrator's interview with X in this third section contrasts with that of Woolf's with von X.—we move out of an academic setting into the real world. The reading room of the British Museum becomes a private dining room in a first-class restaurant—although, like the British Museum, it is "in the center of town"—a place of pleasure, of lavish eating and smoking, rather than a place of discipline and study, dark and warm like a body at odds with the head of the domed British Museum. As Woolf's narrator interrogates von X. et al., London streets crawl with workers, housepainters, nursemaids, the woman who keeps the greengrocer's shop (26, 39); as Colette's narrator questions X, beyond the heavily curtained window extends "a strip of Paris, animated and silent, calling to mind a swarm of fireflies on a lake of asphalt, and I am enveloped in the facile illusion of danger lurking in the night outside, of safety within the old walls warm with secrets" (28).[32]

Like Woolf's von X., Colette's X writes. Colette's narrator expresses surprise that X has not written a Don Juan play and reveals her plan to write her own, with a specific actor, Édouard de Max, in mind. Her companion advises against it, citing her provincial roots as a handicap. Don Juan, whom he characterizes as a tactful, diplomatic sort, who seduces and then becomes bored, has, he claims, never been properly understood (except, he implies, by himself). Colette's decision to use this archetypal figure—symbol of cruelty, enemy of the female sex—underscores the fact that her subject, like Woolf's, is the relationship between the sexes. A later comment (quoted below) regarding the humble origins of the Don Juan name, the relatively few pages of Molière's play that secured its fame as at odds with its eternal quality, suggests that Colette, again like Woolf, is calling into question the stereotyping of both sexes.

Before Colette's narrator is able to explain her approach to Don Juan, her interlocutor has grown tired and they part. A second meeting—the coming and going of Colette's narrator recalls the meandering of Woolf's—finds X poised to leave town. He boasts of outwitting his old lover who, out of malice, has become involved with his new one, offering her overblown stories of their sexual exploits. When Colette's narrator inquires as to whether the new lover seeks sensuality or whether she is merely in competition with her predecessor, she watches with pleasure the expression on his face shift from "defiance" to "cunning" to "primordial hostility," reminiscent of Woolf's von X. doodle.

At the same time, she conjures in her head a scene from "Célimare le bienaimé," a play by Eugène Labiche, written in 1863, where a cuckolded husband is outwitted by his wife and pitied by his servant. Following this, the narrator comments: "I changed, or at least appeared to change the subject" (34).

Colette's narrator continues interrogating X, who plans to welcome a fellow writer from the north named Maasen (a name perhaps inspired by that of Norwegian playwright Henrik Ibsen [OC 3: 1536]). Her subject has not changed; Don Juan continues to dominate in this chapter. Maasen, according to the narrator, is another famous womanizer. X is impressed by the figures cited discreetly by his companion, but sees this habit of Maasen's as in no way detracting from the stature of "ce magnifique édifice humain" (42) ("that magnificent human edifice" [35]). In a man, it is suggested, conduct and art are separate. X tells Colette's narrator: "'I don't care whether or not the edifice includes a room with mirrors and the appurtenances of a brothel.'"[33] To which Colette replies, "Naturellement" (42) ["Of course" [35]).

At this point in the book, Colette admits her collusion with X. While he speaks, she listens; she follows and goads him. In this sense, Colette, like Woolf in the second chapter of A Room, turns the tables on her male interlocutors. She encourages them to speak about themselves, and in so doing they more often than not condemn themselves.

As Woolf's narrator moves along the shelves of the British Museum, so Colette's moves on to de Max, her aging Don Juan, then on briefly to Francis Carco (a contemporary writer and friend of Colette) and Charles S., all of whom claim that the greatest pleasure one can gain from a woman lies in abstinence (46/39). De Max, like X, is transformed in the narrator's imagination (47/40). Tempted by the part of Don Juan, his eyes sparkle with the colors of the water salamander; his hair, a magnificent mane, trembles as he moves his shoulders and reaches for the imaginary hilt of his sword.

From this Don Juan ("that name, of humble origin really, born of a very few pages, but eternal" never replaced by any other name in any other language [41]) Colette's narrator turns to another Don Juan, whom she names Damien, a name reminiscent, she tells us, of his own (49/42). Damien, a possible model for Colette's Chéri, is nonetheless rejected as such—he is too stiff, too limited, lacking "la fantaisie ployante, [. . .] l'impudence et [. . .] la puérilité indispensables à Chéri" (49) ("the indulgent whimsicality, the impudence and boyishness indispensable to Chéri" [42–43]). "I liked being with him, as I liked being with swift animals who are motionless when at rest. He talked little, and

I believe he was second-rate in everything except the performance of his mission on earth" (43).[34] Colette's narrator meets Damien in the lobby of a provincial hotel, an anonymous place—like the opium den of the first chapter—appropriate to the revelations of this lonely figure (one who in a number of ways anticipates Colette's description of La Chevalière in the next section of *Le pur*). Colder and even more "fatuous" than X and de Max, Damien is tied to his *métier*—"une science qu'il inventait" (61) ("a science he had invented" [53]), the seduction of women. However, his conversation with Colette's narrator suggests his disdain for and disconnection from women. His motto, "'ne donne rien—n'accepte rien'" (60) ("'Give nothing—take nothing'" [53]), at once shocks and delights Colette's narrator. What interests Colette's narrator about this unusual man is informed by her taste for "le vide mystérieux" (62) ("the mysterious void" [54]), the paradoxical balance of his sensual code of honor and the frisson of attraction that draws her, against her will, to him. Recalling Woolf's von X., whose superiority rests on an uncertain foundation, that is, women's inferiority, Colette characterizes Damien's concern with his own power, his own ability to please as less important than its opposite, his powerlessness, his failure to please. She asks: "Can his obsession with potency ever equal, for a lover, his obsession with impotence?" (57).[35] Like Woolf's Professor von X., it is Damien's lack of power that motivates him.

Colette's Hermaphrodisme Mental and Woolf's Androgynous Mind

In chapters 4 and 5 of *A Room*, Woolf turns her interrogation onto women, as does Colette in sections 4 through 7 of *Le pur*. Both mix the names of real women with those of fictional or unknown women. Woolf's chapter 4 covers women's writing of the seventeenth, eighteenth, and nineteenth centuries (Lady Winchilsea, Margaret of Newcastle [Margaret Cavendish], Dorothy Osborne, and Aphra Behn; Jane Austen, Emily and Charlotte Brontë, and George Eliot) and chapter 5 the work of contemporaries, including that of fictional fiction writer Mary Carmichael. Colette's fourth chapter introduces actress Marguerite Moreno and La Chevalière (based on Colette's former lover Missy, La Marquise de Belbœuf); chapter 5 the British-American poet Renée Vivien; chapter 6 Amalia X and Lucienne de . . . ; and chapter 7 the Ladies of Llangollen. In each case, the writer builds a generational history of sorts (one with which to oppose the patriarchal history constructed in the earlier chapters) of woman's expression and creativity. Marking a separation of ways, in Woolf's case, the focus is on the relationship of woman to a language and form that proves an inadequate receptacle for the expression of her experience; in Colette's work the emphasis is on the relationship of woman to a body and a set of social mores at odds with her own desires.

This break in terms of focus is accompanied by a structural reversal in this second half of the text—Colette (much like *A Room*'s Mary Carmichael) tampers with the order of things in this section. Where Woolf ends, with a description of her conception of what she terms "the androgynous mind," Colette begins, with an explication of what she calls "hermaphrodisme mental," or "mental hermaphroditism." This reversal, the resituating of this pivotal section, suggests a sequence that takes the reader from Woolf's text to Colette's, supporting the contention that the later text follows or responds to the earlier.

Not commonly read together, these two theories about sex and the mind are remarkable in their similarity and bring the two texts together. These discussions sum up the focus of the latter section of the book in Woolf's case and set the stage for the same in Colette's. Woolf precedes her exposition on mental androgyny with a series of portraits of women writers in chronological order. Progressing from the seventeenth century to the present day, Woolf constructs a platform for the launching of women's literature, a new sentence, a woman's sentence (76). Colette follows her discussion of mental hermaphroditism with a series of portraits of same-sex relationships, both sexual and platonic. Following no particular chronological logic (although there is a general sense that the text moves back into the past rather than forward), leaving out the dates, as she does with Lady Eleanor's diaries, Colette explores the possibility of a same-sex relationship that involves no masquerade, no fiction.

Colette introduces her conception of mental hermaphroditism early in her fourth chapter. Whereas in the third section of *Le pur* Colette's narrator plays the role of spectator, here the text takes an autobiographical turn as the narrator interrogates herself. In conversation with actress Marguerite Moreno, a fellow performer and one of Colette's closest friends in real life, Colette's narrator explores the existence of a virile side of certain women, one that threatens men like Damien with homosexuality. The comfortable setting of this conversation—one is tempted to imagine Woolf's Chloe and Olivia or the Ladies of Llangollen speaking here—provides the two women with a certain liberty:

> We had the comfortable habit of leaving a sentence hanging midway
> as soon as one of us had grasped the point [. . .] No one can imag-
> ine the number of subjects, the amount of words that are left out of
> the conversation of two women who can talk to each other with
> absolute freedom. They can allow themselves the luxury of choosing
> exactly what to say [. . .] I burst out laughing—it does one good,
> when at a safe distance from the claws that have wounded us, to laugh
> at them, even when the old wounds are still raw and gaping.
> (61–62)[36]

Moreno, who, like Colette's narrator, physically combines the male and
female, Chimène and Le Cid of Pierre Corneille's *Le Cid,* in a single
body ("[a]sleep, she rather resembled Dante, or a refined hidalgo, or
Leonardo da Vinci's Saint John the Baptist" [63]),[37] argues for the superiority of a double self, part male, part female, in response to the doubts
of Colette's narrator, who, at the point in her life when the conversation
took place, she tells us, craved to be completely a woman (67/71;
63/59). Moreno distinguishes between the physical androgyny of
which Colette admits she is afraid and a "virilité spirituelle" ("a spiritual virility"), a mental hermaphroditism that is the domain of "highly
complex" men and women alike (67/60). When Colette's anxious narrator asks, "who will take us for women?" Moreno counters with the
response: "Des femmes" ("other women"), and anticipating the shape
of the rest of *Le pur,* she adds, "Regarde dans ta mémoire" (68) ("Think
it over" [61]). Recognizing the inevitability of her own hermaphroditism and the "ambiguity," the "flaws and privileges" it entails
(67/60), Colette, closing this section with a return to work, marks the
split in herself in terms of eyes and hand: "Then I resumed my post at
the side of a worktable, where my woman's eyes followed, on the pale
blue bonded paper, the hard and stubby hand of a gardener writing"
(64).[38]

    Woolf introduces her conception of a mental androgyny in her last
chapter. Contemplating the eddy and flow of pedestrians and traffic in
the London street seen from her window, Woolf's narrator sets about
wrapping things up and drawing things together. Her efforts of the previous days to see one sex as distinct from the other, she says, have tam-
pered with the unity of mind. London appears indifferent to her dilem-
ma (95). A sense of isolation reigns in London streets peopled by
individuals: "each seems bound on some private affair of his own" (95);
"all seemed separate, self-absorbed, on business of their own" (96). To
this is added a momentary sense of stillness: "[n]othing came down the

street, nobody passed" (96). A single leaf falling at this moment signals to Woolf a convergence—a girl, a young man, and a taxicab (a sign of progress?)—a vision that eases Woolf's narrator's mind of the strain of thinking of one sex as distinct from the other (an effort which "interferes with the unity of the mind" [97]).

This leads Woolf's narrator to consider the mind, which she calls "a very mysterious organ" marked by severances and oppositions, similar to those, she says, that exist in the body (97). The mind, she concludes, is quite flexible: it can separate itself from others or it can think with others, it can think back through things, it can be split, as is the mind of a woman who finds herself at once part of and separate from the culture in which she lives (97). But certain states of mind are more comfortable than others; certain states of mind require "nothing [. . .] to be held back," according to Woolf's narrator, among them the union of male and female (97). From here, Woolf embarks on an "amateurish" plan of the soul, imagining it to be part male and part female, the female part dominating in the woman's brain, the male in the man's brain (98). Anticipating Colette's discussion with Moreno, Woolf suggests that "[t]he normal and comfortable state of being is that when the two live in harmony together, spiritually co-operating" (98). Woolf ascribes this idea to Coleridge (in so doing authorizing her theory with reference to a forefather in a way that Colette does not), who, she says, claimed that a great mind is androgynous, an assertion that she understands to mean that an androgynous mind is *"resonant and porous; that it transmits emotion without impediment, that it is naturally creative, incandescent and undivided"* (my emphasis; 98) (and she cites first Shakespeare as a possible candidate, then adds Keats, Sterne, Cowper, Lamb, Coleridge, and lastly Proust [103]). Woolf considers a heightened sex-consciousness a feature of her own age, perhaps at its root the suffrage movement ("a few women in black bonnets"), which put men unused to challenge on the defensive (99).

Woolf's description of the androgynous mind reads as a caveat following on an analysis of how one writes as a woman: write as a woman, but don't forget your male side, as the best writers combine the two. Colette's description of mental hermaphroditism is a code of how to read the pages that follow: I'm not condemning those who imitate the other sex, I'm just suggesting another way to do it. In each case, they suggest that the mixing of sexes is an inevitability, a positive one.

In her fourth chapter, first reviewing the poetry of Lady Winchilsea, born in 1661, Woolf's narrator notes the anger in her poetic voice: she bursts out "in indignation against the position of women," her mind "harassed and distracted with hates and grievances" (59). Little, Woolf's narrator writes, is known about the life of Lady Winchilsea, and what there is is dismissed as gossip (61). Next Woolf's narrator turns to Margaret of Newcastle—hers a "wild, generous, untutored intelligence." "In both," suggests Woolf's narrator, "burnt the same passion for poetry and both are disfigured and deformed by the same causes" (61). She then moves on to the letters of Dorothy Osborne before turning last to Aphra Behn, with whom, she asserts, "we turn a very important corner on the road." With Behn we leave the solitude of the country and "come to town and rub shoulders with ordinary people in the streets" (63). Behn, Woolf suggests, was the first professional woman of letters, and by her example (and those of Winchilsea and Cavendish) middle-class women began to write. They pave the way, Woolf's narrator suggests, for Jane Austen, the Brontës, and George Eliot, anticipating her comments regarding continuing presences: "for masterpieces are not single and solitary births; they are the outcome of many years of thinking in common, of thinking by the body of the people" (65).

Thus, the nineteenth-century section of the British Museum has several shelves of books by women—not the poetry of the seventeenth and eighteenth centuries, but all novels. Woolf's discussion turns to form. Why novels? asks Woolf's narrator. When George Eliot, Emily Brontë, Charlotte Brontë, and Jane Austen have so little in common, what was it about the novel that appealed to all of them? Is it that the interruptions inevitable in the single common sitting room in which these women wrote made the form that required the least concentration—the novel, rather than poetry or a play—the more popular? Is it that the activity particular to that same sitting room, which meant that a woman became trained in observation of character and analysis of emotion, sharpened her eye in a way most appropriate to the novel? The question of why these women wrote novels when they had talent for other literary pursuits ceases to be of import, Woolf's narrator suggests, when one recognizes the quality of the novels these women wrote. Here, she writes, is Austen in about 1800 "writing without hate, without bitterness, without fear, without protest, without preaching" (68). Woolf cites (Colette, too, quotes from the works of others—specifically the *Hamwood Papers* and Francis Carco) a passage from Charlotte Brontë's *Jane Eyre* in which Jane muses about women and freedom but breaks off with "'When thus alone I not unfrequently heard Grace Poole's laugh . . .'" This "jerk," this "indignation" means that Charlotte Brontë, according to Woolf's narrator, "will never get her genius expressed whole and entire. Her books will be deformed and twisted. She will write in a rage where she should write calmly" (69). Woolf's narrator considers Brontë in her own position (as does Colette the Ladies of Llangollen)—what difference might three hundred pounds a year have made? Would it have perhaps provided a greater knowledge of the busy world, towns and regions full of life, more practical experience? Despite the poverty that plagues the lives of these women, Woolf's narrator reminds us of the caliber of the novels they were able to produce: *Middlemarch, Villette, Emma, Wuthering Heights*. Next Woolf's narrator considers whether the sex of the author interferes with the integrity of the novel. In Charlotte Brontë's case, Woolf's narrator contends that it does. Brontë's imagination, she argues, "swerved from indignation and we feel it swerve." The portrait of Rochester is "drawn in the dark": "[w]e feel the influence of fear in it" (73).

Anticipating Colette's assessment of the detrimental effects of a woman's efforts to imitate the man she rejects, Woolf describes the difficulty a woman will face when she writes according to the "patriarchal society," when she "alter[s] her values in deference to the opinion of others" (74). Austen and Brontë, Woolf contends, avoided this compulsion; they "ignored the perpetual admonitions of the eternal pedagogue—write this, think that" (75)—miraculously so, suggests Woolf's narrator, at so early a date. "One must have been something of a firebrand to say to oneself, Oh, but they can't buy literature too. Literature is open to everybody. I refuse to allow you, Beadle though you are, to turn me off the grass" (75–76).

This, however, Woolf's narrator adds, was only half of the problem. The other consisted in the fact that women writers lacked a tradition—"there was no common sentence ready for her use" (76)—the tools provided for her were too scarce and inadequate. Further, the shape of the book "has been made by men out of their own needs for their own uses" (77). Only the novel, Woolf's narrator suggests, is young enough and pliable enough for her use. The future of fiction, women's fiction in particular, is a topic that Woolf's narrator is reluctant to address. However, she does hazard one comment again relating to the physical conditions, the material things, that will affect the shape of women's writing—"women's books should be shorter, more concentrated, than those of men, and framed so that they do not need long hours of steady and uninterrupted work." She suggests a somewhat scientific approach to this question, for, she says, the nerves that feed women's brains differ from those that serve men's brains. Thus one must discover "what treatment suits [women] [. . .] what alternations of work and rest they need." Without these considerations, material considerations, the question of women and fiction has not been fully addressed. She ends this section (echoing/anticipating Colette's claim to at least appear to change the subject) with "[h]appily my thoughts were given another turn" (78).

Chapter 5 finds Woolf's narrator approaching the conclusion of her investigatory journey—she arrives at "the present moment" (*Orlando* 298): "I had come at last, in the course of this rambling, to the shelves which hold books by the living" (79). This chapter again draws Woolf and Colette together. Woolf's description of the work of a fictional contemporary, her comments and questions regarding both style and content, appear to anticipate in a number of ways Colette's fiction. This last set of shelves holds books by both men and women, books of all sorts— women are no longer relegated to the realm of the novel, and the novels they do write do not resemble those that they used to write (79). Woolf's narrator takes down one in particular, the latest, "at the very end of the shelf," "published in this very month of October" (80). Its title, *Life's Adventure*, recalls Colette's *Aventures quotidiennes* of 1924.[39] Woolf's narrator reads it not as Mary Carmichael's first work but as the latest volume in a series of works written by women, a number of whom Woolf has mentioned in the course of her inquiry. What has Carmichael done, asks Woolf's narrator, with the "characteristics and restrictions" inherited from her literary foremothers? Just as Colette is careful in imagining the Ladies of Llangollen one hundred years on in chapter 8 of *Le pur,* so Woolf's narrator approaches this question with some apprehension. Her first strategy is "to get the hang of her sentences," "to [try] a sentence or two on [her] tongue" (80). Carmichael's writing disconcerts Woolf's narrator; it fails to provide her with a firm handhold. However, Woolf's narrator dutifully reads on, recognizing that despite certain irregularities and innovations (perhaps her efforts to counter stereotypes about women's writing), Carmichael succeeds. As Woolf's narrator describes the mechanical swerving and breaking of Carmichael's narrative, so Woolf's own prose swerves from one topic to another, moving from the shape of Carmichael's work—which breaks with order and tradition—to the unconventional subject matter it treats. Before embarking on a description of the book's contents, Woolf's narrator jokingly asks that the doors of the lecture hall be closed and barred—making reference at this point to the presiding judge at the *Well of Loneliness* trial—so new and so potentially inflammatory is Carmichael's writing. Drawing her audience (of women) closer to her in this way, Woolf anticipates the content of Carmichael's work. She cites a first sentence: "'Chloe liked Olivia,'" and then a second: "'They shared a laboratory together'" (82, 83). Woolf's narrator's first reaction is short and to the point. "Sometimes women do like women," she suggests, even though the history of literature would seem to suggest otherwise, and she cites several antipathetic relationships between women, among them that of Cleopatra and Octavia (82). We know women, writes Woolf's narrator, only through the eyes of men, and the women that men (even men like Proust) know are "peculiar," simple beings, usually representative of one extreme or another. In order to better explain her position, Woolf's narrator offers a contrary scenario (one that brings to mind the texts of Colette, such as *Chéri* and *La vagabonde*): "Suppose, for instance," she suggests, "that men were only represented in literature as the lovers of women, and were never the friends of men, soldiers, thinkers, dreamers; how few parts in the plays of Shakespeare could be allotted to them; how literature would suffer!" (83).

The volume of questions that Woolf's narrator asks suggests again her apprehension, the tentative nature of her inquiry regarding the future of women's fiction. What if, Woolf's narrator asks, warming to Mary Carmichael's work by degrees, this new woman writer were to continue writing in this vein? If she had a room of her own and five hundred pounds a year, what might this mean for women? Does Carmichael's work, Woolf's narrator asks, signal a new approach to the representation of women in literature? Has she succeeded in bringing women out of the obscurity to which they have been relegated? Has she succeeded in capturing "those unrecorded gestures, those unsaid or half-said words [. . .]" (84)?[40] If she is to do so, Woolf's narrator contends, she will have to see double, to see differently (anticipating her comments about androgyny):

> [T]o talk of something else, looking steadily out of the window, and thus note, not with a pencil in a notebook, but in the shortest of shorthand, in words that are hardly syllabled yet, what happens when Olivia [. . .] feels the light fall on it [the window?—the referent is unclear here], and sees coming her way a piece of strange food— knowledge, adventure, art. And she reaches out for it, I thought, again raising my eyes from the page, and has to devise some entirely new combination of her resources, so highly developed for other purposes, so as to absorb the new into the old without disturbing the infinitely intricate and elaborate balance of the whole. (85)[41]

At this point, Woolf's narrator stops herself short, thus underscoring the centrality to the work of her last comment (cited here) and reminding herself—lightly ironically here—that she did not want to do what she had recently criticized male writers for doing, that is, "praise [one's] own sex" arbitrarily, to the exclusion of the other (85). However, although she can find nothing to verify her terms "'highly developed'" and "'infinitely intricate'" on the shelves of her library, she looks beyond the books (biographies of men) resting there and envisions woman's role as "stimulus" and as renewer of creative power celebrating her unique relationship with words (86).

As a prelude to a final return to Mary Carmichael and the future of women and fiction, Woolf's narrator contends that this uniqueness should be promoted. Anticipating Colette, she argues that women do not need to write like men, live like men, or look like men, "for if two sexes are quite inadequate, considering the vastness and variety of the world, how should we manage with one only? [. . .] we have too much likeness as it is [. . .]." Woolf wants Carmichael to keep on watching, contemplating, for "[t]here are so many new facts for her to observe" (88). In comments that again anticipate Colette's work (in general), Woolf suggests that Carmichael broaden the scope of women's writing:

> She will not need to limit herself any longer to the respectable houses of the upper middle classes. She will go without kindness or conde-scension, but in the spirit of fellowship into those small, scented rooms where sit the courtesan, the harlot and the lady with the pug dog. There they will sit in their rough and ready-made clothes that the male writer has had perforce to clap upon their shoulders. But Mary Carmichael will have out her scissors and fit them close to every hollow and angle. (88)

Her purview will be the lives of the obscure—those who occupy all of those long streets somewhere south of the river—violet sellers, match sellers, old crones, drifting girls (89), shopgirls (90). Mary Carmichael will learn to laugh at the vanities of the other sex, and her humor, sug-gests Woolf's narrator, will educate.

Again here, Woolf's narrator checks herself; she looks down at the page of Mary Carmichael's book rather than beyond it. Taking us back to the beginning of this chapter, Woolf's writing again mimicking that of Carmichael, Woolf repeats her description of the disruptive nature of Carmichael's writing—things are not to be found in their usual place (91). While Carmichael perhaps lacks the genius of some of her fore-mothers, according to Woolf's narrator, she enjoys a liberty unavailable to those same women writers. Again, Woolf comes remarkably close to a description of Colette's writing:

She had a sensibility that was very wide, eager and free. It responded
to an almost imperceptible touch on it. It feasted like a plant newly
stood in the air on every sight and sound that came its way. It ranged,
too, very subtly and curiously, among almost unknown or unrecorded
things; it lighted on small things and showed that perhaps they were
not small after all. It brought buried things to light and made one
wonder what need there had been to bury them [. . .]. [S]he wrote
as a woman, but as a woman who has forgotten that she is a woman,
so that her pages were full of that curious sexual quality which comes
only when sex is unconscious of itself. (92–93)

Woolf tests Mary Carmichael with "a situation," a challenge to which
she rises quite admirably. Woolf's narrator suggests returning to material things, considering she writes "her first novel in a bed-sitting-room,
without enough of those desirable things, time, money and idleness"
(94).

In the remainder of chapter 4 and in chapters 5, 6, and 7 of *Le pur*,
Colette offers a number of portraits of friendship among women. In her
fourth section, Colette continues her interrogation of her masculine and
feminine sides—her androgyny or hermaphroditism, that which takes
her over the line designating where official sex ends and clandestine sex
begins—with a brief visit to the studio of the painter Boldini (Giovanni
Boldini, 1842–1931). Offended by what Colette later recognizes as his
perceptive casting of her as confused about her sexual status, she leaves
him behind (adjusting the knot of her mannish necktie indignantly as
she goes) to rejoin "a strange company of women who led a marginal
and timorous life, sustained by an out of date form of snobbishness"
(63).[42]

What follows is a description of an older set of lesbians, wealthy and
titled for the most part, who frequented the margins of good society, discreetly veiling their male attire with a second mask, a nondescript cloak.
Like Lady Winchilsea, Margaret of Newcastle, and even George Sand,
George Eliot, and Currer Bell, these women veil their transgressions.
Among these women, Colette focuses on one she names La Chevalière,
a character based on a real-life figure, her lover, the Marquise de Morny.
These are "mannish women" who imitate men—backgammon, bezique
(75/68), darkened rooms, gambling and indolence (77/69), mono-
cles, carnations in buttonholes; they take God's name in vain, discuss
horses competently (80/72), and smoke cigars (83/75). Many have
protégées—one among them refers to hers as her spouse. Many, too,
have a taste for "below-stairs accomplices and comrades-in-livery"

(bringing to mind young Stephen's first love, Collins, in Radclyffe Hall's *The Well of Loneliness*) (70). Salvaging La Chevalière from among them, Colette "[salue] le déclin de ces femmes" (81) ("hail[s] the decline of these women" [73]). She portrays the lot of "a person of uncertain or dissimulated sex" as a poor one: "Anxious and veiled, never exposed to the light of day, the androgynous creature wanders, wonders and implores in a whisper . . ." (76).[43] These women, like Winchilsea, Margaret of Newcastle, and even Behn, are "inquiètes, traquées par leur propre solitude" (86) ("uneasy women, haunted by their own solitude" [77]).

In her fifth section, Colette offers a personal portrait of contemporary poet Renée Vivien (Pauline Tarn), about whom Colette also writes in her *Aventures quotidiennes* (*Œuvres* 3: 136–38). In a gesture characteristic of Colette, sparse reference is made to Vivien's work, with attention focused rather on the life of the poet. Here Colette does as Woolf suggests: breaking with convention, she enters into Vivien's life, into her apartment, and cuts the cloth closely about her shoulders (much of her description of Vivien is physical; the descriptions of Vivien's occupation of space are central to Colette's portrait); she draws Vivien out of the chaos of her setting. Following on from the pessimistic description of the doomed life of the androgyne, Colette offers a dystopic vision of Vivien's existence. The poet is addicted to alcohol, suffers from anorexia, and is dominated by an unseen (and perhaps nonexistent) lover. The claustrophobia of Vivien's apartment, half lit, airless, her windows nailed shut (93), her universe "padlocked" ["son univers cadenassé" (96)], mirrors the oppressive atmosphere of Vivien's existence and the narrowness of her relationships (purely sexual, according to Colette).

Colette's choice of imagery to describe Vivien again brings to mind Woolf's descriptions of Mary Carmichael's writing.[44] Vivien gives things away, necklaces and bracelets, like a tree shedding its leaves ("elle semblait s'effeuiller" [91]); the laughing countenance of Vivien saddens Colette, as does that of blind children who laugh and play with agility without the security of light; this tall young girl empties her glass with the nonchalance of a bridesmaid at a country wedding (91).

Colette opens chapter 6 with a description of a rakish lesbian, Lucienne de . . . (an assumed name, Colette tells us), as recounted to her by an old actress acquaintance, Amalia X. (The distancing of Lucienne de . . . , her story mediated by Amalia X, the teller of the story, pushes her back in time.) Lucienne's photograph, Colette's only firsthand knowledge of this woman, shows her in a man's suit, its traces of feminine taste (lapels too wide, the wrong shoes) alone betraying the incongruous

body contained within it—an incongruity matched by the false signature on the photograph. "One feels that a feminine imagination, imprisoned beneath the bared forehead of a spurious man, regrets having been
unable to let itself go in jabots, ribbons, silky fabrics" (100).[45] Why did
a woman, asks Colette, whose mission was to rival and defraud men, try
so hard to look like one? Colette's narrator's subsequent turn in this section to the character with whom she began the section, Amalia X, who
is now poised over a set of tarot cards (reading her own future), suggests
a step forward or a step closer to the narrator. Amalia, while she covets
the possibility of the illusion that she was once "the equal of a young
man," denies that she ever had had to or had wanted to stop being a
woman. Anticipating the Ladies, she asserts that "'when a woman
remains a woman, she is a complete human being'" (102).[46] Having finished her questioning of Amalia, the narrator writes, "j'allais plus loin
. . ." (118) ("I pursued the subject further" [108]).

Colette's celebration of the calm and consistency of the union of the
Ladies of Llangollen parallels Woolf's celebration in *A Room* of the
work of Mary Carmichael, of a woman writing as herself. The utopic
relationship of Lady Eleanor and Lady Sarah contrasts with the dystopic
atmosphere of Renée Vivien's life, mirrored in her oppressive prison of
a dining room, the scents and tastes and wealth of which nauseate
Colette's narrator, and the destructive disjunction of Lucienne's feminine body and masculine mask. Colette's narrator celebrates the bond
that is possible between two beings, the sameness of whose bodies defies
separation—"the pudicity that separates two lovers during the hours of
repose, of ablutions, of illness never insinuates itself between two twin
bodies that have similar afflictions, are subject to the same cares, the
same predictable periods of chastity . . ." (111).[47] She contrasts the
union of the Ladies with the conquests of Renée Vivien, whose dis-
traught cynicism denied her the possibility of a bond based on anything
other than sensuality (here providing a parallel for Woolf's contrasting
of those women who wrote with anger and those without). Colette
claims that what ties two women together is kinship ("parenté"), similarity ("similitude," "l'étroite ressemblance"), not passion. A woman,
she writes, "se complaît dans la certitude de caresser un corps dont elle
connaît les secrets" (121) ("finds pleasure in caressing a body whose
secrets she knows" [111])—a recognition of herself as herself. Why,
Colette suggests readers will ask, is the feverish pleasure of the senses
absent from a chapter "où passent et repassent, liées par paires, des
femmes" (122) ("where women pass and pass again, two by two"
[112–13]). Sapphic libertinage, she replies, is the only unacceptable

one. The sensuality among women is an unresolved and an undemand-
ing one. This, she claims, is what makes the half-century-long alliance of
the Ladies possible.

"Think of things in themselves"

In the concluding chapter of *A Room* (anticipating an autobiographical
turn in Colette's *Le pur* in section 8) Woolf dispenses with her narrator
in order to end "in my own person" (105). This turn emphasizes, while
seeming to observe it, the arbitrary nature of the line dividing fiction
and reality. Woolf anticipates objections to her approach to the question
at hand. She has not weighed the comparative merits of male and female
writing, her detractors will say, a project that she dismisses as of no
value: "[p]raise and blame alike mean nothing" (106). She has placed
too much emphasis on material things. This second objection she counters with a quote from Sir Arthur Quiller-Couch, editor of the *Oxford
Book of English Verse* (1900), who, reviewing the opportunities available
to "'great poetical names'" like Coleridge, Wordsworth, and so on, concludes that "'the poor poet has not in these days, nor has had for two
hundred years, a dog's chance'" (107). "Intellectual freedom," Woolf
sums up, "depends upon material things," hence her "stress on money
and a room of one's own" (108). A third question foreseen by Woolf
concerns the importance of a woman's voice in the field of literature.
Why, if it is so much trouble, do women need to write? Woolf's motives
for encouraging them to do so, she suggests, "are partly selfish" (108).
She wants variety in what she reads, and she encourages her audience to
write all kinds of different things, "books of travel and adventure,"
"research and scholarship," "history and biography," "criticism and philosophy and science," not just fiction (109).

   While contemplating her motives for encouraging her audience to
write, Woolf turns to a discussion of reality, which she defines as "very
erratic, very undependable." It is the business of the writer, she asserts,
to find this reality "and collect it and communicate it to the rest of us."
Great books, she suggests, in doing this cause one to "[see] more
intensely afterwards"; they "perform a curious couching operation on
the senses" (110). If women can earn money, have a room of their own,
live in the presence of this reality, whether they impart it or not, Woolf
will be satisfied.

   Woolf ends with a modest proposal. Don't dream about influencing
others, she says; rather, "[t]hink of things in themselves" (111). She

repeats her assertion that women are hard on women, and she tries to find something disagreeable to end on—but nothing will come. Instead she says: "I often like women. I like their unconventionality. I like their subtlety. I like their anonymity. I like—but I must not run on in this way" (111). Her last "I like" is broken by a dash, denoting the silence in her work around questions of homosexuality, suggested here by her second covert reference to the *Well of Loneliness* trial (to Bodkin). Her closing words are challenging: "you are, in my opinion, disgracefully ignorant [. . .] What is your excuse?" (112). Yes, she admits ironically, child rearing has taken up some of women's time, but the right to vote, to education, to own property are all theirs now. Use them!

In order to reinforce this last point, in her closing paragraph Woolf reverts appropriately to the realm of fiction, to the story of Shakespeare's sister. She repeats the unfortunate circumstances of Judith's early demise, her burial at the crossroads "where the omnibuses now stop, opposite the Elephant and Castle," this location emphasizing her centrality and her proximity (113). However, Woolf contends, this poet lives on; she is a "continuing presence" in the speaker and the audience, the narrator and the reader. And if Woolf's audience has the courage to stand up, or rather sit down, and write, Judith Shakespeare, according to Woolf, "will put on the body which she has so often laid down" (114).

In an Orlandoesque moment at the beginning of her penultimate chapter, Colette, like Woolf in closing, moves speedily to the present day, envisioning the Ladies of Llangollen one hundred years on. Like Woolf, Colette is tentative in her approach to the question of the future of women and of women in fiction. Can we possibly, she asks, echoing Woolf, imagine "*sans appréhension*" ("*without apprehension*") "deux Dames de Llangollen de 1930?" (my emphasis; 142) ("two ladies of Llangollen in this year of 1930?" [130]). Colette builds a picture: short hair, a car, dungarees, cigarettes, a liquor bar in their apartment. Would Sarah, she goes on to ask, still know how to remain silent? Perhaps, she says, "les mots croisés aidant" (142) ("with the aid of crosswords" [131]). Eleanor Butler curses as she jacks up her car and has her breasts amputated. She no longer greets the village blacksmith, but she chats informally with the garage man, armed, thanks to Marcel Proust, with scandalous appetites and habits and a vocabulary to match (142–43). But Proust is wrong to characterize her in this way, contends Colette, in so doing setting herself up to write in opposition to him. While, like Woolf, she considers Proust a great writer, again like Woolf, she questions his knowledge of women. Colette recognizes Proust's unsurpassed skills as a guide through Sodom, but asserts that Gomorrah, as Proust envisions it, peopled by "insondables et vicieuses jeunes filles" (143) ("inscrutable and depraved young girls" [131]), does not exist. She characterizes Proust's vision of the origin of female homosexuality— puberty, boarding school, solitude, prisons, aberrations, snobbishness— as a foundation too weak to support something so powerful ("un vice nombreux, bien assis, et sa solidarité indispensable" [143]).

In this chapter, Colette turns, as does Woolf, to the material circumstances of writing. She describes her days as a ghostwriter in Willy's atelier accompanied by her mostly homosexual colleagues. Whereas Woolf looks to her female audience, Colette looks to her male colleagues: "I was faithful to their concept of me as a nice piece of furniture and I listened to them as if I were an expert" (138).[48] Colette finds reality, collects it and communicates it, as Woolf suggests in *A Room* (110). Her descriptions of her homosexual colleagues (many of them English; see note 8) are sympathetic and laudatory—hers a privilege to witness and participate in this scene she names "pure" (161/148), usually inaccessible to the female sex. Her stories depict a utopian society (one that she dates as turn-of-the-century)—an interesting contrast to her earlier description of Sapphic women. Colette's gay men (contrary, she suggests, to popular belief) are dignified, well educated: "A kind of austerity overlaid it which I can compare to no other, for it held nothing of parade or precaution, nor did it spring from the morbid fear that galvanizes more often than it checks so many among those hounded by society" (147).[49] These men—who Colette affectionately calls "monsters"— shielded her, shared in her fear and her grief, and demonstrated with their paradoxical normalcy the abnormality of the situation in which Colette found herself, we presume, with respect to her first husband, Willy.

Colette ends this penultimate section with a vignette describing an old friend, a Spaniard called Pepe, who sought out young workmen on the Paris streets. Pepe's poetic imagination, suggests Colette, could not be matched: "No one has ever talked to me as he did of the color blue or of golden hair curling like shavings around a reddened ear" (150).[50] Pepe's is a story of disappointment in masquerade. Having been prompted by a beautiful young man to follow him home—the delicious fear that Pepe experiences (he may kill me, but what better way to die is there?) is shattered when the young man emerges in a woman's chemise, pompom roses in his hair—an image that pursues Pepe to his death at his own hand.

In the final section of *Le pur,* Colette continues (providing a bridge, or so it appears) on the subject of her homosexual coworkers and her own literary apprenticeship. So adept are they (and here she is unclear who) at the art of dissimulating (recalling the focus of her work introduced via Charlotte in the first two sections of the book), she suggests, that "tout semble imparfait" (168) ("everything else seems imperfect" [155].[51] Her first story here is about the revenge a homosexual man takes on a gossiping woman who has revealed his relationship: he finds a female lover for her husband. Colette confesses what she learned from these friends—how to dissimulate and how to recognize dissimulation in others. Insight, Colette claims, gave her an edge—the ability to do harm, to take from those who trusted her. Softened by contact with children and animals, Colette says she is nevertheless still "de taille à gaspiller, comme à piller" (172–73) ("strong enough to be lavish with my gifts as well as to plunder the riches of others" [160]). Her pleasure is to give and take, play the robber one minute and the spendthrift the next, a pleasure only possible when in combat with an equal. Among these is D . . . , a Polynesian painter engraver (his name recalls Woolf's introduction of Mr. A and Mr. B in her last chapter). D . . . , like Colette, and others of their kind, keep a distance from each other, never daring to admit that they need one another. Colette recounts an elaborate (fabricated?) apology made by D . . . , who had failed to honor a dinner engagement. Her narrative then takes a sudden turn. Bored by the likes of D . . . and D . . . 's pretense, Colette waxes nostalgic about love: "Arrange for me, in the last third of my life, a clear space where I can put my favorite crudity, love. Merely to have it before me and to breathe it in, merely to touch it with hand or tooth, it keeps me young" (164).[52] She interrogates her own relationship with love and, nestled at love's side "comme un œillet noir" (177) ("like a dark carnation" [164]), jealousy. She recalls her grandmother's lifelong suspicion of love, one from which she, too, suffered as a young woman. She suggests the creative breadth of the mind of a woman spurned, the sharpening of her faculties that results from a challenger in love. Jealousy, she writes, is "a kind of gymnast's purgatory, where the senses are trained, one by one" (166);[53] "[c]hecked, then released briefly like an elastic band, it almost has the virtue of an exercising apparatus" (167).[54] She also recalls, however, the destructive nature of such a passion, which when acted upon provides little joy. In a comical moment, Colette thinks back to her own feud with a rival, whom she calls Madame X. Neglecting her side of the bargain, failing to respond in kind to the curses aimed in her direction, busy with writing, Colette was brought down by her rival: she fell in a ditch, caught bronchitis, lost part of a manuscript, and was cheated by a cab driver. This is an antagonism that, Colette claims, did not last in any real form:

"I have ceased," she writes, "to exchange, shall never more exchange because of a man and through a man that menacing thought" (171).[55]

Colette's narrator ends *Le pur* with a discussion of the feasibility, or lack thereof, in her opinion, of sexual permissiveness and of a relationship involving three people. Laughable, she suggests, is the belief that sexual permissiveness can work. It is passionless, "lukewarm"; "on respire un air fade de fausse famille" (187) ("[it] reminds one of the stuffiness of a closed room" [173])—the spatial figure of the translation here taking us back to *A Room*. The *ménage à trois,* sanctified in literature as "'harmonie ternaire de l'amour'" (187) ("'the eternal triangle'" [173]), she adds, is equally unworkable—and often the worst hit is the man who orchestrates it, a result of the fact, she suggests, that "women pair off," frequently in secret (174). They form a union that is impenetrable. Again using an example, Colette describes the reaction of one woman at the death of her rival, her lover's lover. In contrast, suggests Colette, to the Ladies of Llangollen, whose "voies célestes" ("celestial ways") were not known to these other women, these two women—perhaps like Woolf and Colette—kept their union secret, a pure union, which the women come to conceive of as disconnected from the man via whom their bond was formed. The characterization of this relationship as "pur" (188) ("pure" [174]) provides closure, although not finality, to Colette's work. For Colette, the word has no boundaries: she takes the word apart, the plaintive "u," "l'r de glace limpide" (188–89) ("the icy limpidity of the 'r'" [174–75]). While the sound provides no "intelligible meaning" to her (it is without limits), she longs to hear it again and to drink it down deeply, revel in its expansiveness and possibility. In this way, Colette's conclusion echoes Woolf's call to women to venture out and to work together.

Conclusion: Ces Deux Opiniâtres Amies

Reading *A Room* and *Le pur* together suggests a reciprocity or dialogue between the two writers. Colette's *Le pur* functions as a sequel to *A Room,* one that Woolf projected but never undertook. Mimicking its treatment of the story of the Ladies of Llangollen, *Le pur* liberates and builds on *A Room,* as it puts into practice that which is prescribed by the earlier text. However, while *Le pur* follows Woolf's *A Room,* it also runs counter to it; its contents run up against *A Room,* away from it. *Le pur* and *A Room* thus sit side by side like two "opinionated friends" in conversation, like Lady Sarah and Lady Eleanor, Chloe and Olivia, Colette and Charlotte, Mary Beton and Mary Seton, Moreno and Colette, the female students of Woolf's audience, Woolf and Colette.

The deconstruction of the word "pur" in Colette's last paragraph takes us back to the opening page of Woolf's *A Room* and her (tongue-in-cheek) suggestion that it is the "pure oil of truth" she seeks. Colette's sounding out of the letters that make up "pur" remind us of Woolf's distillation of her advice to her audience to "think of things in themselves." Each closing suggests an openness to the other. In this way, Woolf's text provides a key to Colette's and Colette's to Woolf's, one that I explore further, in terms of spatial form and women's writing, in the next chapter.

3

In Pursuit of Woolf's 'Woman's Sentence' in Colette's *La vagabonde, Duo,* and *Le toutounier*

VIRGINIA WOOLF gave careful consideration to the spatial form of the text.[1] Her diaries, letters, and notebooks are full of musings about how she might change the shape of the text to alter the texture of the work. Perhaps the most striking example is her diagram of the structure of *To the Lighthouse* (figure 11). The two boxes resemble two rooms, linked by a narrow passageway that represents the middle "Time Passes" section of the tripartite novel.

Just prior to the completion of *Mrs Dalloway*, Woolf uses another spatial image to describe her writing. She writes of her attempts to create a novel that is tiered, ending on three notes, narrated, she suggests, from three different points on the staircase. Her aim is to retain the quality of a sketch in her writing, even when in finished form, and, in so doing, to undo the univocal quality and finality of a conclusion to her novel. Here the ellipsis of the fragmentary response ("Peter, Richard, Sally Seton perhaps . . .") figures the possibility of this refusal:

> It is to be a most complicated spirited solid piece, knitting together everything & ending on three notes, at different stages of the staircase, each saying something to sum up Clarissa. Who shall say these things? Peter, Richard, & Sally Seton perhaps [. . .] Suppose one can keep the quality of a sketch in a finished & composed work? That is my endeavor. (*Diary* 2: 312)

And, in a letter to her friend Jacques Raverat, the French painter, again in reference to *Mrs Dalloway*, Woolf points to the ties between the

Figure 11
Woolf's diagram depicting the structure of To the Lighthouse.

novel, traditionally deemed a temporal art, and painting, its spatial counterpart. The novel, she suggests, is not motivated simply by a central, linear narrative strain, but instead, like a painting, it is textured, layered, spacious, "all over the place" at once:

> In fact I rather think that you've broached some of the problems of the writer's too, who are trying to catch and consolidate and consummate (whatever the word is for making literature) those splashes of yours; for the falsity of the past (by which I mean Bennett, Galsworthy and so on) is precisely I think that they adhere to a formal railway line of sentence, for its convenience, never reflecting that people don't and never did feel or think or dream for a second in that way; but all over the place, in your way. (*Letters* 3: 135–36)[2]

Woolf interrogates questions of gender and sexual difference via a questioning of space. Supporting this contention is the recurrent appearance across the length of her opus of the figure of a woman entering or exiting a room. In each case, this figure is tied up with questions of women and writing, women and a pursuit of form. Thus, we recall Mary Carmichael of *A Room of One's Own,* unshaken by the chorus of chiding voices, of bishops, deans, professors, and patriarchs, entering a different room without hesitation, her intrusion tied to a new form of women's writing (see chapter 2). In *To the Lighthouse,* the line dividing Mrs Ramsay's inner life from her outer life, the poetic from the domestic, is figured in terms of her frequent crossing or occupation of a threshold "coming into the room" (117), leaving a room (111), and sitting in the window "which opened on the terrace" (15).[3] And early in Woolf's last novel, *Between the Acts,* Isa Oliver, the poet who disguises her work as an accounts book, by entering unexpectedly, breaks the threshold of her father-in-law's library (18).

In much the same way, Colette uses the concept of space, both physical and textual, in her novels to raise questions about where a woman
stands in relation to the literary tradition in which she writes. The pursuit of form, one appropriate to the woman writer, is couched in her
work in terms of a pursuit of space. Representations of physical spaces—
gardens, houses, rooms—are used to illustrate not only the constraints
to which women were subject but also the confining, male nature of
conventional literary form and the potential for breaking free of those
confines. At the same time, textual space, that is, punctuation, grammatical structures, and typographical arrangement of phrases on the
page, shows the closed nature of traditional prose and the possibility for
it to be opened up. These reconceptualizations of literary space function
together in Colette's writing to critique and recast inherited forms.

There is a suggestion in Colette's work of how form might be
"adapted to the body" (78), as Woolf describes it in *A Room of One's
Own,* and of how the woman writer might create a sentence "ready for
her use" (76). In *A Room,* Woolf bemoans the inadequacy of the language and form of the nineteenth-century novel to properly accommodate women's voices. "Perhaps the first thing she would find, setting
pen to paper," writes Woolf, "was that there was no common sentence
ready for her use" (76). Traditional form constitutes a "clumsy weapon
in her hands," according to Woolf (77). In response she advocates for a
woman's sentence, one that would better accommodate the specificities
of a woman's life: "women's books should be shorter, more concentrated, than those of men, and framed so that they do not need long
hours of steady or uninterrupted work" (78). This other sentence, as
Woolf envisions it, is shaped according to the different physical and
mental spaces occupied by women, the "different order and system of
life" within which women operate (86). Indeed, Woolf expresses her
notion of what is specific to women in writing in terms of space:

> One goes into the room—but the resources of the English language
> would be much put to the stretch, and whole flights of words would
> need to wing their way illegitimately into existence before a woman
> could say what happens when she goes into a room. The rooms dif-
> fer so completely; they are calm or thunderous; open on to the sea,
> or, on the contrary, give on to a prison yard; are hung with washing;
> or alive with opals and silks; are hard as horsehair or soft as feathers—
> one has only to go into any room in any street for the whole of that
> extremely complex force of femininity to fly in one's face. How
> should it be otherwise? For women have sat indoors all these millions

of years, so that by this time the very walls are permeated by their creative force, which has, indeed, so overcharged the capacity of bricks
and mortar that it must needs harness itself to pens and brushes and
business and politics. (87)

Taking my cue from Woolf's emphasis on space, a number of different questions shape my reading of Colette's work. How does Colette
use the space of the text to develop a more open and accessible style?
How does the stylistic change make room for different voices, women's
voices, in her novels? What makes space, as a principle, so fertile a place
from which to launch an inquiry into women's writing? Why is a continual questioning rather than a resolution of the problem of space preferred
by the female imagination? And lastly, in what sense does Colette's work
provide a response to Woolf's call for a woman's sentence?[4]

Woolf knew Colette's work. She read several of Colette's novels and
was at once fascinated and mystified by her French contemporary. Writing to her friend Ethel Smyth, Woolf expresses her admiration for what
she calls elsewhere, in reference to Colette's novel *Sido*, "a shape I
haven't grasped," "a new combination" (*Letters* 6: 301):

> I'm almost floored by the extreme dexterity insight and beauty of
> Colette. How does she do it? No one in all England could do a thing
> like that. If a copy is ever going I should like to have one—to read it
> again. and see how it's done: or guess. And to think I scarcely know
> her books! Are they all novels? Is it the great French tradition that lifts
> her so serenely, and yet with such a flare down, down to what she's
> saying? I'm green with envy. (*Letters* 6: 49)

In Colette's work Woolf finds a fluidity of form that she has not
encountered before. In 1939, on reading Colette's *Duo,* Woolf writes:
"And I'm reading Colette, 'Duo' [1934]; all about love; and rather too
slangy for my vocabulary, but what a born writer! how she walzes [*sic*]
through the dictionary" (June 18, 1939; *Letters* 6: 341).[5] Woolf marvels
at the wealth of Colette's vocabulary and the apparent ease with which
she makes her way through the dictionary, comparing Colette's writing
to a dance. This choice of metaphor fittingly anticipates the unraveling
of a closed system that I argue is characteristic of Colette's writing. The
turning movement of the waltz, a simultaneous progression and rota-
tion, suggests a dance through the dictionary, a continual uprooting and
overturning of words, an irreverent play with words—to waltz around
an issue is also to skirt it, to refuse to take up a single perspective on that

issue. Like the dancer, Colette's writing, thematically and stylistically, wrestles with an imperative to keep time, to keep up with traditional narrative form.[6]

In order to explore further this notion of linguistic mobility that so intrigued Woolf, I will turn first to Colette's *La maison de Claudine,* published in 1922. This experimental semi-autobiographical novel will function here as a spatial poetics of sorts, as an exploration and partial exposition of the "new combination" to which Woolf refers. In this novel Colette describes the child narrator's experimentation with words and with form. In this novel, which opens and closes on a question of space, the child's play at the parameters of language is bound up with an exploration of the limits of personal space, in the family home and about its borders. The first fragment is entitled "Où sont les enfants?" (9) ("Where are the children?"[7]), an interrogative repeated several times in this opening piece; in the last piece the mother asks her daughter, "Mais où étais-tu?" (158) ("But where were you?" [114]). Within this progression from being one of the children to being absent and alone, and from the present to the past, "where are the children?" becomes "where were [singular] you?" and suggests a step forward in the child's relationship to language across the length of the text.

The work is composed of fragments (thirty-five in all), like beads in a necklace, shiny items in the magpie's nest (30), or objects found in a pocket (157–59), which relate a series of loosely related events from the narrator's childhood. Each piece turns around a word or phrase, often that of the title of that particular episode. In each case the narrator approaches her finding from a number of different angles, builds on it, picks it up, and takes it out of context. The narrator dances around the word—a name or nickname, a phrase or word overheard: "'Mode de Paris'" ("'The Rage of Paris'"), "La 'Merveille'" ("The 'Marvel'"), or a pair of words, one of which is often the mother: "Ma mère et les livres" ("My Mother and the Books"), "Ma mère et le curé" ("My Mother and the Curé"), and so on. As the titles indicate, it is often the mother who provides the child narrator with words.

In the seventh episode, "Ma mère et les livres," the narrator describes the family library, "cette pièce maçonnée de livres" (31) ("those walls faced with books" [27]), and indeed the title suggests that the mother rules in this domain, as her "logis natal" (33) ("my home" [29]). The narrator remembers how she used to make a home for herself amidst the volumes of the Larousse, an encyclopedic dictionary: "I would curl up into a ball, like a dog in its kennel, between two volumes of Larousse" (27).[7] The shelves lining the walls contain the great names of the French and English tradition—"Musset, Voltaire and the Gospels gleamed in their leaf-brown sheepskin. Littré, Larousse and Becquerel displayed bulging backs like black tortoises [. . .] d'Orbigny [. . .] Camille Flammarion [. . .] Elisée Reclus, Voltaire in marbled boards, Balzac in black, and Shakespeare in olive-green" (27).[8] These books provide the young narrator with a landscape (note the colors—greens, browns, blacks) from within which she seeks her own form of expression, hidden like the pattern in a colored carpet: "Beautiful books that I used to read, beautiful books that I left unread, warm covering of the walls of my home, variegated tapestry whose hidden design rejoiced my initiated eyes" (29).[9] The narrator characterizes her first experiences with reading, and by extension writing (she builds a word), as a movement around the periphery of the book, of tradition, of the space of the library. Rather than immerse herself in her own French tradition, embodied by her mother's library, she works at its borders, exploring the relationships between the volumes of the dictionary and the resonances (smells, tastes, textures, etc.) that develop around them. What draws the narrator to these volumes is as much that which lies on the outside, their texture, color, and smell, as that which lies within their pages.

> Perhaps those most hermetically sealed were the dearest. I have long forgotten the name of the author of a scarlet-clad encyclopedia, but the alphabetical references marked upon each volume have remained for me an indelible and magic word: Aphbicécladiggalhymaroid-phorebstevanzy. (28)[10]

Following the chain of letters inscribed on the spines of the encyclopedia, the narrator rearranges the alphabet and creates a new vocabulary, a new combination. She dances her fingers back and forth across the spines of the books as across a keyboard (recalling Woolf's characterization of Colette's waltzing through the dictionary): "I never took a lamp when I went at night to choose one, it was enough to feel my way, as though on the keyboard of a piano, along the shelves" (27).[11] This suggests a conception of writing and reading as the creation of new combinations from a set of keys or terms. Letter is piled upon letter to create a word without specific referent (a set of empty syllables), but one that is transformative and magical.[12]

In "Le curé sur le mur" ("The Priest on the Wall"), a word is rifled by the narrator. This fragment, the sixth of Colette's *La maison de Claudine,* turns around the question of naming. The piece opens onto an exchange between the narrator (the mother) and her daughter,

Bel-Gazou, a name derived from the *patois, beau gazouillis,* which means *beau langage* ("beautiful language"), a name first given to the narrator herself, by her father. The mother's intrusive inquiry with which this piece begins, "A quoi penses-tu, Bel-Gazou?" (28) ("What are you thinking about, Bel-Gazou?" [24]) is immediately shut down by the child, who builds a wall of words impenetrable to her mother tongue: "A rien, maman" (28) ("Nothing, mother" [24]). The mother is put back in her place. The narrator recognizes her daughter's right to refuse to admit (to) her mother, staging it in terms of space, a common place: "tout temple est sacré" (28) ("All temples are sacred" [24]).

Having achieved literally nothing, recognizing the folly of her attempted infraction, the narrator steps back to a moment in her own past. She reconstructs her own wall of words, the wall of the fragment's title, figuring it as a liminal space, a slice of solid ground, all her own, where she is afforded the freedom to be herself, "[être] devant elle-même" (29) ("[to appear] to herself" [24]), a possibility that is figured spatially. The difference between one and oneself, self and other, suggested by this phrase, figures the capacity of language to take one elsewhere.

This wall, the paved surface of which serves as both *piste* ("promenade") and *terrasse* ("terrace"), draws a line that separates *le jardin* ("the garden" with flowers and fruit) from *la basse-cour* ("the farmyard"). Here, the narrator first divests the title *Curé* of its sacred quality and takes it for herself. She doubles it, transforming it, making of it not only a noun but an adjective, connoting a physical state:

> At her age—not quite eight years old—I was a priest on the wall, the thick wall that divided the garden from the farmyard, and of which the flat tiled summit, broad as a pavement, served me as a promenade and terrace, inaccessible to the ordinary run of mortals. Yes, I mean it; a priest on a wall. Why should it seem incredible? I was a priest without religious duties or parish, without any irreverent travesty, but nonetheless, unknown to all, a priest. A priest just as you, sir, happen to be bald, or you, madam, arthritic. (24–25)[13]

It is to this wall that the narrator takes the word "presbytère," which is let slip by an anonymous source, unaware of its potential. Falling on her sensitive ear, it wreaks havoc, "des ravages" (29). Instead of seeking clarification from her parents in the form of a definition, the narrator picks up the word and runs with it, taking it to her wall.

Far from me the idea of asking one of my relations: "What kind of a thing is a presbytery?" I had absorbed the mysterious word with its harsh and spiky beginning and the [protracted and dreamlike final syllable]. Enriched by a secret and a doubt, I slept with the *word* and bore it off to my wall. (25)[14]

The narrator explores the shape and surface, and the sound, of the word. She imagines its first letters embroidered with a harsh, spiky relief, its last syllable protracted and dreamlike. She finds, unwittingly, that her ignorance of its contents (meaning)—which are indeed sacred, it is *le curé*, the priest—opens the door to a wealth of possibility. Her choice of alternatives takes her into two different areas that are perhaps most at odds with the sacred referent. She makes of the word first a curse, then a scientific designation for a type of snail.

"Presbytery!" I would shout it over the roof of the henhouse and Miton's garden, towards the perpetually misty horizons of Moutiers. From the summit of my wall, the word rang out as a malediction: "Begone! You are all presbyteries!" I shouted to invisible outlaws. Later on the word lost some of its venom and I began to suspect that "presbytery" might very possibly be the scientific term for a certain little yellow-and-black striped snail. (25)[15]

The ellipsis with which this citation ends in the French, one in a series at this juncture in the fragment, leaves open, although only for a time, the excursus of the narrator. This break can be found again in the closing chapter of the book, "La noisette creuse" ("The Hollow Nut"), as the narrator crushes three shells that she finds in her pocket—"She admires the mother-of-pearl petals, then drops them and crushes them under her espadrille" (113).[16] Here it marks the momentary fracturing ("l'effraction"—house breaking, breaking and entering) of a certain possibility, of an accommodation. At the same time, it deepens the divide separating child and adult, a certain freedom in not knowing from the constraint that results from knowing too much: "What becomes in later life of that tremendous determination not to know, that quiet strength expended on avoidance and rejection?" (28).[17] The narrator, as child, is forced "to learn" that a "presbytère" is in fact "la maison du curé," "the priest's house"; she is enjoined "to call things by their name." "I still tried to react . . . I fought against the intrusion, closely hugging the tatters of my absurdity. I longed to compel Monsieur

Millot, during my pleasure, to inhabit the empty shell of the little 'presbytery' snail . . ." (26).[18] Momentarily forced back from her "voyage
out," her extravagance, onto the straight and narrow, the road home, an
injunction accompanied by another to close her mouth and breathe
through her nose, the narrator crushes her snail shell, her once "presbytère." However, undaunted by the obstacle of the dictionary definition that suddenly looms before her, she does not dispense with the
word completely but instead compromises, finally pulling it back up to
the surface, taking the "beautiful word" back to her narrow terrace.
This space she in turn baptizes "Presbytère" and here designates herself
"the priest on the wall," hence the title of the fragment. Frustrated in
her attempts to force the priest to inhabit the snail's shell, to subordi-
nate the content to her form, she instead elects to inhabit the presbytery
herself. The wall, a passage of writing of sorts, with its wide, paved surface, like a page, contrasts with the closed *maison de curé*, suggesting a
preference for remaining on the move, out in the open.

The style and form of *La maison de Claudine* itself mirrors the
experimentation suggested in these episodes. The fragmented text
incorporates diverse genres and themes—ghost stories, journalistic
pieces, and reminiscences cover topics ranging from politics ("Propa-
gande" ["Propaganda"]) to religion ("Ma mère et le curé" ["My Mother and the Curé"]), death ("Epitaphes" ["Epitaphs"]), birth ("Mater-
nité" ["Maternity"]), and marriage ("L'enlèvement" ["The
Abduction"]). Verbs and adjectives are piled one on top of the other in
snakelike sentences that extend from one end of the paragraph to the
other ("Musset, Voltaire, et Les Quatre Évangiles brillaient sous la
basane feuille-morte. Littré, Larousse et Becquerel bombaient des dos
de tortues noires [. . .] D'Orbigny [. . .] Camille Flammarion [. . .]
Élisée Reclus, Voltaire jaspés, Balzac noir et Shakespeare olive . . ."
[31]). Verbs are exchanged one for the other ("Des romans bourraient
les coussins, enflaient la corbeille à ouvrage, fondaient au jardin, oubliés
sous la pluie" [69] ["Novels were stuffed among the cushions, wedged
into the work-basket, or languished forgotten in the garden, soaked by
the rain" (59)]). Metaphors predominate. Attention to detail gives texture to Colette's writing, adding smell, color, taste, and body. Syntactic
elements, such as the dash and the ellipsis (frequent, for example, in the
section "L'enlèvement," which is not discussed here), depict typo-
graphically notions of escape and of infraction in the work.

What results is a dictionary or encyclopedia of sorts, in several volumes. This is not a book, however, that might be found by the narrator
of *La maison de Claudine* on the shelves of her mother's library, her

"logis natal," among the great masters. Instead it is a decoder that will enable both Colette's stepson, Bertrand, for whom this piece was originally written (Jouve, *Colette* 114), and the reader to navigate a route through Colette's work, and in so doing gain access to another language, a different form, a form that is being developed in terms of space: Claudine's/Colette's house.[19] Here *La maison de Claudine* provides us with a map with which to approach or a key with which to open Colette's work.

One of Colette's best-known novels, *La vagabonde,* and a lesser-known pair of novels, *Duo* and *Le toutounier,* explore the relationship between space and writing in a more conventional literary form. I examine these novels in terms of the spatial poetics I have identified in *La maison de Claudine.* In the first novel, *La vagabonde* (1910), the protagonist Renée Néré, a music-hall performer, returns to writing as she rejects the home of a husband in favor of work and the road and as she regains her own room. The childhood home of the husband represents in Colette's work a place inhospitable to the (potential) wife in novels such as *La chatte, Duo,* and *La vagabonde.* In the second, a novel in two parts, *Duo* (1933) and *Le toutounier* (1939), Alice writes her way out of a stifling marriage, embodied in *Duo* by the provincial home of her husband, and back into the linguistically rich home of her childhood. In these works Claudine's/Colette's own family home (at Saint-Sauveur-en-Puisaye) is reworked. We are no longer at Claudine's house per se but in Renée's apartment (*La vagabonde*) or at the home of Alice and her sisters (*Le toutounier*), the home of the narrator now grown, a home of her/their own. While none of the novels are epistolary fictions in the conventional sense, in each case the letter is a form central to the novel. The centrality of this form of a writing that travels, I will argue, underscores the importance of space and writing to Colette's work.

In *La vagabonde* letters are embedded within a first-person narrative. The protagonist of *La vagabonde,* Renée Néré, is a woman of letters and a writer of letters, one who has taken a wrong turn, turned out badly, one who does not write: "A woman of letters who has turned out badly: that is what I must remain for everyone, I who no longer write, who deny myself the pleasure, the luxury of writing" (126).[20] As the name of the protagonist suggests, this text is about a renewal: *renée* means "reborn" in the feminine. However, it is the rebirth of an errant (*néré-erré*), echoed semantically by the title of the work, which is being celebrated here. The collapsing of the first name of the protagonist onto the last (almost its anagrammatic double) suggests an ambivalence and at once the inextricability of these two names that marriage would separate. It also recalls the name of the author: Colette (Sidonie Gabrielle Colette) adopted her last name as her first at the beginning of her writing career, on the advice of Willy.

Colette's *La vagabonde* turns (the verb *tourner*, "to turn," recurs across the length of the work) around Renée Néré's decision either to forego the freedom she has gained having finally left her first husband, by letting herself fall in love and set up home with Max Dufferein-Chautel, or to remain alone. Initially Renée rejects this either/or proposition, exclaiming to her friend Hamond:

> You want me to act like everyone else? To make up my mind? Him or someone else, what's it matter! You want to upset my newly-discovered peace, to make me exchange the keen, invigorating, natural care of earning my living for a care of a different kind? Or perhaps you're advising me to take a lover for health reasons, as a blood-purifier? But what for? I'm in good health and, thank God, I love no one, no one, and never again will I love anyone, anyone, anyone!" (190)[21]

The refusal of the female protagonist to remarry and to set up home in this case, I will suggest, is also that of the woman writer to become part of a tradition. It is a refusal that is staged in terms of space. Thus, Renée's rejection of Max's offer of marriage is accompanied by a return to writing, specifically the writing of letters, and a return to her own home. The repetition of the negative *personne* ("je n'aimerai plus personne, personne, personne" (97) in the last citation echoes the recurrent three dots of the ellipsis as well as the tripartite structure of *La vagabonde,* and it anticipates the three steps Renée takes away from a marriage that threatens to entrap her: "I am leaving, each turn of the wheel takes me further from Paris, I am leaving, while an icy spring adorns the tips of the oak branches with frozen pearls; all is cold and damp, with a mist which smells of winter still, and I am leaving when I might at this hour be lying, relaxed with pleasure, against the warm side of a lover" (264).[22]

Renée muses early in the novel on the incompatibility of writing and a lifestyle like her own. Economic necessity, she says, renders works of Balzacian proportions out of the question for her.

> To write is the joy and torment of the idle. Oh to write! From time to time I feel a need, sharp as thirst in summer, to note and to describe. And then I take up my pen again and attempt the perilous and elusive task of seizing and pinning down, under its flexible double-pointed

nib, the many-hued, fugitive, thrilling adjective . . . The attack does not last long; it is but the itching of an old scar.

It takes up too much time to write. And trouble is, I am no Balzac! The fragile story I am constructing crumbles away when the trades- man rings, or the shoemaker sends in his bill, when the solicitor, or one's counsel, telephones, or when the theatrical agent summons me to his office [. . .] (127)[23]

However, money and time do not foreclose access to different kinds of writing. As Woolf suggests in *A Room of One's Own,* women need a sen- tence that allows for the breaks that are necessarily part of their lives. Indeed, *La vagabonde* traces Renée's (and Colette's) search for a sen- tence that will fit her or into which she might fit. This search is under- taken in terms of space. Renée's suggestion that the text crumbles (*s'émietter*) recalls the dismantling of the façade of the family home in the opening chapter of *La maison de Claudine.* The reality of a home disintegrates as the text moves forward. A metonymical use of space, space as such, is replaced by one that is more metaphorical, space repre- senting something else—home is no longer somewhere with a roof and four walls, and an *homme,* a man ("'Enfin! voilà dans la maison *un homme*—voilà L'HOMME'" [93] ("'At last *a man* in the house— behold THE MAN'" [187]), but somewhere her own.

While she contemplates the marriage plot in parts one and two of the novel, Renée ultimately dispenses with it; she writes herself into and then rapidly out of it, eventually refusing Max's proposal. Her tempo- rary consideration of marriage is described in terms of language, of a dis- pensing with conjunctions, with escape routes: "J'ai envoyé au diable [. . .] mes *si,* mes *car,* mes *mais,* mes *cependant . . .*" (147) ("I have sent to the devil [. . .] my *ifs* and *fors* and *buts* and *howevers*" [228]). Her final decision against this future is figured in a recuperation to the text of these qualifiers or conditionals and is matched grammatically: Renée signs her name with a question mark and the text closes on an ellipsis.

The collapsing of author and protagonist, paralleled by an overlap- ping of form and content here, is supported by the structure of the nar- rative. The use of a first-person narration suggests the autobiographical nature of the work—the collapsing of the authorial and the narratorial "I" (even though our protagonist is not named Claudine, as she is in the more explicitly autobiographical works of Colette). Although letters appear only in the third part of the novel, we can understand the whole piece as a letter, one in which the protagonist engages with herself. This engagement with herself is suggested by the scene with which the novel opens, where Renée contemplates and engages with her own reflection in the mirror. This other self is returned to again and again throughout the text as "'une femme de lettres qui a mal tourné'" (15) ("A woman of letters who has turned out badly" [126]). This initial engagement with herself throws into question the destination of Renée's letters to Max reproduced in the third part of the narrative. "[T]hat painted mentor who gazes at me from the other side of the looking-glass [. . .] She gazes at me for a long time and I know she is going to speak to me. She is going to say: 'Is that you there? [. . .] Why are you there, all alone? And why not somewhere else?'" (119).[24]

This other self asks questions of space and of agency (both structure and content). Bound up with questions of space, of "where to?" are questions of "who decides?" Renée must decide about the terms of her performance contract: "'Come on now, either make up your mind or don't. Does it seem to you all right, or doesn't it?'" (198),[25] says her friend Hamond. She must also decide whether to commit herself to another marriage or not, whether or not to let another decide for her: "'You're going away, darling? Whoever decided that? [. . .] But I haven't yet given my consent'" (236).[26]

Renée's attempts to put off responding to these requests consist in the implementation of a space, a silence, an ellipsis (paralleled by her decision to go on tour) between herself and that person or thing that is asking her to decide on or commit to a direction to be taken. "I look as if I'm reflecting, but I am not reflecting. Hesitating is not reflecting" (198).[27] This hesitation, in a sense, constitutes the novel.

> Ugh! All that manœuvering, those elaborate preparations for love, for a goal that one cannot even call love, am I to encourage and even to imitate that sort of thing? Poor Dufferein-Chautel! Sometimes it seems to me that it is you who are being deceived here, and that I ought to tell you . . . to tell you what? That I have become an old maid again with no temptations, and that the four walls of my dressing room at the music-hall are for me a cloister?
>
> No, I shall not tell you that because, like those who have got to the tenth lesson at the Berlitz School, we only know how to exchange elementary phrases where the words *bread, salt, window, temperature, theatre* and *family* play a great part.
>
> You are *a man*, so much the worse for you! Everyone in my house seems to remember it, not in the way I do, but in order to congratulate you because of it, from Blandine who gazes at you with a never-wearying satisfaction, to Fossette whose wide doggy smile says just as

clearly: "At last *a man* in the house—behold THE MAN!"
I don't know how to talk to you, poor Dufferein-Chautel. I hesi-
tate between my own *personal* language, which is rather brusque,
does not always condescend to finish its sentences, but sets great store
on getting its technical terms exact—the language of a one-time bluestocking—and the slovenly, lively idiom, coarse and picturesque,
which one learns in the music-hall, sprinkled with phrases like: "You
bet!" "Shut your trap!" "I'm going to hop it!" "Not my line!"
Unable to decide, I choose silence. (187)[28]

Renée expresses her ambivalence toward marriage in terms of
space: her choices are bound up on a literal level with her work as a
music-hall dancer. She describes herself as cloistered ("une vieille fille"),
but in the most unusual of places, the music-hall dressing room, a space
in some senses associated at this time more with the emancipation of
women than their subjugation. Renée rejects traditional choices offered
to women—"[L]a couture, [. . .] la dactylographie, ou le trottoir?"
(161) ("Sewing, or typing, or street-walking?" [239])—which reinforce
traditional divisions of inside and outside, public and private. With these
conventions, she puts aside the myths associated with love, again in
terms of space, revealing instead its repressive side. "'Let me stay alone
in my closed bedroom, bedecked and idle, waiting for the man who has
chosen me to be his harem'" (243),[29] she suggests, ironically; "'the loving couple, imprisoned in a warm room, isolated by four walls from the
real world—the normal dream of any young girl very ignorant of life'"
(243).[30] Love, Brague tells Renée, is not compatible with the freedom
afforded by work: "l'amour et le métier, ça ne va pas ensemble" (185)
("love and work don't go together" [256]).

At the end of the first part of *La vagabonde,* Renée reveals, however, that this incompatibility contributes to the contradiction at the heart
of her vagabond spirit. She is the "bohême ordonnée," "[une]
vagabonde, soit, mais qui se résigne à tourner en rond, sur place" (83)
("an orderly gipsy," "[a] vagabond, maybe, but one who is resigned to
revolving on the same spot" [178]). While part of her moves abroad,
another part remains, she suggests, sitting by the fire:

For me the future, whether it is here or there, is . . . My lately
acquired and rather artificial liking for uprootings and travel fits in
happily with the peaceful fatalism natural to the bourgeoise that I am.
A gipsy henceforth I certainly am, and one whom tours have led from
town to town, but an orderly gipsy, careful to mend her well-brushed

garments herself; a gipsy who always carries her slender fortune on her person, but in the little suède bag, the coppers are in one compartment, the silver in another, while the gold is preciously hidden in a secret pocket.

A vagabond, maybe, but one who is resigned to revolving on the same spot like my companions and brethren. It is true that departures sadden and exhilarate me, and whatever I pass through—new countries, skies pure or cloudy, seas under rain the colour of a grey pearl—something of myself catches on it and clings so passionately that I feel as though I were leaving behind me a thousand little phantoms in my image, rocked on the waves, cradled in the leaves, scattered among the clouds. But does not a last little phantom, more like me than all of the others, remain sitting in my chimney corner, lost in a dream and as good as gold as it bends over a book which it forgets to open? (179)[31]

The second part of the novel (the pivot around which Renée's decision turns) explores the contradiction between moving on and staying. Renée is pulled in both directions, backwards and forwards, first by her past and the promise of a future home offered in part one (this second section begins "[l]e joli coin intime!" ("What a charming, cosy nest!"), and then in the third part (centrifugally) around France and ultimately perhaps to South America, and solitude.

Throughout the second section, Renée grows ever anxious to leave: "No, nothing keeps me here, or elsewhere. No dear face will rise from the mist, like a flower emerging from dark water, to beg tenderly 'Don't go away!' [. . .] it is as if I already left" (201).[32] In the background we hear "le tic-tac de ma petite pendule de voyage" (138) ("the tick-tock of my little traveling-clock" [221]). At the suggestion of the tour, Renée cannot contain her joy. For her, associated with a move out of Paris is a retrieval of the freedom that is the privilege of anonymity (anticipating the refusal of yet another name that marriage will bring).

My sudden laugh, instead of undeceiving him, bewilders him still further, but this evening I feel in a gay and teasing mood, and as lighthearted as if we had set off already. Oh, how lovely to go away, to move from one place to another, to forget who I am and the name of the town which sheltered me the day before, scarcely to think, to receive and retain no impressions but that of the beautiful landscape which unfolds and changes as the train runs past, of the lead-coloured pool in which the blue sky is reflected green, and the open-work spire of a belfry encircled with swallows. (194)[33]

Prior to her actual departure, Renée feels as if she has already departed;
she is carried away by her imagination.

> How far away I feel, as if I had already left, cut adrift, and taken refuge
> in my journey! Their voices grow muffled and fade into the distance,
> mingling with the rumbling of the trains, with whistlings and the
> lulling swell of an imaginary orchestra. Ah, what a delicious depar-
> ture, what a sweet sleep, which wafts me towards an invisible shore!
> (204)[34]

The sense of dispersal experienced by Renée is reflected later in the work
in the multiplication of towns, listed one after the other, that Renée visits as she crosses France (102/194).

Dreaming of her voyage, Renée wakes up to find that "[d]ebout
contre moi, le Grand-Serin [Max] barre toute la hauteur de la chambre"
(116) ("[s]tanding beside me, the Big-Noodle [Max] looms as high as
the room" [204]). Max reproaches Renée for her illicit desire to escape
him, a desire that he reads in her face as she sleeps: "'you look as though
you had closed your eyes to hide a joy that is too much for you. You
really do. You haven't the face of a woman asleep, you . . . [. . .]'"
(205).[35] The doubling of the term *femme* as both woman and wife in
French anticipates the limits Max intends to place on Renée, both physical and linguistic.

The barrier between Renée and Max is indeed linguistic—Renée
refers to "my own *personal* language, which is rather brusque, does not
always condescend to finish its sentences" (187);[36] "What would be the
good of writing, and pleading, and discussing? My voluptuous friend
can only understand love" (279).[37] Like new students at the Berlitz
School, Renée suggests, they know only the most elementary words
with which to communicate (93/187). While Max does respond to
Renée's letters, his own are not reproduced. They are characterized as,
for the most part, labored, stilted, flat, at odds with the fluidity of
Renée's pen: "He writes simply but obviously not with ease. His beautiful flowery writing slows up the natural impetus of his hand" (269).[38]
His letters rustle like bank notes, suggesting that he is trying to buy
Renée, trying to entrap her in a cycle of exchange (214/282).

> Does he think? Does he read? Does he work? [. . .] Not a trace of wit,
> a certain quickness of comprehension, a very adequate vocabulary
> enhanced by a beautiful rich voice, that readiness to laugh with a child-
> ish gaiety that one sees in many men—such is my admirer. [. . .] a

look that is sometimes absent and seeking [. . .] He has travelled, but just like everyone else: not very far and not very often. He has read what everyone reads, he knows "quite a few people" and cannot name three intimate friends, in addition to his elder brother. (183–84)[39]

In contrast, Renée's writing lunges forward: "To write, to write, to cover white pages with the rapid, uneven writing which he says is like my mobile face, exhausted from expressing too much. To write sincerely, almost sincerely!" (288).[40] The flatness of Max's writing, with which Renée's own writing is unable to engage, recalls the imposing form that hampers Renée's mobility (a shadow like a black line crossing through Renée's words).

The sedentary nature of Max's life (like his writing style)—he enjoys "sa liberté d'oisif" ("his lazy freedom"), he is "[l']homme inoccupé" (158–59) ("an idle man" [237])—contrasts sharply with that of Renée. A gender reversal is suggested: "c'est lui la courtisane" (159) ("it is he who is the courtesan," "[i]l peut se donner tout entier, jour et nuit, à l'amour, comme . . . comme une grue" [159] ("[h]e can give himself up entirely, day and night, to love, like . . . like a prostitute" [237]). The home offered by Max stands in opposition to Renée's own apartment, which she characterizes as dark and inhospitable. Of her apartment she says: "The whole place gives an impression of indifference, neglect, hopelessness, almost of imminent departure" (181)[41] and "The only thing I take trouble over, for my own sake more than theirs, is the sketchy, deceptive interior where I live so little" (182).[42] To both Max's offer and her own place she prefers the hotels of her tour (here Colette uses the English word "home"): "A shelter, and not a home, that is all I leave behind me"; hotels are "more familiar and more benevolent" (262).[43] The provinces provide Renée with a freedom unavailable to her in the traditionally more liberal capital.

In the third part of *La vagabonde*, Renée writes letters to Max as she tours France. Anticipating Renée's refusal of the marriage proposal, Max has already disappeared from the third section of the novel. Renée moves in a circle: first east, then south, before traveling up to Brittany then back to Paris. As she embarks on her tour, rather than leaving home, Renée is returning there: "'I've just passed through, without stopping, a region which belongs to me because I spent my childhood there [. . .] Perhaps it is only beautiful because I have lost it'" (266–67).[44]

Renée's move from Paris and from Max results in a return to writing, specifically letters. Before meeting Max, she had stopped writing. As she reaches the provinces, the language of the text becomes more animated; metaphors, similes, colors, sounds, and textures replace the black and white of the Parisian episode: "Alive to that excess of scent and colour and warmth, and unable to resist although I had foreseen it, I let myself be taken by surprise, carried away and conquered" (278).[45] As minor characters, peripheral to the central narrative, draw Renée to the edges of the text, so metaphors proliferate, suggesting an exploration of the parameters of language. As she embarks on her tour it is spring; the first letter is dated April 3, suggesting a renewal.

Late in the text, Renée, still undecided as to her future, perches off-balance on the arm of a chair (216). "Why do I feel as though I were rocked on an invisible swell like a ship set afloat by the sea? It is the kind of evening that makes one want to sail to the other side of the world" (276).[46] Sitting at her hotel window, caressing her feet, Renée occupies (voluntarily) a space associated with women and a (frustrated, unrealizable) desire for escape. The ellipses, dashes, and question marks that are predominant at this moment in the novel match this occupation of liminal spaces.

> For just a minute longer, just one more, I cling to what would be the greatest folly, the irremediable unhappiness of the rest of my existence. Clinging and leaning, like a tree which has grown over an abyss, and the weight of whose blossoming bends it towards its destruction, I still resist, and who can say if I shall succeed? (288)[47]

In one of her last letters to Max, Renée, delaying her response to his proposal of marriage, asks if he has any regrets about having had to decide on a single woman, her: "'You are the best of men, and you deserve the best of wives. Will you not regret having chosen only [. . .]'" (286).[48] This letter is signed with a question mark: "Renée Néré?" In a similar gesture that completes her final letter, she questions its integrity, and, by extension, that of the text as a whole, with the question: "But though signed and dated and finally stuck down, it still remains an unfinished letter. Shall I open it again?" (309).[49] These letters plot the protagonist's refusal of the domestic and with it her rejection of the gendered text of history. She will not settle into a repressive marriage; she will not write herself into a literary tradition that determines her trajectory in terms of her gender.[50] In this third section, Nancy Miller argues, "a series of refusals and reversals" results in the replacement of "the fixed identity of woman with *the improvised mobility* of a feminist subjectivity, a feminist modernist whose desires in language remain subject to change" (*Subject to Change* 258). Indeed, the novel ends with an ellipsis.

Renée refuses to see things Max's way: "I refuse to see the most beautiful countries of the world microscopically reflected in the amorous mirror of your eyes" (310).[51]

> You wanted to brighten me with that commonplace dawn, for you pitied me in my obscurity. Call it obscurity, if you will: the obscurity of a room seen from without. I would rather call it dark, not obscure. Dark, but made beautiful by an unwearying sadness: silvery and twilit like the white owl, the silky mouse, the wings of the clothes-moth. (310)[52]

Renée counters Max's efforts to bring her out into the light, to make her known, by characterizing herself as a space that is dark, one teeming with possibility, reflected here by the multiplication of adjectives and similes. Renée's comparison of herself (and of her text) to "a room seen from the outside" parallels her embracing of a text that is multiplicitous, a future made up of many spaces, spaces that enable the creation of a different sentence, a woman's sentence (248/310). That is, a sentence that is broken and double, one that embraces interruption and, as Miller suggests, is "subject to change" (258).

In *Duo* (1934) and its sequel *Le toutounier* (1939), a similar spatial configuration is closely bound up with the relationships of the two protagonists, Michel and Alice, to language. In this pair of novels Alice moves out of her husband's childhood home, following his supposed suicide, and back into her own. In this sequence Michel's search for the truth of the circumstances of a long-finished love affair between Alice and his business partner, Ambrogio, is figured in terms of his relationship to writing, to words, those of Alice and her former lover, and his own. In *Duo* Michel fears the duplicity of language, the fact that language is ambiguous. This is reflected in his inability to write and in his retreat into a closed and isolated space. Michel fears the language that has taken his wife out of the house—the lover's letters—the language of a relationship that his wife dismisses as inconsequential.

Duo opens with Michel's discovery of the removal of a purple leather portfolio, "un buvard de maroquin violet," from Alice's desk. It is the absence of this purple portfolio (which we later learn contains the love letters), the color of which resonates with the orchids set beside it, that brings it to Michel's attention. These letters introduce the lover into the text, this other whose intrusion has violated the sanctity of the monogamous bond joining Alice and Michel: the letters are, then, this other, and this other is in language.

Much of this short novel is taken up with Michel's attempts and ulti-mate failure to reconstruct the truth of the encounter described in the letters he has discovered. Yet words resonate and refuse to stand still; they elude him: "'What an existence!' he thought bitterly, 'if every word, every gesture must bring us up against something hidden, quiv-ering and bleeding'" (413);[53] "The words 'fire,' 'flames,' 'finish' fasci-nated his imagination with their F's, which suggested the rush and smoke of a conflagration" (464).[54] The elusiveness of this other man is expressed by Michel in terms of the slipperiness of words. It is reflected in the novel itself in the proliferation of color imagery that is tied up with writing, specifically the writing of letters. Against the dark dreari-ness of the landscape of Cransac (the provincial town where the novel takes place) and its environs, the blues and purples of the writing uten-sils dominate: "[le] buvard violet" (15) ("[the] purple portfolio" [379]), "une fine écriture violette" of Ambrogio (103) ("fine hand-writing in purple ink" [461]), "un crayon bleu" (105) ("a blue pencil" [463]) that Alice holds between her teeth, are all reflected in Alice's eyes, "le gris verdissant de ses yeux" (7) ("her greenish grey eyes" [371]). The blues and purples of the narrative suggest that the text is somehow bruised or damaged (49, 51). They stain the narrative. The violet color of the ink, with its homonym in French, "violer" ("to vio-late"), prefigures the interruption that has occurred.

Michel's resistance to his wife's duplicity, and to the duplicity of lan-guage, can be seen in his refusal to enter into dialogue with his wife: "Michel suddenly looked up at her from behind his eyeglasses with such a keen, enigmatic expression that she stopped short" (463).[55] Nor will he write. While Alice writes with ease—"the sheets of the pad that Alice was covering with her changeable, elastic handwriting, large at the start of a blank page and smaller as the space grew less" (420)[56]—Michel labors to write. On the evening of his death (an apparent suicide) Michel notes the therapeutic, hence liberating, possibility of writing: "I'm always behind with my correspondence, and the labor of writing, which I detest, will quiet my nerves and makes me sleepy" (462).[57] Bound up with this reluc-tance to write is Michel's fear of the revelation of his wife's infidelity, of a rift in his relations with his wife. Among those he attempts to hide from are "le facteur qui doit être en train de monter la butte" (26) and "la demoiselle de la poste" (27) ("the postman too, probably just coming up the hill" and "the girl at the post office" [390]). Thus tied up with this pursuit for the truth is an isolation of Alice.

The fear and stagnation Michel feels in the face of language is mirrored by the narrowness of Michel's trajectory; the unidirectionality of
his attempt to discover the truth is reflected in the dark passage-like
room, "ce salon-bibliothèque" (11) ("this combination study and living
room" [375]), where the majority of the action in the novel takes place.
While Alice's desk sits between the French window and the fireplace at
one end of the room, Michel occupies the other, flanked by two "sullen-
looking" ("revêches" [37]) bookcases, which are matched by the twin
beds in which the two sleep when in Michel's childhood home.

This sense of claustrophobia is reinforced by Alice's dream toward
the end of the novel. Escaping from the towering, sullen bookcases, the
repressive quality of which is doubled by the low towers of Cransac,
Alice imagines herself caught up in a flurry of colored paper, which she
gathers together, before fleeing.

> The scattered elements of a dream jumbled together the picture of
> the squat towers at Cransac, a swarm of many-colored papers and
> Chevestre's tall, black silhouette ("Just like a priest, just like a priest,"
> Alice kept mumbling to herself) and submerged all of this in the black
> darkness that hung heavily between the two gigantic, impassive book-
> cases. It seemed to Alice in her dream as if she got up, gathered the
> papers together and fled. (449)[58]

Like two sentries Michel's bookcases—their authority substantiated by
Cransac history (its fortifications)—and the dominating silhouette of
the elderly servant, Chevestre, who has spent his life tending the master's land, suggest a tradition stretching back into the past, of which
Alice is not a part. The multicolored swarm of paper resonates with that
of the love letters, suggesting a second infidelity, this time to a literary
tradition, a provincial history, one in which women did not write.

Following Michel's death, Alice escapes back to her own childhood
home, one inhabited only by women: the father has died, and the mother is not mentioned. We move from the pair of *Duo,* to the three, or
four, or all (the *tout*) of *Le toutounier,* whom Alice has written about
midway through *Duo* (56–57/419–20). In *Le toutounier,* the
"toutounier" (the "doggy-bed") of the title provides Alice a space of
linguistic possibility. Infused with the shared past of the four Eudes sisters, this space or backdrop gives rise to a proliferation of metaphors and
images. This is a past in which she has participated, as opposed to that
of Cransac, where she is a visitor, an outsider in a place where women,
such as the servant, Maria, are silent. "The toutounier. . . . The hideout,

the cave, with its signs of humanity, its humble marks against the walls, its untidiness which isn't dirty. No one is happy there, but no one wants to leave it . . ." (178–79).[59]

The sofa has codes and conventions of its own ("leur code partic-ulier" [124, 131, 176] ["their individual code" (146)]; "the convention of frivolity, silence and irony that governed their relationship" [146][60]) and its own tone. Its very name is idiomatic (*tout/toutou* means "doggy nest" [Jouve, *Colette* 140]), as is the language that springs up around it: *la busette* is *la clé* (the key), *les sisibècques* are *les cigarettes* (cigarettes) (128/151).

> Finally she abandoned herself to the "native toutounier," a huge, indestructible sofa of English origin, battered down like a forest road in the rainy season. The back of Alice's neck encountered a cushion whose leather cover was cold and soft as a cheek. She sniffed the old morocco which smelled of tobacco and the scent of hair, and kissed it lightly. (137)[61]

The *toutounier* bears scars, dips; its walls are infused with memories, smells, stains, wounds and scars, odds and ends. It is trampled down like a forest path, "défoncé autant qu'une route forestière dans la saison des pluies" (117) ("battered down like a forest road in the rainy season" [137]), vast like a river bed, one bank invisible to the other (117–18/137). One has to bend and squeeze to get around it: "She automatical-ly pulled in her tummy in order to pass between the baby grand piano and the wall, and made contact again with the big sofa in the old way; in other words, she sat astride the upholstered back, swung herself over and let herself roll down onto the seat" (135).[62]

Alice's contact with *le toutounier*—she rides sidesaddle, suggesting that it is a vehicle of sorts, then tips over and rolls on the seat cushions—implies an ease and irreverence, similar to that noted by Woolf on read-ing Colette's work. This contact gives rise in the text to a proliferation of imagery. Figures, metaphors, and stories abound around it. While the *toutounier* is a private, protected space, divorced from the outside world, it is one where "real life" is experienced, is written and can be read in the sharpest detail.

Among women, at home, Alice regains a freedom of expression that was denied to her in Cransac. The multiplication of the "I," effected by the multiplication of characters (Alice's others), divided and yet at once united, contrasts with the closing out of others in *Duo*. Le toutounier suggests a space where differences coexist in harmony: "'Paragraph seven of the toutounier code . . . ' 'What's yours is mine, what's mine is yours'" (210).[63] While Alice insisted upon twin beds when sleeping with Michel, at home she is happy to sleep intertwined with her sisters on the *toutounier*. "[L]e vivant voisinage" ("the feeling of someone close to her" or literally "the living surroundings") in which she finds herself in the second of this pair of novels bears no resemblance to that of her marriage (177/212).

Renée's rejection of stability and her refusal of a home in favor of the road in *La vagabonde* parallel Alice's escape from a stifling marriage in a provincial town in *Duo* and her embracing of diversity at home in the city among her sisters in *Le toutounier*. In each case, a change of place and a reconfiguration of boundaries, boundaries that are less impermeable, are accompanied by a return to writing on the part of the female protagonist. Accession to a space of her own enables each woman to explore a new form of expression, as it does for Bel-Gazou of "Le curé sur le mur" in *La maison de Claudine*. However, for both women this new form is one that is open and shifting, reflected in the space to which they have acceded: for Renée the music-hall and the tour, for Alice a tumultuous space shared with her sisters. Along with the marital home, each woman rejects the marriage plot in favor of a new, less conventional narrative: Renée's on the music-hall stage and the tour, among errant performers, Alice's fractured narrative intertwined with the uncertainties of those of her sisters. In tandem with the interweaving of different narrative strains with that of the protagonist, the nature of the prose changes. The plot thickens and with it the language; as the novels move forward, Colette employs more metaphors and similes, adding greater color and texture to the works.

Colette's pursuit of a form of expression, of a style of her own, like that of Renée and Alice, consists in the creation of a new space, one that is continually "subject to change," to return again to Miller's term. Rather than occupy a static, closed room, the dimensions of which are prescribed by husband and tradition, the female protagonists of her novels, like Colette, elect to remain on the move. Thus, instead of matching a fixed form that admits no commonality with another that is equally inflexible, Colette creates spaces that are fluid and necessarily incomplete. In this sense, Colette answers Woolf's call for a woman's sentence in *A Room of One's Own* (76) with a question, retaining rather than resolving the problem of space: the question of how a book might be "adapted to [a woman's] body" (78).

4

Fathers in the First Fictions
of Woolf and Colette

QUESTIONS OF the daughter writer's relationship to a tradition of writing initially appear to put Colette and Virginia Woolf in different camps. Colette was the daughter of a patriarchal tradition. Devotee of nineteenth-century French literary great Honoré de Balzac, she wrote in the absence of a tradition of middle-class women writers in France.[1] By contrast, Woolf was heir to a strong matriarchal tradition; she is famously the originator of the call to "think back through our mothers" and, in *A Room of One's Own,* writer of a history of women's writing that includes Jane Austen, George Eliot, and the Brontë sisters.[2]

However, an examination of the writers' own comments on the issue of literary inheritance suggests that both realized the indispensability to the text of a matriarchal *and* a patriarchal tradition. Both acknowledged, as Woolf put it herself in *A Room,* that a text—and here she refers specifically to poetry—must have "a mother as well as a father" (103). However, while in the work of Colette these two strains, the paternal and maternal, reached a comfortable equilibrium—in her own words, "lyrisme paternel" and "humour, spontanéité maternels" ("father's lyricism" and "mother's humor and spontaneity") are mingled and superimposed in her work (*Sido* 37)—in the work of Woolf the two sit uncomfortably together. According to her nephew and biographer Quentin Bell, Woolf "believed that she was the heiress to two very different and in fact opposed traditions [and] that these two rival streams dashed together and flowed confused but not harmonised in her blood" (18). While her father's family, the Stephens, "were all writers; they all had some gift, some pleasure in the use of the English language [. . .] wrote like men who are used to presenting an argument [. . .] seeing in literature a means rather than an end," her mother's kin, the Pattles, were "an altogether less intellectual race than the Stephens [. . .] chiefly remembered for their faces" (Bell 19). Bell labels the two sides (albeit, he says, unsatisfactorily) paternal and maternal, "sense and sensibility, prose and poetry, literature and art, or, more simply, masculine and feminine" (20).

This chapter treats Woolf's first novel *The Voyage Out* and the series of four books that mark Colette's debut as a writer, the *Claudine* novels, in the light of these two opposed conceptions of or reactions to literary inheritance, the one harmonious, the other conflictual. Via an analysis of the female protagonist's negotiation of familial relationships and her reading choices, I trace the daughter writer's engagement with a tradition of writing and her efforts to define herself in terms of it. I follow in each case the daughter writer's efforts to come to terms with a predominantly patriarchal tradition, the matriarchal all but absent, and I chart her success in establishing a place for herself there. Contrary to standard readings of the father in *The Voyage Out* and the *Claudines*, which cast him as menacing and threatening in the first and insignificant in the second, I read the father as an at least temporarily constructive figure, one who provides the daughter with access to a tradition otherwise closed to her.[3]

In their capacity as first fictions, Woolf's *The Voyage Out* and Colette's *Claudine* series are novels of apprenticeship in a double sense. Not only do they follow the maturation of the protagonists, but they also represent the authors' first published attempts at writing. In both cases, critics have characterized these first novels as flawed and chaotic, the work of an as yet untrained mind. Thus, David Daiches suggests that "[t]here is a hesitancy, even a clumsiness, in *The Voyage Out,* which denotes the writer who has not yet found her proper medium. Again and again we find Virginia Woolf hovering over her subject, undecided where to pounce, until the chapter is filled up with a miscellaneous collection of descriptions and digressions which do not seem to lead anywhere" (10). And Elaine Marks argues that "the mastery of style in [Colette's] *La naissance du jour*—a certain sense of 'distance' which Colette observes while relating her intimate feelings; the psychological subtleties of *Chéri, Le blé en herbe* and *Le pur et l'impur;* the poetry of *La maison de Claudine* and *Sido* are not present or, if present, are not sustained in the *Claudine* series" (*Colette* 74). "Between *Claudine* and *Naissance du jour,*" suggests Simone de Beauvoir, "the amateur became a professional, and that transition brilliantly demonstrates the benefits of a severe period of training" (*The Second Sex* 784).

These were views that both authors shared. Rereading her first novel in 1920, Woolf describes *The Voyage Out* as "a harlequinade," at certain moments strong and at others simpering:

> The mornings from 12 to 1 I spend reading *The Voyage Out*. I've not read it since July 1913. And if you ask me what I think I must reply that I don't know—such a harlequinade as it is—such an assortment of patches—here simple & severe—here frivolous & shallow—here like God's truth—here strong & free flowing as I could wish. What to make of it, Heaven knows. The failures are ghastly enough to make my cheeks burn—& then a sentence, a direct look ahead of me, makes them burn in a different way. On the whole I like the young womans mind considerably. How gallantly she takes her fences—& my word, what a gift for pen & ink! I can do little to amend; & must go down to posterity as the author of cheap witticisms, smart satires & even, I find, vulgarisms—crudities rather—that will never cease to rankle in the grave. (February 1920, *Diary* 2: 17)

In her *Mes apprentissages,* Colette regrets the immaturity of her early works and the submissiveness it reveals:

> Time has not changed my opinion, and my judgement on all the *Claudines* is still severe. They frisk and frolic and play the giddy girl altogether too freely. The work reveals, indeed, an irrepressible youthfulness, if only in its lack of technique. But I do not like to rediscover, glancing through these very old books, the suppleness of mood that understood so well what was required of it, the submission to every hint and the already deft manner of avoiding difficulties. (60)[4]

While not an automatic choice for a comparative analysis, several details about these two works, both first fictions, both semi-autobiographical, suggest connections and intersections.[5] Both are books about books, and about reading, specifically the daughter's reading. Both are *bildungsromane,* albeit unusual ones, stories of the daughter's education and stories of voyages, real and metaphorical, as their titles suggest.[6] Claudine of the *Claudine* series leaves her *pays natal,* Montigny, in the Burgundy region of France, a double for Colette's own *pays natal,* Saint-Sauveur-en-Puisaye, also in Burgundy, for Paris; Rachel Vinrace of *The Voyage Out* leaves England for the Amazon aboard her father's ship. Rachel never returns home; Claudine does so only for a brief visit. The father, present at the beginning of the voyage in each case, retreats and is replaced by a husband/lover figure: for Rachel, Terence Hewet, and for Claudine, Renaud. In each case the biological mother of the heroine is absent, as are, for the most part, mothers in general.

In both *The Voyage Out* and the *Claudine* series, the protagonist's relationship with tradition can be traced both via her choice of reading material and in terms of her family history. Thus, the absence of the mother from both works—Rachel's mother, Theresa Vinrace, has been dead for some ten years, and the absence of Claudine's "bien désagréable" ("remarkably unpleasant") mother (*Claudine à Paris* 207/338) is never explained—suggests the absence of a tradition of women's writing. The centrality of the father in both novels (both open their worlds to their daughters) and their preoccupations—Willoughby Vinrace leaves his daughter with her aunt and uncle while he pursues his business interests, and Claudine's father, Claude, is too engrossed in his study of slugs to supervise his daughter in any meaningful way—can be understood in the first case as a gesture that *excludes* the daughter writer from a patriarchal tradition she desires to be part of and in the latter case one that *frees* the daughter from a tradition to which she considers she does not belong.

Real Parents: The Stephens and the Colettes

As suggested above, both novels might be read autobiographically. Real fathers inform the portraits of fictional fathers in both *The Voyage Out* and the *Claudine* series.[7] Both writers emphasize the instrumental role played by the real father in the process of their coming to writing. In *Le Képi* and *Sido*, for example, Colette traces her love of the tools, the materials of writing, back to her father; in her late memoir "A Sketch of the Past" (*Moments of Being*, 1939), Woolf credits her father with the breadth of her literary education. However, in each case the father poses a significant obstacle to the daughter's accession to writing; the father-daughter relationship is marked by a rift or absence.

Woolf's father, Leslie Stephen, was descended from a long line of literary people. A prolific writer, he was author of some sixty-three volumes of literary biography and other literary historical work. He educated his daughters, paying particular attention to Virginia, whom he ultimately provided, critics suggest, with as good an education as the one she might have received at either Oxford or Cambridge, which she, as a woman, was unable to attend at the time (Hill 351).

Figure 12
*Woolf and her father, Leslie Stephen. G. C. Beresford. By courtesy of the
National Portrait Gallery, London.*

However, Leslie Stephen also bullied and intimidated his daughter. According to Quentin Bell, Woolf felt that the volumes of her father's extensive *Dictionary of National Biography* had "crushed and cramped" her and her younger brother Adrian in the womb (38–39). The father's work threatened to silence the daughter. In 1928 she wrote of her father in her diary:

Father's birthday. He would have been [here she does a short calculation] 96, yes, today; & could have been 96, like other people one has known; but mercifully was not. His life would have entirely ended mine. No writing; no books;—inconceivable. I used to think of him & mother daily; but writing The Lighthouse, laid them in my mind. And now he comes back sometimes, but differently [. . .] He comes back now more as a contemporary. (*Diary* 3: 208)

Colette's father, Jules Colette, by contrast, is an *auteur manqué*, whose love of the trappings of writing—the pens, the paper, the bindings, the titles and dedications—so preoccupied him that he never made it beyond page one. "My father, a born writer, left few pages behind him. At the actual moment of writing, he dissipated his desire in material arrangements, setting out all the objects a writer needs and a number of superfluous ones as well" (*The Tender Shoot* 302).[8] Thus, in contrast to Woolf's weighty legacy, Colette's heritage is an "immaterial" one (*Sido* 56). In the semi-autobiographical novel *Sido,* when, subsequent to his death, his children take down the volumes of his work, bound and titled, from a shelf in his office, they discover only blank pages. The father's work is an illusion, an imaginary work, the mirage of a writer's career: "Une œuvre imaginaire, le mirage d'une carrière d'écrivain" (*Sido* 55). His legacy is a blank slate, hundreds and hundreds of blank pages: "des centaines et des centaines de pages blanches" (*Sido* 55).

In terms of writing, the mother's engagement is less clear. Woolf's mother, Julia Stephen, wrote children's stories, as well as unpublished tracts on "the morality and work ethic of 'agnostic women' and on the current debate on domestic service" (Lee 83). Although Julia Stephen certainly played a role in her daughter's education, her death when Woolf was just thirteen limited her impact on her daughter's life. Colette's mother, Sidonie Colette, corresponded by letter intensively with her daughter at certain periods of her daughter's life. In this sense, Sido was a much-valued reader of and commentator on the daughter's work, rather than a writer in her own capacity. Sido represents an interlocutor to whom Colette turned as a muse of sorts.[9]

> Thirty, then, and a most unusual dearth of feminine companions, of feminine complicity and support. The ideal accomplice, the true helper, I had them both in "Sido," in "Sido" so far away and yet so near. Every week I wrote her two or three long letters, full of news of things that had happened, or not happened, of descriptions, of boasting, of myself, of her. She died in 1912. Still, now, twenty-three years later, I sit down at my table, or at a hotel writing-desk if I'm travelling, and pull off my gloves, and ask for picture postcards with 'views of the neighborhood,' which were the sort that she liked best . . . And why should I stop writing to her? Why be checked by such a futile, vainly questioned obstacle as death? (*My Apprenticeships* 103–4)[10]

While the nature of the paternal literary legacy sets Woolf and Colette apart—Woolf's literary patrimony is ample, Colette's nonexistent—it also brings the two writers together. The juxtaposition of these two family stories highlights the complications of both. When one considers the freedom afforded Colette due to the absence of a literary

Figure 13
Colette with her mother and father, Sido and Jules Colette.

legacy, one is led to question the privilege enjoyed by Woolf as a result of her eminent ancestors. Conversely, when one considers the wealth of Woolf's education, one begins to understand Colette's lack of literary forebears as a handicap rather than an advantage.

Both writers recognized these contradictions. Colette repeatedly laments and celebrates her absence of vocation:

> Vocation, holy signs, childhood poetry, predestination? . . . I can find nothing of the sort in my recollections [. . .] No, I did not wish to write. When one can enter the enchanted kingdom of reading, why write? [. . .] But in my youth, I never, *never* wanted to write. No, I did not get up at night in secret to write verses in pencil on the lid of a shoebox! No, I did not get nineteen or twenty for style in an exercise between the ages of twelve and fifteen! For I felt, more so every day, I felt that I was made precisely *not* to write. (*Looking Backwards* 15–16)[11]

Her genesis as a writer, she suggested when being honored at the Académie royale belge de langue et de littérature françaises, was purely accidental.

I became a writer without noticing, and without anyone suspecting I
would. Exiting from an anonymous shadow, author of several books,
some of which carried my name, I was still surprised when people
called me a writer [. . .] and I attributed these recurring coincidences
to indulgent chance, chance that from landing to landing, from meeting to marvel, led me here. (My translation)[12]

In a similar way, Woolf interrogated her privilege with a certain degree
of irony:

Who was I then? Adeline Virginia Stephen, the second daughter of
Leslie and Julia Prinsep Stephen, born on 25th January 1882,
descended from a great many people, some famous, others obscure;
born into a large connection, born not of rich parents, but of well-to-
do parents, born into a very communicative, literate, letter writing,
visiting, articulate, late nineteenth century world; so that I could if I
liked to take the trouble, write a great deal here not only about my
mother and father but about uncles and aunts, cousins and friends.
(*Moments of Being* 65)

"Full fathom five thy father lies": The Voyage Out

Woolf completed *The Voyage Out* ten years after the death of her father
in 1904. According to DeSalvo, Woolf suffered considerably at the loss
of her father. Indeed, Woolf wrote to Violet Dickinson shortly after her
father's death of a desire to resurrect him and to make amends: "I cant
believe our life with Father is over and he dead. If one could only tell
him how one cared, as I dreamt I did last night" (March 1904, *Letters*
1: 133). While this regret resulted in part from her guilt at having alter-
nately loved and hated her father during his lifetime, it stemmed in large
part from the more general problem identified by DeSalvo, citing Woolf
herself, as "the 'emotions and complications' of her family history"
(303).[13] As Lee contends, concurring with DeSalvo: "When [Woolf]
looked back on her family life she thought of it not as a single thing but
marked by dramatic splits. Lines of division criss-cross her memoirs.
Childhood was cut in two between Cornwall and London. An end to
childhood came with the violent division made by her mother's death.
The household was fragmented" (55). *The Voyage Out*, which Woolf
dedicated to the man who would in some senses replace her father, her

husband Leonard Woolf, represents an initial attempt to address these emotions and complications.

The Voyage Out traces the maturation of the central character, twenty-four-year-old Rachel Vinrace, over the course of a voyage from London to the Amazon aboard the *Euphrosyne,* the ship captained by her father, Willoughby Vinrace. When her fellow travelers, her maternal uncle Ridley Ambrose and his wife Helen, stop off in Santa Marina, Rachel remains with them while her father goes on. In Santa Marina, Rachel and her aunt join up with a group of English tourists, among them Rachel's fiancé-to-be, Terence Hewet. After one of several excursions up the river, Rachel falls ill and eventually dies.

The setting of the novel at sea, aboard a ship in which, Helen Ambrose notes, "the whole course of their lives was now put out of order" (61), sets the stage for Rachel's attempts to come to terms with the disorder of her family. As Lucio Ruotolo has suggested in terms of *The Voyage Out:* "Sea voyages are by their nature parenthetical. Between the acts of departure and arrival, accustomed roles and routines seem often implausible if not unreal" (20). Rachel's mother having died when Rachel was eleven (recalling Woolf's own loss at age thirteen), her father frequently absent on business, the young woman is being raised by her father's sisters. Rachel's early education is described as having been somewhat slapdash. In the care of her paternal aunts, she has received a bit of information here and a bit there: "[k]indly doctors and gentle old professors had taught her the rudiments of about ten different branches of knowledge [. . .] But there was no subject in the world which she knew accurately. Her mind was in the state of an intelligent man's in the beginning of the reign of Queen Elizabeth" (26). While Rachel has not learned anything very useful, neither has she learned anything that will hamper her. In this sense, Rachel's relationship with her father, like that which Claudine shares with hers in Colette's first novels, is not characterized as limiting to the daughter in any fashion, although Rachel's lack of knowledge about men and women is viewed by her aunt Helen as potentially very dangerous. "'She's been brought up practically in a nunnery. Her father's too absurd,'" Helen Ambrose tells St John Hirst (149).

Willoughby Vinrace is an ambiguous character. He is both businessman and scholar. His rather rough-and-ready countenance—"[h]e is big and burly, and has a great booming voice, and a fist and a will of his own," (17) according to Helen Ambrose—appears to hide a softer side. While his voice is the voice of authority at the London home of Rachel's aunts, his sisters and daughter run the house in an altogether different fashion, in their own way. "He was a great dim force in the house, by means of which they held on to the great world which is represented every morning in the *Times*. But the real life of the house was something quite different from this. It went on independently of Mr Vinrace, and tended to hide itself from him" (201). Helen Ambrose suspects that Willoughby may have bullied his wife and his daughter. Indeed, she believes him guilty "of nameless atrocities with regard to his daughter, as indeed she had always suspected him of bullying his wife" (17)—a moment in the text that many read as a reference to sexual abuse. However, she recognizes that he has a real affection for his daughter. Likewise, the daughter has a real affection for the father. She admires her father, a little too much for her aunt's liking: "Rachel seemed to get on very well with her father—much better, Helen thought, than she ought to" (25). The strength of the tie between daughter and father is emphasized by the fact that Rachel is initially reluctant when Helen suggests that the girl should break her trip and remain with her and her husband, Ridley, in Santa Marina.

The Voyage Out contains a number of other father figures, figures who double and complicate the father-daughter relations in the work. As well as Willoughby Vinrace, we find Ridley Ambrose, Rachel's maternal uncle, who resembles Woolf's real father, Leslie Stephen, in his capacity as a classical scholar—he edits Pindar. Like Leslie Stephen, Ridley also likes to read aloud. A brief fellow traveler aboard the *Euphrosyne*, Richard Dalloway plays an ambiguous paternal role, shifting from father to lover, almost without warning, when he fumbles an embrace with Rachel, perhaps in this way anticipating Hewet's replacement of Willoughby Vinrace (66–67). Both St John Hirst and Terence Hewet, in their capacity as educators for Rachel, a role cast for them by Helen, and in their resemblance—mentally and physically—to the older generation of men in the text, are also fathers of a kind.

Much of what Rachel reads in *The Voyage Out* involves parent-child relations and suggests her efforts to understand who she is and how she fits into the family structure. Reading recommendations can be divided along gender lines, with Rachel taking more seriously the recommendations made by the men in the text. Rachel's father gives her *Cowper's Letters*—perhaps suggesting an attempt to maintain a correspondence with his daughter—however, she finds them "dull" (49), although she does have a positive response, "entering into 'communion' with 'the spirit of poor William Cowper there at Olney,'" as Beverley Ann Schlack has noted in her thorough analysis of literary allusion in the works of

FATHERS   105

Woolf (17). Cowper, who lost his mother at the age of six, struggled with
mental illness for most of his life, again suggesting a tie with Woolf herself and perhaps anticipating Rachel's demise at the close of *The Voyage
Out*. (The fact that it is Rachel's father's choice of text that is tied to madness supports my later contention that it is his withdrawal that leads to
Rachel's demise.) Many of the other texts suggested involve the rise and
fall of empire, conquest and revolution; most, like *Cowper's Letters*, are
nonfiction. The historical nature of many of these texts might reflect the
choices of Woolf's own historian father, Leslie Stephen. For example,
Richard Dalloway is indecisive as to whether Rachel might gain more
from reading Edmund Burke's speech on the French Revolution or his
speech on the American rebellion (66). Hirst recommends she read Gib-
bon's *History of the Decline and Fall of the Roman Empire* (141). She
tries but cannot bring herself to enjoy it ("'it goes round, round, round,
like a roll of oilcloth'" [184]). Ridley Ambrose suggests a French novel,
Honoré de Balzac's *Cousine Bette*, as an alternative (157–58).[14]
     By contrast, the reading recommendations made by the women in
the text are for the most part dismissed by the daughter. Clarissa Dalloway recommends that Rachel read Jane Austen. However, Rachel says
she does not like Jane Austen, judging her work to be "like a tight plait"
(49). While Helen Ambrose wishes that Rachel would read Maupassant,
Defoe, or "some spacious chronicle of family life," her niece instead
chooses modern texts with shiny covers, such as Ibsen's *Three Sisters* or
a novel "whose purpose [according to Helen Ambrose] was to distrib-
ute the guilt of a woman's downfall upon the right shoulders," which
she reads, suggests Helen, with "the curious literalness of one to whom
written sentences are unfamiliar" (113). As a challenge to Rachel's dis-
missal of the mother's texts, two other texts appear in the novel, both
associated with Clarissa Dalloway, and both of which deal with a rupture
in paternal-filial relations. Thus, Clarissa Dalloway mentions a staging of
Antigone,[15] an archetypal tale about the daughter's defiance of the
father's will (37), one that appears frequently in Woolf's work, and Mr
Grice reads to Clarissa Dalloway from Shakespeare's *The Tempest*, a text
in many ways central to *The Voyage Out*—specifically, Ariel's false words
to Ferdinand regarding his father's whereabouts: "Full fathom five thy
father lies" (Act I, scene 2, 78). This line is part of Ariel's song: "Full
fathom five thy father lies, / Of his bones are coral made; / Those are
pearls that were his eyes; / Nothing of him that doth fade, / But doth
suffer a sea-change / Into something rich and strange, / Sea-nymphs
hourly ring his knell: / (*Burden*) Ding dong. / Hark! Now I hear
them—Ding-dong bell."

Echoing Rachel's resistance to the maternal text, the maternal relationship is not dwelt upon at any length in this novel. Jane Novak
explains this omission, pointing out the fact that as Woolf revised *The
Voyage Out* (originally called *Melymbrosia*) she deleted references to
Rachel's dead mother, Theresa, and her power over Rachel's life.
Novak suggests that Woolf removed the references to the mother
because

> to arouse compassion publicly for Rachel's orphaned state might have
> seemed to Virginia Woolf 'obviously not good manners.' It might
> also have dangerously touched the deep spring of her own grief for
> the mother who died suddenly when Virginia Stephen was thirteen.
> Although she dealt triumphantly with these memories in *To the Light-
> house*, their inclusion in *The Voyage Out* was perhaps not possible for
> her. (81)

Rachel appears to know very little about her mother, whose portrait
hangs over her father's desk. Theresa Vinrace is portrayed as a spirited
woman who, while revered by her husband, cannot quite get him to
engage with her: "the head of an individual and interesting woman, who
would no doubt have turned her head and laughed at [her husband] if
she could have caught his eye" (76). Willoughby thinks of his business
as an offering to his deceased wife and tries to educate his daughter as
his wife would have wished him to. "[A]lthough he had not been particularly kind to her while she lived, as Helen thought, he now believed
that she watched him from heaven, and inspired what was good in him"
(76). Helen Ambrose characterizes Willoughby's relationship with his
wife as somewhat ambiguous. In the course of the novel we learn, via
Helen (who is perhaps attempting to present a positive maternal image
to her niece), that Theresa Vinrace was not treated particularly well by
either her husband or his sisters during her lifetime. Helen characterizes
Rachel's mother as possessing a special kind of power that drew people
to her—more men were in love with her than with any other woman
Helen Ambrose knew (171). Helen also provides Theresa Vinrace with
an emotional past, a life independent of Willoughby Vinrace, in an
engagement to a man named Maurice Fielding prior to her marriage to
Rachel's father. This first love ties Theresa Vinrace to Julia Stephen, who
had been married to Herbert Duckworth prior to her marriage to
Woolf's father.[16]
Although both Helen and Clarissa are mothers (the book opens
with Helen's lament over having to leave her children in England;

Clarissa expresses her regret at being without her children when aboard the *Euphrosyne*), when we meet them they are without their children. While Helen is, in some senses, a mother substitute for Rachel—it is she who chaperones Rachel and who writes to Willoughby to get his consent for Rachel's engagement to Terence Hewet—she takes on that role only reluctantly. She asks that Rachel not call her "Aunt"—"'"Aunt's" a horrid name; I never liked my Aunts'" (74). She also later acknowledges that she is *not* the motivating force behind Rachel's maturation. As David Daiches has suggested, Helen's figure, having been developed to a degree where we expect her to be central to the work, ultimately fades into the background (11).

The disagreement in the text over Rachel's resemblance to her mother, Theresa, again suggests that the daughter's relationship with her mother is unclear. While Rachel's father Willoughby and her aunt Helen see a resemblance between mother and daughter, perhaps demonstrating their desire to make Rachel part of the family text (echoing Helen's desire that Rachel read spacious family chronicles) and to see her follow in her mother's footsteps (Willoughby hopes Helen will make an accomplished hostess of his daughter during her stay in Santa Marina), Rachel herself and Theresa's brother Ridley, Rachel's uncle, disagree. While Willoughby tells himself "'There is a likeness?'" (the question mark, however, suggesting uncertainty) (76) and Helen thinks "She was like her mother, as the image in a pool on a still summer's day is like the vivid flushed face that hangs over it" (18), when Clarissa Dalloway asks Rachel: "'Are you like your mother?'" Rachel responds forcefully: "'No; she was different'" (52). When Ridley expresses his opinion of the lack of likeness between mother and daughter in the daughter's presence ("'Ah! she's not like her mother'"), Helen tries to drown out his comment by thumping her tumbler on the table (8).

The instability and confusion resulting from parent-child relationships is everywhere in this novel. There are, in fact, very few characters who do not have some unpleasant family secret to reveal. Terence Hewet's description of his father's death suggests an emotional disconnection between father and son: "'My father was a fox-hunting squire. He died when I was ten in the hunting field. I can remember his body coming home, on a shutter I suppose, just as I was going down to tea, and noticing there was jam for tea, and wondering whether I should be allowed—'" (131). This recalls Delia's reaction to her mother's death in *The Years*—dinner would be ruined—and Woolf's own impulse to laugh at her mother's funeral, described in "A Sketch of the Past." Hewet blames his mother for his failure to play a musical instrument. Music was not manly enough for his mother; "'she wanted me to kill rats and birds,'" he tells Rachel (207). Hewet's friend, St. John Hirst, a character based on fellow Bloomsbury writer Lytton Strachey, is the son of the Reverend Sidney Hirst, who, along with his wife, the son laments (half comically, we presume), is still living: "'Parents both alive (alas)'" (131–32).[17] When Helen asks Hirst whether his relationship with his family is strained, he describes it as "'intolerable'" (147); they want him to be a peer and a privy councillor. Of his mother, Hirst adds, "'there's something to be said for my mother, though she is in many ways deplorable'" (148). Further, Richard Dalloway confesses to Rachel: "'I didn't get on well with my father [. . .] He was a very able man, but hard. Well—it makes one determined not to sin in that way oneself. Children never forget injustice'" (59). Again this is a comment echoed in later novels. In *To the Lighthouse*, Mrs Ramsay's youngest son, James, will never forget his father's repeated refusal of the trip to the lighthouse. Children never forget such things, says Mrs Ramsay. Another visitor in Santa Marina, Arthur Venning, is waiting for the death of his widowed mother (she is "of strong character" [127]) so that he can quit his job as a barrister and take up flying (despite the suspicion that Venning's marriage to Susan Warrington might once again hold up his aeronautical aspirations) (108). Another minor character, Raymond Oliver, another hotel guest, is not treated well at home, having been forced into the mining trade by his parents (173).

Daughters fare equally poorly in *The Voyage Out*. Evelyn Murgatroyd, a flirtatious and confused young Englishwoman whom Rachel meets in Santa Marina, expresses her regret at not having had the opportunity to get to know her own father (her parents did not marry). Evelyn resembles her father, not her mother, according to Rachel after contemplating photographs of both parents (237):

'I'm the daughter of a mother and no father [. . .] It's not a very nice thing to be. It's what often happens in the country. She was a farmer's daughter, and he was rather a swell—the young man up at the great house. He never made things straight—never married her— though he allowed us quite a lot of money. His people wouldn't let him. Poor father! I can't help liking him. Mother wasn't the sort of woman who could keep him straight, anyhow. He was killed in the war. I believe his men worshipped him. They say great big troopers broke down and cried over his body on the battlefield. I wish I'd known him. Mother had all the life crushed out of her [. . .]'
(174–75)

The husband of another English tourist in Santa Marina, Alice Flushing, describes his wife's upbringing as "very unnatural—unusual": "They had no mother [. . .] and a father—he was a delightful man, I've no doubt, but he cared only for racehorses and Greek statues" (260). Mrs Flushing goes on to describe forced bathing in icy winters in a stable-yard (which some of her twelve brothers and sisters survived and others did not), a practice Mrs Flushing claims she would repeat had she children of her own (260). Helen Ambrose gives only a brief description of her family, mentioning only the father and omitting the mother: "[H]er father had been a solicitor in the city who had gone bankrupt, for which reason she had never had much education—they lived in one place after another—but an elder brother used to lend her books" (131). Miss Allan, the literary scholar, is concerned about her brother; she has her father's watch—suggesting perhaps that she keeps order in the place of her father (104).

While Rachel initially flourishes in the absence of her father—she and Helen join up with the English in Santa Marina, where Rachel falls in love with Terence Hewet—I want to suggest that it is the realization of the permanence of the father's absence, because she will marry Hewet and live away from the father, that results in Rachel's illness. Rachel's fever and subsequent death occur rather suddenly in the novel.[18] Having returned from an excursion of several days, Rachel develops a headache while listening to Hewet read an extract from John Milton's masque *Comus*:[19] "There is a gentle nymph not far from hence," he read, "That with moist curb sways the smooth Severn stream. / Sabrina is her name, a virgin pure; / Whilom she was the daughter of Locrine, / That had the sceptre from his father Brute" (308). The lines he reads involve fathers and daughters, a short genealogy, suggesting that it is Rachel's memory of her father's absence that sets the illness in motion.

> The words, in spite of what Terence had said, seemed to be laden with meaning, and perhaps it was for this reason that it was painful to listen to them; they sounded strange; they meant different things from what they usually meant. Rachel at any rate could not keep her attention fixed upon them, but went off upon curious trains of thought suggested by words such as 'curb' and 'Locrine' and 'Brute,' which brought unpleasant sights before her eyes, independently of their meaning. (308)[20]

Indeed, Rachel locks onto three words from the extract, the latter two of which are fathers' names (one of these Brute, or brute, suggesting

ambivalence toward the father figure; Brute might also suggest nostalgia for home [as might the mention of the river Severn], as Brut is the
name of British chronicle histories); the first word, "curb," suggests a
change of direction or, in another sense, a prohibition.[21]

Woolf had mixed feelings about Milton. In 1918 in her diary she
writes of the "sublime aloofness and impersonality of the emotion" of
Paradise Lost. While she admires the "wonderful, beautiful and masterly
descriptions of angel's bodies, battles, flights, dwelling places," the
poem, she feels, sheds no light on "one's own joys and sorrows." Milton's epic poem offers her no help, she asserts, in "judging life" (*Writer's
Diary* 5). While Hewet significantly does *not* choose *Paradise Lost,* as
Lisa Low demonstrates in her reevaluation of the significance of this passage, I want to argue that Rachel's reaction to Milton's poetry is similar
to that which we see in Woolf's diary and supports my contention that
these lines remind Rachel of her father, who, while he introduced her as
a child to much great literature, left her to fend for herself in the real
world.[22] In support of this assertion, one might also note the tie between
Milton's *Comus* and Shakespeare's *The Tempest,* cited earlier in *The Voyage Out.* The lines Woolf chose from *The Tempest,* a text on which Milton modeled *Comus,* involving Ferdinand's loss of his father, can be read
as prefiguring the later text. The inclusion of these lines then connotes
regret, and confusion perhaps, rather than fear.

The suggestion that Rachel falls ill in part due to the father's absence
is supported by Rachel's unexplained repeated exclamation during her
illness: "'Why doesn't he come?' 'Why doesn't he come?'" (320).[23]
Willoughby Vinrace is not referred to during Rachel's illness. Indeed, he
is not mentioned until after Rachel's death when Mrs Thornbury asks,
"'Has the father arrived? Could one go and see?'" (338). Rachel's words
recall an earlier moment in the novel when Helen Ambrose worries
about her sanctioning of Rachel's engagement to Terence. She asks herself what might Rachel have done if she "had been left to explore the
world under her father's guidance. The result, she was honest enough to
own, might have been better—who knows?" (287).[24]

Thus, Rachel's reaction to Hewet's reading of *Comus* and Helen
Ambrose's rhetorical question encapsulate a central theme of Woolf's
first novel, that is, the ambiguous role played by the father in the daughter's literary apprenticeship. Helen asks: What role does the father, or
more generally patriarchy, play in the process of the female writer's coming to writing? How does he help, and how does he hinder, the daughter's accession to the realm of language and literature? This question of
what might be called "the temporary efficacy [. . .] of patriarchal par-

adigms," to borrow Elizabeth Kowaleski-Wallace's phrase from her study of two lesser-known nineteenth-century writers, Hannah More and Maria Edgeworth, suggests interesting insights into Colette's *Claudine* series (13).[25] Woolf's *The Voyage Out* asks in what sense is an identification with the father a step indispensable to the process of the daughter's differentiation from the mother and from the negatives associated with her role. Further, it asks how identification with the father, as Kowaleski-Wallace suggests, might provide the daughter access to a literary tradition not available via the mother.

"Une Jolie Instruction": Colette's Claudine *Series*

The four novels of Colette's *Claudine* series (1900–1904) consist of the diaries of Claudine, who has just turned fifteen as the first novel opens.[26] For the purpose of this comparative analysis I will treat the Claudine novels as four parts of a single project. All of the novels are written in the first person. In the first three in the series, Claudine is the narrator; in the last in the series, *Claudine s'en va* (*Claudine Takes Off*), a second narrator, Annie, is introduced. These novels trace the somewhat unconventional education and maturation of the young motherless Claudine, from the freedom of the woods surrounding her hometown, Montigny, in the Burgundy region of France, into the drawing rooms of literate turn-of-the-century Parisian society. These novels also trace the evolution of the writer-reader Claudine/Colette and her relation to the father's text.

The *Claudine* series is an appropriate place in which to locate a study of paternity, in part because it was itself the subject of a paternity suit. Colette began the *Claudines* in collaboration with her first husband, Henry Gauthier-Villars, better known as Willy, in the late 1800s. She was one of a number of writers who ghostwrote for Willy in his literary factory.[27] There has been much debate over the degree of involvement of Willy and Colette in the composition of the *Claudines*, which appeared first under Willy's name, then under both of their names. After the death of Willy, Colette went to court and had Willy's name removed from the *Claudines*. After Colette died, Jacques Gauthier-Villars, Willy's son from a liaison prior to his marriage to Colette, sued for the right to have his father's name restored to the book alongside Colette's and won (Thurman 106–7).[28]

Although Colette does not use real names as she does elsewhere in her fiction (in *La naissance du jour*, for example), the semi-autobiographical

nature of the *Claudines* is apparent even at a superficial level.²⁹ Like
Colette, the young Claudine leaves the provinces for Paris and sets up in
the capital with an older man—Willy was Colette's senior by fourteen
years. Like Jules Colette, Claude, the father of Claudine, a scholar,
struggles with his writing; however, whereas Jules Colette could not
start, Claude cannot finish.³⁰ Like Colette and Willy, Claudine and her
husband, Renaud, become rivals in the course of the third novel in the
series: in the former case, rivals in literary matters, and in the latter, rivals
in love. Claudine is named for her father, Claude (*Claudine à Paris* 40),
as Colette is named for her father, Jules Colette. The autobiographical
nature of these novels makes the mother's absence all the more striking.
While Jules Colette died shortly after the appearance of the last *Claudine* novel in 1905, Colette's mother, Sido, was very much alive when
the *Claudines* appeared. She died in 1912. Claude Abastado explains
Sido's absence by suggesting that Colette refused to "travestir" ("mis-
represent") her mother; "elle a voulu, de son enfance, préserver la part
la plus pure" (32) ("she wanted, from her childhood, to preserve the
purest part"). Marks argues that "it is not too difficult to imagine why
Colette excluded from these novels Sido, the person she most loved.
Sido was still alive in the opening years of the twentieth century and
Colette obviously did not wish to associate her mother with the scandalous antics of her other characters" (*Colette* [1960] 76).

    Like Woolf's *The Voyage Out*, Colette's *Claudine* series presents a
young woman in the process of maturation, in the absence of parental
supervision. When we first meet Claudine in *Claudine à l'école* (*Claudine at School*), she is at play in the woods of her hometown, and at
school among the daughters of local farmers, grocers, and policemen.
Her father, so buried in his own scholarship, so out of touch with cultural and social norms, is unable to see the inappropriateness of the situation—these other girls are of a social status inferior to that of Claudine. While a mother would have known better and would not have
allowed her daughter to remain in Montigny, Claudine suggests,
Colette has conveniently written her out of the novels.

> If I had a Mamma, I know very well that she would not have let me
> stay here twenty-four hours. But Papa—*he* doesn't notice anything
> and doesn't bother about me. He is entirely wrapped up in his work
> and it never occurs to him that I might be more suitably brought up
> in a convent or in some Lycée or other. There's no danger of my
> opening his eyes! (*The Complete Claudines* [hereafter *CC*] 4)³¹

Juliette Rogers argues that "Colette uses the teachers' (Mlles Sergent and Lanthenay) relations in *Claudine à l'école* to dismiss the traditional maternal role model from her fictional provincial school; she replaces it," argues Rogers, "with a different ideal—a lesbian role model" (50).

Just as Willoughby Vinrace sanctions Rachel's stay in Santa Marina with her aunt and uncle, where he believes she might learn something useful from her aunt Helen, so Claudine's father unwittingly sanctions Claudine's love relationship with her young instructor, Aimée Lanthenay, allowing Claudine to use his library for extra English lessons with Aimée, the girl's pretext for spending more time with the object of her affections (*Claudine à l'école* 39). Indeed, throughout *Claudine à l'école*, Claudine invokes her father's authority as a foil to the objections of her schoolmistresses.

Like Rachel in *The Voyage Out*, Claudine learns to read in her father's library. "I'm a book-worm in Papa's library" (*CC* 146), asserts Claudine.[32] As Marie-Françoise Berthu-Courtivron suggests: "This room appears from the start as the privileged space of all transgressions" (my translation).[33] Claudine reads within the parameters set by the father, but at her own will and discretion, "à [sa] guise." She is a self-confessed book maniac, suffering from "[une] bibliomanie" (*Claudine à Paris* 101). She reads the books and articles that her father does not have time to read for himself, in his library, which numbers 2,307 volumes (*Claudine à l'école* 39/*CC* 28). Unlike Rachel of *The Voyage Out*, however, Claudine reads inside and outside the canon: "I read, I read, I read. Everything. Anything."[34] When questioned on her reading habits, and on challenging the canon and defying authority, by the shady District School Superintendent, Monsieur Dutertre (who is sleeping with one of her teachers)—he asks: "'What do you read? Everything you can lay your hands on? Everything in your father's library?'" (17)[35]— Claudine responds that she does not read those things that bore her.

Thus, Claudine—an "after-school" reader, to borrow Rogers' term (58)—reads contemporary texts (many written by friends and acquaintances of Colette and Willy) that she selects herself.[36] The focus of a number of them on the sexual maturation of a female protagonist suggests that they have an educational function for Colette's precocious protagonist. She reads the lightly erotic work of Pierre Louÿs, *Aphrodite* (1896)[37]—the story of Chrysis, an ambitious courtesan—and *La femme et le pantin* (1898), experimental novelist Paul Adam's *L'année de Clarisse*,[38] Léon Daudet's *Suzanne* (1897) (*Claudine à l'école* 64), and *La carrière d'André Tourette* by Lucien Muhlfeld (*Claudine à Paris*

100). When the school inspector appears in the classroom in *Claudine à l'école*, Claudine's friend Anaïs hides her magazine, *Gil Blas illustré*, between the pages of her *Histoire de France*, and Claudine covers up her copy of the "marvelously told animal stories" of Rudyard Kipling ("en voilà un qui connaît les animaux!" [116]). Claudine also reads Michelet's *Histoire de France:* "la folle *Histoire de France* de Michelet, écrite en alexandrins" (*Claudine à l'école* 130). In *Claudine à Paris* (*Claudine in Paris*) she declares Voltaire's *Dictionnaire philosophique* boring—she learns only about nasty, shocking things from Voltaire (25–26). A dog-eared copy of Honoré de Balzac, Colette's favorite, full of crumbs from a snack of another day, provides Claudine consolation on a rainy day (103).[39] Claudine's father does not understand his Molière as his daughter does, according to his daughter. Claudine is not fond of the work of Zola: "Your Zola just doesn't understand the first thing about the country. I don't much care for his work in general" (*CC* 247).[40] In *Claudine à Paris*, Marcel finds a copy of Henri de Régnier's *La double maîtresse* (1900), the story of the seduction of the boy Nicolas de Galandot by his cousin Julie, on Claudine's desk and threatens to tell her father (*Claudine à Paris* 64).[41] Claudine responds with the assertion that her father would not give a damn. (It is unclear whether Colette procured these texts from her father's library or from elsewhere.) While the men in Colette's work make no recommendations, all, with the exception of Claudine's father, express shock and surprise at Claudine's taste.

The disjunction between father and daughter that we find in the *Claudine* series is similar to that of *The Voyage Out*. Like Rachel, Claudine is an only child. Both Willoughby Vinrace and Claudine's father, Claude, are benevolent figures (Claude perhaps more so than Willoughby); however, both are so engrossed in their work that they have little or no time for their daughters. Claude is an absent-minded man, with a red and white beard, busy at work on an interminable study of an obscure topic, the molluscs ("la malacologie") and in particular the slugs ("les limaces") of the Fresnois region of France. "'You haven't read [his study],' exclaims Claudine, 'because it'll never be finished'" (19).[42] So immersed is Claude in his work, he does not have time for paternal affection:

> How could you expect that the budding hope of such discoveries would leave a passionate malacologist any paternal sentiment between seven in the morning and nine at night? He's the best and kindest of men—between two orgies of slugs. (*CC* 20)[43]

The father's absence that results from his preoccupation with his work is not, however, perceived as a lack but rather as an advantage for the daughter. The father of Colette's *Claudine à l'école* opens his library, literally and metaphorically, to the daughter. His love of scholarship fuels Claudine's imagination, although in a very nonprescriptive fashion. In his silence, in his failure to police his daughter's reading, he is complicit with his daughter.

Neither Claudine nor Rachel has a mother to fill the space left open by the father; the absence of Claudine's mother, "an unpleasant woman" according to her father, remains unexplained (207/338). There are mother surrogates in the *Claudines*, as there are in *The Voyage Out*, such as Mélie, a housekeeper and Claudine's wet nurse from Montigny, and Tante Cœur, Claudine's aunt, who is raising her grandson Marcel, in *Claudine à Paris*; however, no attempt is made to suggest that these figures fill in for the real mother in any significant way.

In both *The Voyage Out* and the *Claudine* series, then, the father, by initially stepping aside, frees the daughter to develop as a reader and a writer. Just as Willoughby Vinrace accompanies Rachel on the first part of her journey in *The Voyage Out*—they travel to Santa Marina on his ship—so Claude takes his daughter to Paris at the beginning of the second novel in the series, *Claudine à Paris*. The father's desire to work on his interminable manuscript is the motivating force behind the move.

While Claudine's reaction to her move from her *pays natal* is initially a negative one—she falls ill and remains in the apartment, and she stops writing—she later embraces the change of scene. The father's complicity in this change is hinted at in the third novel, when Claudine suggests that her father has unwittingly done the work of destiny. "Papa is a force of Nature; he serves the obscure designs of Fate. Without knowing it, he came here in order that I might meet Renaud; he is going away, having fulfilled his mission of irresponsible father" (*CC* 412).[44] Indeed, having absolved himself of further responsibility, in the latter part of *Claudine à Paris*, the father hands his daughter over to the husband, a father surrogate of sorts, and heads back to the provinces.

The increase in family size—Claudine's discovery of an aunt, a nephew, and a "cousin Uncle," Renaud—that occurs in *Claudine à Paris* parallels the expansion of Rachel Vinrace's familial and social circle, first aboard the *Euphrosyne* and then in Santa Marina in Woolf's *The Voyage Out*. As in *The Voyage Out*, the dysfunctional family—or in Colette's words the "complicated family" (Renaud tells Maugis that theirs is "une famille compliquée" [*Claudine à Paris* 115])—predominates.

The *Claudines*, like *The Voyage Out*, are full of unconventional families. The mother of Mlle Sergent, the headmistress of Claudine's school in Montigny, lurks in the background in *Claudine à l'école*, complicit in her daughter's irregular activities. Also in *Claudine à l'école*, Claudine's young teacher Aimée and her sister Luce suffer with their parents. While the former finds refuge in the arms of Mlle Sergent, in *Claudine à Paris* the younger sister Luce allows herself to be exploited and kept by her uncle (a parallel to Claudine's story). Mélie functions as a surrogate mother in *Claudine à Paris* and the subsequent *Claudines*, forming an odd pair with Claudine's eccentric father. Marcel and his father Renaud share a strained relationship in *Claudine à Paris*. Marcel's mother, "la pauvre Ida," died young, and Marcel feels that his father fails to treat him as a son. In the absence of his father, Marcel is being raised by his grandmother, Aunt Wilhelmine. Annie of *Claudine s'en va* has a grandfather, a grandmother, and a father, but, like Claudine, she has no mother. Annie's relationship with the paternal Alain is similar to that of Rézi and her husband in *Claudine en ménage* (*Claudine Married*). Alain's sister Marthe mothers her novelist husband, Léon. Their relationship, according to Annie, is "un ménage contre nature" (*Claudine s'en va* 13). In a reversal of Colette's real-life relationship with her husband Willy, Annie's sister-in-law, Marthe, has her husband (who writes novels about adulteresses, suicides, and bankruptcies) writing a fixed number of pages a day so that she can pay her bills and cheat on him (Marthe calls his study the torture chamber [*CC* 536]). This family disorder sets the stage for Claudine's unusual alliance with her uncle Renaud in the course of the second novel.

In contrast to Rachel, Claudine is explicit about her desire to find a father substitute. "It was a father like that that I missed and needed. Oh, I don't want to speak ill of mine; it isn't his fault if he's a little peculiar" (*CC* 285);[45] "Because of that noble, almost lunatic father of mine, I needed a Papa, I needed a friend, I needed a lover" (*CC* 351).[46] She calls Renaud "Renaud-amant" and "Renaud-papa" (*Claudine en ménage* 65) ("Renaud-the-lover" and "Papa-Renaud" [*CC* 404]), as well as "cher grand ami paternel" (*Claudine en ménage* 64) ("great fatherly friend" [*CC* 404]). Unlike her father's text, his thesis on molluscs, which is interminably in process, unfinished, Renaud's story is a little more complex, his past a mystery to Claudine (the inaccessibility of Renaud's life story recalls Terence Hewet's proposed novel entitled "Silence" in *The Voyage Out* [204]). Renaud is a journalist. He writes about foreign politics for the *Diplomatic Review*, a job Claudine characterizes as "frightfully boring [. . .] I mean those are awfully serious articles" (*CC* 285)[47].

Claudine is not sure what she wants from him, liberty or subjugation, a father or a lover: "My liberty oppressed me, my independence exhaust-ed me; what I had been searching for for months—for far longer—I knew, with absolute clarity, was a master. Free women are not women at all"[48] (*CC* 352–53) Like Max of Colette's later novel *La vagabonde* (1914), Renaud is repeatedly portrayed as more feminine than Claudine herself: "il est plus femme que moi" (*Claudine en ménage* 59) ("But how much more feminine he is than I am" [*CC* 400]), "d'esprit plus femme que moi" (*Claudine en ménage* 66) ("much more feminine and house proud than myself" [*CC* 405]). This unresolved question regard-ing Renaud's purpose affects Claudine's reading and writing. As Clau-dine embarks on her romantic relationship with Renaud in *Claudine en ménage*, her reading—which Renaud, like the District School Superin-tendent of *Claudine à l'école* and Marcel in *Claudine à Paris*, questions (Renaud picks up a copy of Lucien Muhlfeld's *La carrière d'André Tourette* in Claudine's room and exclaims "Sapristi. [. . .] Quelle drôle d'idée!" [100])—drops off, as does her journal writing. "A big gap in my diary. I have not put down a daily account of my impressions and I am sure I should get them wrong on a general summing-up" (*CC* 424).[49]

The love relationship in the *Claudines* functions as does the rela-tionship of Rachel and Terence and other male figures in *The Voyage Out*, as a place in which the female protagonist is able to play with or raise questions about her relationship to patriarchy. While in Rachel's case Terence reproduces the father to some extent (his novel will be entitled "Silence," suggesting complicity with patriarchy), Renaud pre-sents Claudine with more of a challenge. His sanctioning of Claudine's lesbian relationship with Rézi and his provision of space for them (an apartment where the two women can meet in secret and in private) can be compared to the father's provision of the library in which Claudine woos Aimée in *Claudine à l'école*. In this sense, both father and hus-band offer Claudine a blank page on which she is free to compose her own story. However, in contrast to the father (at least explicitly) Renaud intervenes in Claudine's story. Claudine discovers toward the end of *Claudine en ménage* that Renaud has embarked on an affair with her lover, Rézi, in the very same apartment he has procured for her use. At this point in the narrative Claudine packs her bags, leaves her hus-band, and returns to her father and her *pays natal*, Montigny. The father welcomes his daughter back without question. This contrasts sharply with Rachel's reaction in *The Voyage Out*. On realizing that the support of the anchoring paternal text has been withdrawn, Rachel becomes disoriented and falls into a delirium. She reaches out for her father ("'Why doesn't he come?' 'Why doesn't he come?'") but he is not there.

Both *bildungsromane* end with a resumption of business as usual. In the last chapter of *The Voyage Out,* subsequent to Rachel's death, we return to the hotel lobby in Santa Marina, where life goes on as usual. The failure of Rachel's death to change the scene suggests that her question has not been answered in any satisfactory fashion, and that it remains as an unresolved query that will resurface in Woolf's later work. Indeed, as Woolf's friend and mentor, Lytton Strachey (incidentally called "papa" by Woolf), suggests, Woolf raised "an enormous quantity" of questions in her first novel, many of which remained unanswered: "There seemed such an enormous quantity of things in [*The Voyage Out*] that I couldn't help wanting still more," he wrote to Woolf. "At the end I felt as if it was really only the beginning of an enormous novel, which had been—almost accidentally—cut short by the death of Rachel" (*Virginia Woolf and Lytton Strachey* 56).

In the last novel in the *Claudine* series, *Claudine s'en va* (literally *Claudine Takes Off,* translated as *Claudine and Annie*), Renaud and Claudine are reunited. Renaud has resumed his paternal-facilitator role. He resembles the father, "ce mari aux cheveux blancs" (28) ("that white-haired husband of hers" [*CC* 527]); he remains in the background, "indulgent à toutes ses folies" (48) ("indulgent to all [his wife's] crazy ways" [*CC* 540]). While it appears that order has been restored, there is a suggestion of compromise: "Voilà, nous nous suivons . . . sans nous ressembler" (130) ("We follow each other . . . without being like each other" [*CC* 592]). They are "married lovers"; theirs is "[un] ménage réellement trop fantaisiste" (9) (they are "too fantastically unconventional a couple" [515]). The introduction of a different narrator, Annie, in this last novel suggests a maturation on the part of the protagonist Claudine and the author Colette. Claudine becomes a character in the novel advising the younger narrator, a younger self, in affairs of the heart. The doubling of Claudine in Annie, and Annie's choice to escape ("[elle] s'évade") from her unfaithful and domineering husband, Alain, while Claudine "s'en va," goes away (the two phrases are balanced, the first at the end of the book, the second at the end of the penultimate chapter), back to Renaud, suggests that Claudine has achieved compromise in her negotiation with patriarchy, where Rachel has been defeated by it.

5

Reading across the Channel: The Reception of Woolf's and Colette's Work in England and in France

> The French today are slightly confused by how seriously English-speaking readers take Colette, a writer they think of as someone their grandmothers read under a hairdryer. (Edmund White, *Le flâneur*, 27)

> [Woolf] has yet to be adequately welcomed and acclaimed by her feminist daughters in England and America. (Toril Moi, *Sexual/Textual Politics*, 18)

AS A NUMBER of critics have noted, in the interwar and postwar period the work of Virginia Woolf became the subject of a backlash among contemporary and subsequent British women writers (Moi 1986; Armstrong 1992). In a move that Elaine Showalter has described using Woolf's own terms—"[t]o borrow her own murderous imagery, a woman writer must kill the Angel in the House, that phantom of female perfection who stands in the way of freedom. For Charlotte Brontë and George Eliot, the Angel was Jane Austen. For the feminist novelists, it was George Eliot. For mid-twentieth-century novelists, the Angel is Woolf herself" (265)[1]—writers like Dorothy Richardson, Rebecca West, Muriel Spark, Doris Lessing, and Angela Carter turned away from their predecessor, characterizing her work as detached, elitist, and inaccessible.[2] At the same time in France, the work of Colette was suffering a similar fate. In the 1930s and on, French writers like Marguerite Yourcenar, Nathalie Sarraute, Simone de Beauvoir, and Marguerite Duras rejected their maternal foremother as representing and perpetuating the image of a certain France to which

119

they felt they did not belong. Colette's work, they charged, was trivial, bloated, and aimed at an audience of men, not women.[3]

Adding an interesting twist to these two stories of influence anxiety (rather conventional ones, according to Harold Bloom's theory of influence), a cross-Channel exchange of sorts appears to have taken place.[4] While the French existentialists and new novelists adopted Woolf's work in place of Colette's, appreciating among other things the experimental quality of texts such as *The Waves* (Yourcenar, Sarraute) and the breadth of Woolf's work (Beauvoir, Duras),[5] a number of British writers turned from Woolf's work—despite being encouraged to do precisely the opposite, according to Joyce Carol Oates—to the work of the more down-to-earth, physical, sensual Colette (West, Carter).[6]

Based largely on anecdotal evidence culled from the letters, memoirs, interviews, and diaries of the later writers—where they describe what they read of the work of their predecessors and how they read it— this chapter traces the terms of this crossing over, characterizing it as in some senses the logical response to the later woman writer's exclusion from her own national canon. I understand this act of literary expatriation as an effort on the part of the woman writer to mark her difference from a tradition that has undervalued the work of women writers—a movement that resembles in certain respects that explored in chapter 1, where women sought the shelter of a foreign city or country less repressive than their own. That it is in each case Woolf and Colette who are cast in the role of institutional representative, Woolf's and Showalter's "Angel in the House," by their female successors—both are rejected because they are perceived to "belong" and because they represent what the patriarchy wants from a woman writer—comes as a surprise when one considers the degree to which both writers were themselves outsiders. Curiously, this analysis, in highlighting exchange, does not overturn that perception but rather supports it: the later French writers confirm the view that the work of their English predecessor was revolutionary, and the English define that of their French precursor as the same. Thus, whereas Duras argues that Colette's writing lacks the violence of an effectual feminine writing, West celebrates Colette's writing precisely for its strength and vigor; and while Richardson condemns Woolf's "docility," Yourcenar celebrates her work as revolutionary in terms of both form and content.

Common to the responses of French women writers of the 1930s, 1940s, and 1950s to Woolf's work is a sense of awe. Writer and Woolf translator Marguerite Yourcenar (1903–87) demonstrates this in the laudatory introduction to her translation of *The Waves*, a ballet-like work, she suggests, that communicates an intense human sentiment:

> If one stops to consider the scintillating depth of the work of Mrs. Woolf, its weightlessness, its clear density, and the icy pulsations of a style that makes one think again and again of that which is crossing and is being crossed, of light and crystal, one realizes that this so subtly singular woman was born perhaps at the precise minute when a star began to think. (My translation; 5)[7]

In this same preface, Yourcenar writes that Woolf is considered a revolutionary at home and justly so, for her work is profoundly different from that of her predecessors, not only in the sense of technical innovation but in "l'affirmation d'un point de vue sur la vie" ("the affirmation of a perspective on life" [my translation, 7]).

During her lifetime, Yourcenar met both Woolf and Colette, declaring the former a virtuoso and describing the latter as too provincial for her tastes. Like a number of her female contemporaries, Yourcenar developed an attachment to England (and a knowledge of English that facilitated that attachment), one that perhaps informed her admiration for the work of Woolf, which she acquired at an early age. In flight from the war, Yourcenar's family (under the original name of de Crayencour, the name from which Yourcenar adapted her own) spent time in England, a country she would later describe as "one of those countries in which one is instinctively at ease with oneself" (Savigneau 43). Yourcenar translated Woolf's *The Waves* and wove British history into her novel *Mémoires d'Hadrien* (1951). As an adult, Yourcenar again looked away from France. She lived in Maine and New York, where she lectured in comparative literature at Sarah Lawrence, and lived with her American-born lover, Grace Frick. In 1974, like both Woolf and Colette, Yourcenar was photographed by Gisèle Freund.

Yourcenar was both a young reader of the work of Woolf and Colette and a writer writing contemporaneously. She was twelve years old when Woolf's first novel, *The Voyage Out*, appeared in 1915, and in her first fifty years she would have seen the almost yearly publication of Colette's work. Yourcenar published her first novel, *Alexis*, in 1929, in the same year that Colette's *Sido* and *La seconde* and Woolf's *A Room of One's Own* appeared. Yourcenar was a close friend and admirer of Natalie Barney, whom she met late in 1951 (only three years prior to Colette's death in 1954).[8] Perhaps via Barney, Yourcenar met Colette in 1952 while in Paris with Grace Frick (on a visit that included a ceremony where Yourcenar was awarded the Prix Femina Vacaresco, an interview with Janet Flanner for the *New Yorker*, and dinner with Ernst Junger); however, little information is available regarding this encounter (Savigneau 223, 236).

Yourcenar and Woolf met in London in 1937, when the French writer visited her British counterpart at her home in order to discuss her translation of *The Waves*, which appeared under the title *Les vagues* in the same year. It appears unlikely that Woolf had read any of Yourcenar's work at this point. Both women cast their fellow writer in (nationally) stereotypical terms. Woolf describes her meeting with Yourcenar in both her diary and a letter to Ethel Smyth, in the latter in somewhat disdainful terms. Reminiscent of her response to photographer Gisèle Freund, Woolf describes Yourcenar as "some intolerable necessary bore" who wasted one of her rare solitary evenings (*Letters* 6: 109). In her diary, Woolf cannot remember the name of her French translator: was it "Madame ou Mlle Youniac(?)" She describes Yourcenar briefly as "a woman I suppose with a past; amorous; intellectual; lives half the year in Athens; is in with Jaloux &c." She remarks on her red lips, describes her as strenuous and as "a working Fchwoman," and remembers that she "wore some nice gold leaves on her black dress" (*Diary* 5: 60–61).

Yourcenar, for her part, found Woolf pale and melancholic: "[S]he seemed very threatened, very fragile," Yourcenar tells Matthieu Galey, in a collection of interviews entitled *Les yeux ouverts* (*With Open Eyes*) (162). She notes that "nothing remains 'in that pale face of a young Fate barely aged but delicately lined with thought and weariness' but a mouth that seemed never to have known how to smile, eyes filled with sadness" (my translation; quoted in Nathan, *Virginia Woolf par lui-même* 47).[9] Yourcenar spent two hours with Woolf talking over the meaning of several phrases from *The Waves*. Yourcenar explains to Galey that she wished to ask Woolf how she wanted her to translate her book (Cliche 324). Woolf's rather flippant response, "Faites ce que vous voulez" ("do as you like"), opens the way for Yourcenar to produce a translation that "appears as much as possible to have been written in the language into which it is being translated," according to Cliche (235), an effect Yourcenar desired for translation of her own work: "'The ideal of the translator,' as she will describe it later to her Italian translator in a letter in 1962, is to give 'the impression that the work has been composed in the language into which one is translating it'" (my translation; quoted in Cliche 325).[10]

Critical discussion of Yourcenar's translation of *The Waves* indeed suggests that she tried to bring Woolf home—a move perhaps entirely appropriate for the work of a Francophile like Woolf, who, as Yourcenar points out in her preface to the translation, boasted of her French ancestry with a certain pride (5).[11] Yourcenar, according to one critic, "seeks to create for the target audience *a new poem that returns to the literary system of the reader*" (my translation and my emphasis; Shields 322).[12] When compared with the later translation by Cécile Wajsbrot (1993), Yourcenar's translation of *The Waves* is judged by critic Vivianne Forrester as too French: "elle *françise* la langue anglaise" ("she frenchifies the English"). Yourcenar, Forrester asserts, makes of Woolf's English *parc* (park or estate) a French garden (quoted in Shields 313–14). Yourcenar does not translate; she "rewrites," according to Michel Cusin, who is preparing a third translation of *The Waves* for a Woolf Pléiade edition (quoted in Renaudin and Toczyski 23). Wajsbrot, on the other hand, who eliminated adjectives, pronouns, and the multiple repetitions integral to Woolf's novel and declined to translate many culturally specific terms (for example, buns, bow windows), produces a translation inaccessible to the French reader, according to Forrester.

In the few references Yourcenar makes to Colette, one notes a respectful distance (one that contrasts with the excessive praise offered Woolf).[13] On her admission to the Académie française in 1980, the first woman to receive the honor, Yourcenar makes reference to her excluded predecessors, "with whom," Yourcenar says, she wrote. Their work, she says, "surrounded" and "accompanied" her own body of work. In the course of the speech, in a rather defiant gesture, Yourcenar sarcastically suggests to her audience that perhaps the professionalization of women's writing in the mid-nineteenth century was too recent a development to interest the Académie française. She names Colette among "the invisible troupe of women who should perhaps have received this honor very much sooner" (my translation; quoted in Savigneau 418).[14] Her survey of the reasons why these women were invisible and excluded, heavy with irony, points to their status as outsiders: Mme de Staël nationally and culturally, George Sand sexually and in terms of class, and Colette institutionally.

> Mme de Staël would have been ineligible as a result of her Swiss parentage and her marriage to a Swede: she was happy to be one of the greatest minds of her century. George Sand would have been a scandal due to the turbulence of her life, as a result of the very generosity of her emotions that made her a so admirably womanly woman; the person more than the writer got ahead of her time. Colette herself thought that a woman should not visit a man to solicit

his vote, and I cannot think otherwise, not having done it myself. (My translation; quoted in Savigneau 418)[15]

This reference perhaps provides a key to Yourcenar's look to England for inspiration. Yourcenar refuses, as did Colette before her, to pander in order to be accepted into the mainstream. Thus, just as Colette wrote on the margins of the tradition to which she was heir, so Yourcenar did the same, ironically rejecting Colette as she emulated her, casting her as to some degree part and parcel of that tradition.

Yourcenar's rejection of Colette on the basis of her tie to France and French tradition can be seen in another reference made by the later writer with regard to a recording of Colette reading her own *Gigi Chéri*, which Yourcenar received from her friend Florence Codman in 1956, following Colette's death in 1954.[16] The two women, according to Codman, had spoken frequently and at length about Colette. Yourcenar's response to the gift of the recording reveals a certain reverence toward her literary predecessor coupled with a degree of condescension:

> Thank you for *Gigi Chéri* [Gigi Darling], which we listened to this morning. [. . .] One can follow her entire life by way of the contours of her voice: the rich and fulsome tones of Burgundy, the street-urchin element from Willy, the literary element, and also, if I might be so bold, the concierge-and-fortuneteller-adored-by-the-little-local-ladies element. For she was all of this. She was incredibly representative of a certain France between 1900 and 1946 with her spicy, vernacular flavor, her affectations (for there are some), her personal notion of the good life, and her code of what is proper and improper, as complicated as ancient China. A France that, deep down, I am not sure I like. (Quoted in Savigneau 240)

While Yourcenar recognizes the complexity of Colette's œuvre, she is ambivalent about the legacy of her predecessor. Yourcenar's association of Colette with "a certain France" of the first half of the twentieth century—a France for which she had little affection—and her somewhat disdainful remarks about Colette's provincialism ("the fulsome tones of Burgundy," "the concierge-and-fortuneteller-adored-by-the-little-local-ladies element"), her class, and her ambiguous moral code anticipate the responses of many of her female contemporaries.

Like Yourcenar, Nathalie Sarraute (1900–99) allied herself with her English rather than her French foremother. While Woolf plays a prominent role in Sarraute's recounting of literary influences, Colette does not figure there. Again, like Yourcenar, Sarraute was an outsider of sorts. Born in Russia of Russian Jewish parents who had met while studying in Geneva and who eventually divorced, Sarraute spent much of her child-hood shuttling between France and Russia. And like Yourcenar, she lived in Britain for a short period in 1920–21, when she studied for an undergraduate degree in history at Oxford University.

A New Novelist, Sarraute sought stylistic direction from the stylisti-cally innovative Woolf. Sarraute makes many references to Woolf in her writing about writing. At first, Woolf's example, along with that of Proust and Joyce, intimidated her. After reading Proust, Joyce, and Woolf in the early 1920s, realizing that the nature of the novel had com-pletely changed and finding she had nothing to write about, she remained silent. Indeed, Sarraute did not begin writing until 1932, at the age of thirty-two. Her first book, *Tropismes,* appeared in 1939 (just two years before Woolf's death).

> It was a time when the novel seemed to be dead—at least the tradi-tional novel. Max Jacob and Valéry were both saying so. As for me, after reading Proust and Joyce, which I did between 1922 and 1924, and then reading Virginia Woolf, I felt that it was no longer possible to write as people had done previously and so, since I couldn't find anything to write about, I didn't write. (Quoted in Brée 138)[17]

Character, she believed, had changed, and one could no longer look to "Tolstoy or Balzac" for guidance (Brée 142).

In her essay "Conversations et Sous-Conversations" (in *L'ère du soupçon* [1956]), which she later describes explicitly as "a defense of psy-chology" (Brée 141), Sarraute opens with another reference to the work of Woolf, this time affirming her debt to the earlier writer. Ironically mimicking the voices of those who "want to read as if the works of Proust, Woolf etc. don't exist," she condemns psychology in favor of behaviorism, suggesting (in a tongue-in-cheek fashion) that Woolf's comments regarding the advent of Modernism and its subversion of a more traditional narrative form are naïve.[18] Affirming her interest in Woolf's formulations about writing, Sarraute again mentions Woolf, along with Proust and Henry James, when asked whether she thinks that a writer can reliably talk about his or her own work. While she ini-tially asserts that the work should suffice in and of itself and that there is nothing to add, she goes on to concede that, with some distance, a writer might be brought to consider why he or she has chosen a particular route

and how his or her work relates to other works, past and present, as had
done Woolf, Proust, and James.[19]

The elliptical nature of Sarraute's *Usage de la parole* (a late text) and
her conception of characters as voices rather than as people with a gender both manifest Woolf's influence. Echoing Woolf in *A Room of One's
Own,* Sarraute asserts that "[a]ny good writer is androgynous, he or she
has to be, so as to be able to write equally about men and women"
(quoted in Barbour 272).[20]

Unlike Yourcenar, Sarraute does not make explicit reference to
Colette in her work. Sarraute's association with the contemporary
French literary scene and with figures such as Jean-Paul Sartre and
André Gide—both of whom read Colette's work—would most likely
have brought her into contact with Colette. Her association with the
new novelists/antinovelists (to borrow Sartre's term for his own *Portrait d'un inconnu*), however, might have led her to look away from traditional narrative forms, which were conventionally (and somewhat
erroneously) associated with Colette, and toward the more experimental work of the Modernists.

While Simone de Beauvoir (1908–86) gives more time to the work
of her French predecessor than do Yourcenar and Sarraute—she refers
to Colette, whose first novels she began reading as a teenager on the
sidewalk outside a Paris bookstore (Thurman xiii), more than twenty
times in her landmark work *Le deuxième sexe* (*The Second Sex*), published
in 1949 (the same year in which Colette published her last works,
among them her memoir *Le fanal bleu*)—she, too, seems to identify
more closely with Woolf in terms of style, and in terms of her writer's
gift.[21] In a *Paris Review* interview, Beauvoir articulates the distinction
that she believes exists between the two writers, echoing Yourcenar in
her characterizing of the work of Colette as limited and provincial and
in opposition to the breadth and timelessness of Woolf's work:

> Virginia Woolf is one of the woman writers who have interested me
> most. Have you seen any photos of her? An extraordinarily lonely face
> . . . in a way, she interests me more than Colette. Colette is, after all,
> very involved in her little love affairs, in household matters, laundry,
> pets. *Virginia Woolf is much broader.* (My emphasis; quoted in *Women
> Writers at Work* 143)

However, in other comments with regard to Woolf's work in the same
interview, Beauvoir betrays the allegiance that ties her to her compatri-
ot, that is, Colette's familiarity, her Frenchness, and the down-to-earth

quality of her work. While she finds Woolf's diaries "fascinating," they are at the same time "too literary," "foreign" to Beauvoir. She feels Woolf herself is "too concerned with whether she'll be published, with what people will say about her" (143). She celebrates *Orlando* and *Mrs Dalloway,* but she is not so keen on the more experimental *The Waves.* Of *A Room of One's Own* (perhaps Woolf's most grounded work and obviously Beauvoir's favorite), Beauvoir says: "it hits the nail on the head. She explains very well why women can't write" (143).

In *The Second Sex* Beauvoir confirms her appreciation of the craftsman in Colette, asserting that:

> It is not only because of her gifts and her temperament alone that Colette became a great writer; her pen has often been her means of support, and she has had to have from it the same good work that an artisan expects from his tools. Between *Claudine* and *Naissance du jour* the amateur became a professional, and that transition brilliantly demonstrates the benefits of a severe period of training. (784)

.

While many women in 1949, according to Beauvoir, "regard[ed] themselves as given," believing "that their merits derive[d] from an immanent grace," Colette realized that "worth [could] be acquired by conquest" (784).

Beauvoir encountered Colette for the first time in 1948 in the company of Jean-Paul Sartre. Also present were the writer and artist Jean Cocteau and actress and director Simone Berriau. Sartre had first met Colette at the home of Berriau in 1945 (Thurman 472) and had given her a copy of his *La nausée* with the following dedication, which pegs Colette in a sense as a writer of autobiography: "To Colette so similar to her books that I love so much with the admiration and if I may be so bold the friendship of J.-P. Sartre" (my translation).[22]

Beauvoir describes this meeting with Colette in *La force des choses.* Despite Colette's cold reception, Beauvoir is happy "just to contemplate [Colette]":

> I had been told that she was not very cordial toward [younger] women and she received me coldly. "Do you like animals?" "No," I say. She looks me over with an Olympian eye. I didn't care. I hadn't been counting on any real contact between us. It was enough for me just to contemplate her. Arthritic, wild-haired, violently made-up, age gave her sharp face and her blue eyes an electric brilliance: between her collection of paperweights and the gardens framed by

her windows, she appeared, paralyzed and sovereign, like a formidable Mother-Goddess. When we dined with her and Cocteau at Simone Berriau's, Sartre had the impression of facing a "sacred monster." She [Colette] had made the effort to come, in large part out of curiosity to see [Sartre], and knowing that for him she was the principal attraction of the evening . . . The Burgundian fullness of her voice didn't blunt the acuity of her words. Her speech flowed from a natural source, and . . . Cocteau's brilliance seemed contrived in comparison. (Quoted in Thurman 484–85)[23]

Beauvoir was not always so kind about Colette, especially when writing to Sartre. In 1935, after badly sunburning her ankles, she writes to Sartre: "So I spent Monday afternoon rubbing myself with ointments and reading Colette's *Sido,* which is pretty awful" (*Letters to Sartre* 6). Several years later, in 1937, Beauvoir recounts to Sartre a "delightful dream" she had "about Maurice Chevalier [who later starred in the film version of Colette's *Gigi* in 1958], who was simultaneously Colette and very surprised by this: 'Isn't she a woman?' he was saying" (*Letters to Sartre* 8).[24]

   In 1948, in a letter to American writer Nelson Algren early in their seventeen-year-long relationship, Beauvoir again describes her dinner with Colette, this time honoring her as "the only great woman writer in France." Her laudatory remarks (which contradict those she makes to Sartre) betray a somewhat condescending view of Colette's work in France and perhaps suggest more about Beauvoir's version of herself as a French woman and writer that she would like to convey to her new American lover than about Colette. Her comments offer an interesting rendering of Colette's biography.

I think you heard of Colette: she is the only great woman writer in France, a really great writer. She was once the most beautiful woman. She danced in music-halls, slept with a lot of men, wrote pornographic novels and then good novels. She loved country, flowers, beasts, and making love, and then she loved too the most sophisticated life; she slept with woman [*sic*] too. She was fond of food and wine—well, she loved all good things, and she spoke beautifully about them. Now she is seventy-five and still the most fascinating eyes and a nice triangular cat face; she is very fat, impotent, a little deaf, but she can tell stories and smile and laugh in such a way nobody would think of looking at younger, finer women. She spoke the whole evening with Cocteau about the neighbourhood where they live, the Palais-

Royal, which is one of the best places in Paris indeed. They described the life of the old whores who live there, the little shops, the little cafés, the people in them with such humanity and such humour that we listened, really fascinated. I hope I shall see her again. I was in love with her, through her books, when I was a girl, so it meant something to me to see her. It's strange an old woman when she has lived so much, so feverishly, so freely, when she knows so much and does not care for anything more because now everything is over for her. (*A Transatlantic Love Affair* 181)

Beauvoir refers to Colette's life and work in *Le deuxième sexe* more than she does any other female author. In her discussion of sexual initiation, she makes reference to Colette's *Le blé en herbe* (435–36); when addressing love, marriage, and abortion, she mentions *Gribiche* (546); lesbianism, *Ces plaisirs* (the earlier title of *Le pur et l'impur*) (465); lesbianism and its analogies with the mother-daughter bond, *Les vrilles de la vigne* (465); and masochism, *Mes apprentissages* (447). Beauvoir notes the particularity of Colette's relationship with and depiction of her mother, Sido: "Rare indeed," she suggests, "are the instances when the mother's authority is as comprehending and discreet as in the case of that 'Sido' whom Colette has lovingly depicted" (331). For Beauvoir, Colette's characters are progressive, rare examples of women and girls who explode stereotypes, such as Vinca, the protagonist of *Le blé en herbe*, Léa in *Chéri*, and Renée Néré in *La vagabonde*. She refers to the fact that it is Vinca's young lover, Phil, not Vinca herself, who feels he has been taken after they first make love:

Colette's Vinca, in *Blé en herbe*, on the day after a rather rough defloration, displays a calmness that surprises her friend Phil: the point is that she did not feel that she was being 'taken'; on the contrary she felt pride in ridding herself of her virginity, she experienced no overwhelming bewilderment; truth to tell, Phil was wrong in being astonished, for his sweetheart had not really come to know the male. Claudine was farther from being unscathed after a mere dance with Renaud. (435–36)

Despite Vinca's early rebellion, Beauvoir suggests that Colette predicts that once Vinca has become a woman, she will conform more closely to stereotypes of the good, passive wife (408).

In contrast, when Beauvoir chooses examples of girls and women from Woolf's work, it is to illustrate the restraints imposed on women and the tempered nature of their epiphanies:

> The moments that women regard as revelations are those in which
> they discover their accord with a static and self-sufficient reality: those
> luminous moments of happiness which Virginia Woolf (in *Mrs Dal-
> loway* and *To the Lighthouse*) and Katherine Mansfield (throughout
> her work) bestow upon their heroines by way of supreme recom-
> pense. The joy that lies in the free surge of liberty is reserved for man;
> that which woman knows is a quiet sense of smiling plenitude. (690)

Beauvoir quotes two passages from Woolf's *The Waves*. In the first,
young Jinny revels in her emergent sexuality: "'I now begin to unfurl,
in this scent, in this radiance, as a fern when its curled leaves unfurl . . .
I feel a thousand capacities spring up in me'" (410); in the second, anxious to become a woman, Jinny embraces a future that is oppressive and
restrictive: "'He will stand under the cedar tree. To his one word I shall
answer my one word. What has formed in me I shall give him. I shall
have children; I shall have maids in aprons [. . .] I shall be like my
mother, silent in a blue apron locking up the cupboards'" (411). Beauvoir uses Woolf to contrast the greater freedom enjoyed by women in
France with that accorded to their English counterparts: "In England,
Virginia Woolf remarks (in *A Room of One's Own*), women writers have
always aroused hostility. In France, things were somewhat more favor-
able, because of the alliance between the social and the intellectual life,
but, in general, opinion was hostile to 'bluestockings'" (120). Again,
returning to what seems to be her favorite of Woolf's works, Beauvoir
also cites Woolf's famous comments in *A Room of One's Own* with
regard to the limits placed on an imaginary sister of Shakespeare compared to the liberty enjoyed by her brother.[25]

Beauvoir returns once again to *A Room of One's Own* in 1966 in a
presentation given in Japan, entitled "La femme et la création," calling
it "un très joli petit livre" ("a very nice little book"). Beauvoir uses
Woolf's work to support her own views on social class and the importance of engagement. In *A Room of One's Own*, according to Beauvoir,
Woolf had asked herself why, in terms of literature, works by English
women were so rare and generally of secondary quality. "The room,"
says Beauvoir, "is at the same time real and symbolic. In order to be able
to write, in order to be able to accomplish something, one must first of
all belong" (my translation; 458–59).[26] She outlines Woolf's contemplation of Shakespeare's sister's fate—"She would have stayed at home,

she would have done the cooking, the sewing" (my translation; 459),[27] and she mentions her own attempts to make a similar argument (to provide a translation of sorts) in *Le deuxième sexe:* "I tried myself in *The Second Sex* a similar analysis using Van Gogh. I tried to show that a daughter born in the place of Van Gogh would not have had the opportunities he had" (459).[28] She is, she says, completely in agreement with Woolf, that "si doué que soit un être au départ, si ses dons ne peuvent pas être exploités par suite de sa condition sociale, par suite des circonstances qui l'entourent, ces dons resteront stériles" ("as gifted as a being might be in the beginning, if her gifts cannot be exploited as a result of her social condition, as a result of the circumstances that surround her, her gifts will remain sterile") or as Stendhal, who Beauvoir (facetiously?) suggests is a great feminist, put it: "tout génie qui naît femme est perdu pour l'humanité" (459) ("all genius that is born woman is lost for humanity").[29]

Marguerite Duras (1914–96), whose major success as a writer post-dated Colette—her first novel, *Les impudents,* was published in 1943, her award-winning autobiographical novel *L'Amant* appeared in 1984, and her last work, *C'est tout,* was published in 1995—echoes Yourcenar and Beauvoir in her criticism of Colette's work. In a 1975 interview Duras mentions Colette when talking about what she calls "feminine literature": "an organic, translated writing . . . translated from blackness, from darkness." "Women have been in darkness for centuries. They don't know themselves" (Marks and Courtivron 174), writes Duras, echoing Woolf's *A Room of One's Own.*[30] Some women, she suggests, "write as they think they should write—to imitate men and make a place for themselves in literature." Colette, she goes on to say, "wrote like a little girl [. . .] So she wrote 'feminine literature' as men wanted it" (Marks and Courtivron 174). This, Duras contends, is not really feminine literature at all—it is the man's view of what feminine literature should be. Colette's work lacked the violence that Duras believed feminine literature required.

> I think 'feminine literature' is a violent, direct literature and that, to judge it, we must not—and this is the main point I want to make—start all over again, take off from a theoretical platform. The other day you were telling me, "Yes, but women can also be ideologues, philosophers, poets, etc., etc." Of course. Of course. But why go over that? That should go without saying. We should be saying the opposite: can *men* forget everything and join women? . . . (Marks and Courtivron 174)[31]

Despite Duras's disavowal of the influence of her predecessor and
the distinction she makes between her own form of feminine writing
and that of Colette's, Hélène Cixous, in her oft-cited essay "Le rire de
la méduse," pairs writings of Duras with those of Colette and Jean
Genet precisely in terms of what she terms their "inscriptions of femininity." In France these three writers alone wrote in the feminine,
according to Cixous. "The Anglo-Saxon countries," she adds in
parentheses, perhaps in reference to Woolf, "have shown resources of
distinctly greater consequence" (Marks and Courtivron 248–49,
n. 3).[32]

Although Duras does not name Woolf among her influences—her
list of all male writers, Michelet, Saint-Just, Stendhal, curiously resembles that of Colette in *La maison de Claudine,* with the exception of
Balzac[33]—critics frequently tie the two together:

> One can't talk anymore about influence, but of intertextuality, or,
> why not, culture. Marguerite Duras "writes with" since no writer
> advances in undiscovered territory [. . .] Very far from her, Balzac,
> very close, Virginia Woolf or Louise Labé, evoked in *L'amant de la
> Chine du nord.* (My translation)[34]

Duras is cited as having claimed Virginia Woolf and Emily Dickinson as
sisters to her protagonist Emily L. of the novel of the same name. In a
story about women and madness, Emily L. is a poet whose husband,
named the Captain, destroys the poem she most covets. Like Woolf's Isa
Oliver of her last novel *Between the Acts,* who disguises her notebook as
an account book (*Between the Acts* 15), Emily L. writes poetry in secret.
Again, like *Between the Acts, Emily L.* is a layered text, framed by a second narrative.

Thus, Duras's dissatisfaction with Colette and her turn to Woolf
echo that of Yourcenar, Sarraute, and Beauvoir. Looking for something
bigger and broader than the narrow realm of what they perceived to be
Colette's provincial, domestic fiction, they embraced Woolf's work, celebrating her version of feminism and what they saw as the more progressive nature of her writing. Considering themselves outsiders—and
one notes Yourcenar's address to the Académie française, the violence of
Duras's writing—the French women writers looked away from France
for their female influences.

Meanwhile, in England writers like Rebecca West, Antonia White,
Dorothy Richardson, A. S. Byatt, Margaret Drabble, and Angela Carter
were looking the other way. They sought an alternative to the elitist

patriarchal structures of which they believed Woolf was an anomalous, but nevertheless a well-established, support. In contrast to their French contemporaries, many English women writers felt that Woolf failed to speak for them. Common to the British writers' responses to Woolf's work is a sense that something is missing, something is absent from her work. In Colette's work, by contrast, the English writers found the force and substance lacking in Woolf's. They found the strength usually yoked to the body, yoked to the mind, to paraphrase West.

Like Yourcenar, West met both Woolf and Colette. West and Woolf moved in similar social circles and met on numerous occasions. In 1922, prior to meeting West, Woolf described her novel *The Judge* in disparaging terms: "[I]t bursts, like an over stuffed sausage," asserts Woolf. "She pours it all in; and one is covered with flying particles" (*Letters* 2: 548). In a letter to Vanessa Bell in May 1928, Woolf describes a first meeting with West in more positive terms:

> Rebecca was much the most interesting, though as hard as nails, very distrustful, and no beauty. She is a cross between a charwoman and a gipsy, but as tenacious as a terrier, with flashing eyes, very shabby, rather dirty nails, immense vitality, bad taste, suspicion of intellectuals, and great intelligence. She gave me the true history of Isadora Duncan's life—(I sent you the life, by the way, which is rather valuable, as libraries are banning it). Rebecca has knocked about with all the mongrels of Europe. She talks openly of her son [Anthony], who has got consumption: They say she is a hardened liar—but I rather liked her. (*Letters* 3: 501)

Several years later, in December 1932, Woolf wrote of West in her diary: "oh yes a very clever woman, rather rubbed about the thorax: with a good supply of worldly talk: & much go & humour; a silky careening society voice" (*Diary* 4: 131–32). On another occasion, in 1933, Woolf describes tea with West and Ethel Smyth as "a screaming howling party." She portrays "Old Ethel" meandering, deaf, as "so violent" but "shrewd," and she compares West, "although she is tenacious and masterful and very good company," to "an arboreal animal grasping a tree, and showing all her teeth, as if another animal were about to seize her young" (*Letters* 5: 259). Her later comments about West were not so flattering. In 1939, in a letter to Vita, Woolf calls West "preposterous and fat"; she "[dillydallies] with the world and the flesh" and "she's too distorted one foot on sea and one on land," suggests Woolf, citing an ancestor of Vita Sackville-West (*Letters* 6: 351).

West's view of Woolf is similarly mixed. Like Beauvoir, West distin-guished between Woolf's texts, praising some and dismissing others. In 1929 she praises the recently published *A Room* (in which West herself, incidentally, gets two mentions) in her essay "Virginia Woolf and Autumn" (included in *Ending in Earnest*). In this essay West portrays Woolf as a "genius," and she calls *A Room* "an uncompromising piece of feminist propaganda: I think the ablest yet written" (211). "She proves her case," which West understands to be a defense of women "from the accusation of inferiority that is laid against them on the grounds that they have failed to be geniuses," "in passages that in their perfect, rounded form, and in the warm yet restrained colour of their imagery, remind one of the great chrysanthemums seen these days in the florists' window" (211).[35]

In 1972, in Joan Russel Noble's *Recollections,* and in 1981, in a *Paris Review* interview (the latter significantly conducted after the pub-lication of Woolf's collected letters and diaries in the late 1970s), West criticizes works like *The Waves* and *The Common Reader.* In Noble's col-lection, West begins by marking her distance from Woolf. She and Woolf, she suggests, were "no more than acquaintances," and "[t]he Bloomsbury Group did not like me, and," she adds, "I did not like them" (89). West describes Woolf as possessing "a phantom-like quali-ty": "Though she sat opposite one, the impression left was as hard to recall as if she were one of those ghosts who are only seen as they turn the corner of the passage" (89). While West admires Woolf's originali-ty—*Orlando,* she contends, is an exquisite book, although ruined, she asserts, by the addition of "those terrible photographs" of Vita/Vir-ginia, Orlando, and Sasha (93)—she is skeptical about whether Woolf's work merits the approval it has received: "*The Waves,*" she opines, "is Pre-Raphaelite *kitsch* and should be forgotten. *A Room of One's Own* is on the right side and is a good piece of craftsmanship, but it is hardly worth teaching it in schools, and indeed I think too much is made of *The Common Reader*" (92).[36] She continues these comments in the later of the two interviews, telling Marina Warner:

> It's an absurd error to put modern English literature in the curricu-
> lum. You should read contemporary literature for pleasure or not read
> it at all. You shouldn't be taught to monkey with it. It's ghastly to
> think of all the little girls who are taught to read *To the Lighthouse*. It's
> not really substantial food for the young because there's such a strong
> feeling that Woolf was doing a set piece and it didn't really matter
> very much. She was putting on an act. Shakespeare didn't put on an

act. But *Orlando* is a lovely original splash, a beautiful piece of fancy. (Quoted in *Women Writers at Work* 93)

West goes on to criticize the Bloomsbury group as a whole. She says that Leonard Woolf had "a tiresome mind" and describes Vanessa Bell's paintings as "awful muddy decorations." She also hates, she adds, Duncan Grant's artwork. West describes the reaction of her butler to a scene at dinner when the Bloomsbury group were discussing, in a "terribly subtle" way, a scene from Faulkner where a cob of corn is used in the course of a rape. The pretentiousness of the group is highlighted by the reaction of the butler, who runs to find Faulkner's work, understanding that it must be "saucy" (Quoted in *Women Writers at Work* 93–94). West closes the discussion of Woolf and Bloomsbury by conceding that "Virginia Woolf's criticism was much better than criticism others were writing then" (94). And in a gesture that suggests an effort to take back Woolf, West writes: "It is odd how the French writers who think they are carrying on her method simply show they do not read English very well. She did not catalogue, as the nouvelle vague does, she, I repeat it, perceived" (93).

West was, on the other hand, an admirer of Colette. In *Ending in Earnest* she describes her first sight of Colette, standing on the platform of the St. Raphael train station in Paris. The imposing French writer, who assumed the "stance of a Spanish fighting bull," had a face that "suggested the muzzle of a very fierce animal," according to West, and eyes "prolonged by blue lines till the proportion they bore to the rest of her features was queerly non-human" (180). Colette's strength of character, she goes on to suggest, is unmatched. She even leaves Radclyffe Hall, to whom West was, according to Cline, a "literary mentor-friend" (Cline 29), in the dust:

> In thirty years she has been putting into infallible artistic form her gross, wise, limited, eternal view about life, at times leaving [Radclyffe Hall's] *The Well of Loneliness* beaten at the post, at times producing little candid pearls of innocence, since these too are aspects of the universe. It is one of the peculiar virtues of the French race that it can take the kind of sturdy long-lived strength which in other countries remains dedicated to the body and yoke it to the service of the mind. (181)

In the same *Paris Review* interview in which she had harsh words for Woolf and the Bloomsbury group, West praises Colette's skills as a

writer while questioning a number of her personal traits, particularly her
lack of engagement with contemporary politics:

> I think she was repetitive and I hate all her knowing nudges about
> men, but I think she was a good writer on the whole and she was very
> good on landscape. She did a wonderful book called Trio [author's
> note: does she mean *Duo?*]. She was really more egotistical than you
> could possibly imagine, and she was outside a lot of experiences in a
> most curious way. I was taken to see her in Paris with a man who was
> a judge at Nuremberg. She didn't pick it up at all. (Quoted in *Women
> Writers at Work* 82)[37]

A similar response to Woolf's and Colette's work is that of Antonia
White (1899–1980, born Eirene Botting), a counterpoint to Yourcenar
as the translator of a number of Colette's works into English, including
the *Claudines* (*Claudine at School* in 1956, *Claudine in Paris* in 1958,
and *Claudine Married* in 1960[38]), *Bella-Vista,* and *La chatte.* White's
translation credits also include Maupassant's *A Woman's Life,* Voltaire's
The History of Charles XII: King of Sweden, and Georges Simenon's *The
Glass Cage.* Like Yourcenar, White also wrote: her first novel, *Frost in
May,* the story of Nanda, a new pupil at a Catholic girls' high school,
appeared in 1933 and is often compared to Colette's *Claudine à l'école.*
Woolf appears to have read *Frost in May;* however, her response to it is
unclear. She wrote to Quentin Bell in late 1933: "The one I admired
[. . .] is Ordinary Families; the other [book], Night in May no Frost
she calls it [21 words omitted]. She is a friend of Logan's, a Chelsea
pensioner, and I daresay worthless; but the erudite say she's full of sup-
pressed ardour, virtue and it's her own story. So let me have it back"
(*Letters* 5: 213–14). It is unclear whether the latter sentence applies to
White.

Unlike Yourcenar, who sat down with Woolf to discuss her translation of *The Waves,* White never met Colette; her translations postdate
the author's death in 1954. The Colette whom White met via her translations, however, often exasperated her: "I really don't think ANY
woman was as much in love with herself as Colette . . . She is so overwhelming! I am worn out having to live in her personality, translating
her! I love her . . . but I need a rest from her" (in a letter to Emily Cole-
man, quoted in Dunn 379).

White looked abroad for her literary models. She admires American
writers: "Eudora Welty, Martha Gelhorn [who, incidentally, married
Bertrand de Jouvenel, Colette's stepson-turned-lover], and of course

Djuna [Barnes]." However, it is with the French that she allies herself: "I belong to the French line and there I'm well outdistanced . . . Mauriac, Colette, Julien Green" (White 282). While among the ancients White says "she [feels] a minnow," she is not threatened by her English contemporaries: "there are very few," she thinks, "who are definitely 'better'" (282).

White's biographer, Jane Dunn, tells us that Woolf (two decades older than White) was "the hero-writer of Antonia's youth" (70). Indeed, White wrote a fan letter to Woolf. In 1939, at the age of forty, however, as White reads *Jacob's Room*, she views Woolf in a more critical way, describing it as lacking structure, leaving her as a reader empty and dissatisfied:

> It exasperated yet charmed me. Here was an attempt to relate day and night. She [Woolf] lays her little strands side by side instead of working them into a pattern. But perhaps it is because there is no solid structure underneath that it leaves me with this curious empty and dissatisfied feeling. In the last book it is beaten out so thin that it is threadbare. Life may be entirely meaningless and yet I feel that in art you must impose a form on it. The most beautiful reproduction of sounds and colours and atmospheres is somehow unsatisfactory . . . (White 164)

This is a sentiment that was echoed by White's and Woolf's contemporary, Dorothy Richardson (1873–1957), whose work and whose use of stream of consciousness narrative is frequently compared with Woolf's. When asked to review *The Years* in 1937, Richardson refused, stating in a letter that Woolf's writing "does not deeply move me" (330). Richardson appears to have resented what she perceived as Woolf's snobbery and the elitism of the Bloomsbury group, issues that also bothered West.[39] When reading Woolf's last novel, *Between the Acts*, she has a sense that there is something missing from Woolf's prose. Woolf's "heritage" and her "upbringing in academic circles," Richardson suggests in a letter to fellow writer Bryher, are detrimental to her work:

> What upset me, I think, in V. Woolf is a sort of, I mean the *kind* of disillusionment that somewhere in each book approaches paralysis. In the essays too, it is there, overshadowing each statement. Movement ceases of mind & spirit. Less than usual in this book [*Between the Acts*], which in certain directions, particularly in the significant matter of what people draw from just being together, reveals the ripening

of a perception that in *The Voyage Out* has not begun to dawn. One side of the trouble, of what at any rate so troubles those who enormously admire & yet deprecate her work, is, I believe, her docility, due perhaps to an upbringing in academic circles, to certain kinds of generalizations. The closing page of this book reveals her reciting a lesson from an extremely dubious text-book. She obviously doesn't herself believe it adequate, but has nothing, given her own so very specialist angle of vision, to substitute. All her avenues have the brief perspective of the good Pagan, so that her adorable, wonder-working talents show, in the end, like peacocks in a prison. Peacocks is the word. Because sometimes they strut & strike attitudes. But always with drooping wings. Still, in this book, she *was* escaping the burden of her heritage. (Richardson 424)[40]

She goes on to describe *Between the Acts* in a second letter to Bryher as "poetry moaning in a vacuum. Patronage, too, always, rather than vital concentration. Life seen, from a balcony, through a lorgnette. Nerves & brain, these only, operative . . ." (425). Woolf reviewed the fourth of Richardson's *Pilgrimage* sequence for the *Times Literary Supplement* in 1919 and the seventh for the *Nation & Athenaeum* in 1923. She refused to review several others. In her diary in 1920, Woolf wrote that both Richardson and Joyce "were ruined by the damned 'egotistical self'" (quoted in Hussey 229). In the *Nation* review she attributed to Richardson the invention of "'a sentence which we might call the psychological sentence of the feminine gender'" (quoted in Hussey 229).

This anti-Woolf sentiment, largely based on her class status, carried over to another generation of writers that includes Doris Lessing (1919–), Margaret Drabble (1939–), A. S. Byatt (1936–), and Angela Carter (1940–92). When Lessing mentions Woolf she does so in terms of her own and Woolf's inclusion and exclusion as a writer. While Lessing admires Woolf, according to Woolf and Lessing scholar Dorothy Brewster, she "feels that Virginia Woolf's experience must have been too limited, 'because there's always a point in her novels when I think "Fine, but look at what you've left out"'" (quoted in Brewster 158).[41] Lessing explains in an interview that growing up away from England— she was raised by English parents in southern Rhodesia (now Zimbabwe)—broadened her own experience and enabled her to see things a little differently: "I'm extremely lucky. Both my parents were quite excessively British. I have that as absolute bedrock. But I also have the other eye because I was brought up outside England" (quoted in Blume).[42] In the same interview, Lessing cites Woolf's comments about the restrictions imposed on such writers as Charlotte Brontë in comparison to her Russian contemporary, Tolstoy. Lessing considers her own work to be more closely allied with the Russian novel than with the English, although, as Brewster points out, many English and American novelists, Woolf among them, were themselves influenced by Russian literature.[43] When asked directly, Lessing scoffs at the suggestion that either Woolf or Colette "influenced" her work. However, she writes that she enjoys the physicality of Colette's work (personal correspondence).[44]

A. S. Byatt (1936–), author of *Possession* (1990) and *Angels and Insects* (1992), suggests that she writes to some degree "against" Woolf. In the introduction to an early novel, *The Shadow of the Sun* (1964), Byatt says that she struggled with "the form of the novel" for which she could find no satisfactory model. While she found "Elizabeth Bowen, Rosamund Lehmann, Forster [and] Woolf" "too suffused with 'sensibility,'" the alternative, "the joky social comedy of [Kingsley] Amis and [John] Wain," was even less satisfactory. She looked to France for stylistic influence—she cites French novelist Françoise Sagan's *Bonjour tristesse,* a novel she describes as "against sensibility"—and found in the work of Marcel Proust and Iris Murdoch "a kind of toughness [combined with] a sensuous awareness" that suited her.[45] Byatt cites as her influences "Proust [. . .] Balzac, Dickens, Eliot, Thomas Mann and James, Iris Murdoch, Ford Maddox Ford, and Willa Cather [. . .] Leo Tolstoy and Fyodor Dostoevsky" (quoted in Kelly 2).[46]

In a 1972 *Ms.* article, entitled "How Not to Be Afraid of Virginia Woolf," Margaret Drabble (1939–), author of many novels and short stories, including her first novel, *A Summer Bird Cage,* in 1964, explains the vicissitudes of her own relationship with Woolf and her work.[47] At first resistant to Woolf, whom she believed to be "a 'difficult' writer overfond of technique, self-important about her use of stream of consciousness, a somewhat disdainful creator of a literary avant garde," "an elitist," writing "for a minority about a minority," "a dull dilettante," "out of date," and "out of touch" (68), Drabble's attitude changed when she stumbled upon *A Room of One's Own.* Here Drabble found a work that spoke to her own condition. In Woolf's other essays and polemic works, she also found "a good fighter, a brave speaker, and a loyal addresser of envelopes" (70). On turning to the novels, Drabble describes her initial disappointment. What did Mrs Ramsay of *To the Lighthouse* and Mrs Flanders of *Jacob's Room* have to do with "the brave new world of liberation," she asks? However, she also softens to the novels, appreciating them for "the living detail and variety of life" contained therein (70). Woolf's influence, Drabble contends, is pervasive; her style has changed the form of the novel:

> Seascapes, holidays, dinner parties. A trivial domestic world, maybe, unworthy of the pen of a militant. It was for these preoccupations that she was rejected by succeeding generations. *But there is hardly a writer who has not been affected by her.* Her fluid sentence structure, her poetic prose, her perception of the slightest connection, her lack of interest in a heavy conventional narrative, her passion for the inconsequential psychological detail—*all these things have gone into the novel and remained there.* (My emphasis; 72)

Perhaps the most forthright of this group of more recent writers is Angela Carter, who attacked Woolf for her elitism and embraced Colette for her break from tradition. Carter published her first novel, *Shadow Dance,* in 1966 and her last, *Wise Children,* in 1991. She also translated the fairy stories of Charles Perrault. When asked by critic Elaine Jordan about feminist attacks on her work—Jordan ties the two writers together in terms of their perceived lack of feminist credentials—Carter responds by explaining that her story "The Bloody Chamber" (the title story of the collection of the same name and a Bluebeard rewrite) is "a homage to Colette": "'I wanted a lush fin-de-siècle decor for the story, and a style that . . . utilizes the heightened diction of the novelette, to half seduce the reader into this wicked, glamorous, fatal world'" (quoted in Jordan, "The Dangerous Edge" 197).

Confirming further Colette's presence to Carter's work, Carter has Colette appear briefly as a character in her novel *Nights at the Circus* (1989). While in Paris, Carter's protagonist Fevvers dines with Colette and Willy. She coaches the former while the latter feeds her:

> On that European tour of [Fevvers's], Parisians shot themselves in droves for her sake; not just Lautrec but *all* the post-impressionists vied to paint her; Willy gave her supper and she gave Colette some good advice. Alfred Jarry proposed marriage. (11)

An appropriate choice of visitor, Colette, like Fevvers, embodies "all the *éclat* of a new era about to take off"(11).[48]

Carter writes at length about Colette's life and work in a review of Michèle Sarde's biography of Colette, *Colette: Libre et entravée.*[49] Highlighting the life of Colette over her work, Carter says that she admires Colette first and foremost for her tenacity: "Magnificently," writes

Carter of Colette, "she did not know her place" (*Shaking a Leg* 525). Colette lived at the limit: according to Carter, her life "was as picaresque as a woman's may be without putting herself in a state of hazard" (520). Her (single) name and her renown, writes Carter, attest to her uniqueness: "Colette is one of the few, possibly the only, well-known woman writer of modern times who is universally referred to simply by her surname, *tout court*. Woolf hasn't made it, even after all these years, Rhys without the Jean is incognito, Nin without the Anaïs looks like a typo. Colette, Madame Colette, remains in this as much else, unique" (519). For Carter, Colette is a mystery, a constant contradiction. Echoing the title of Sarde's biography, Carter contends that "not one but two writers are growing within Colette"—Colette, author of *La vagabonde*, creator of Renée Néré, who says no to marriage and remains free; and Colette, writer/journalist for *Le matin* who marries its editor, Henri de Jouvenel (521). Despite the impressive breadth of Colette's provincial culinary expertise—"'she knew a receipt for everything, whether it was for furniture polish, vinegar, orange-wine or quince-water, for cooking truffles or preserving linen and materials'" (524)—Carter questions the authenticity of Colette's "paysanne" persona; she believes this quintessential French provincialism was as manufactured as British cookbook writer (and frequent butt of Carter's jokes about elitism) Elizabeth David's book on French country cooking and as much intended for publication. This capacity for dissimulation is a quality that Carter admires in Colette: "The passionate integrity of Colette's narcissism," Carter contends, "rendered her indestructible" (524).

Carter describes Colette's work as "a peculiar kind of strip tease": "Colette never tells you about herself," writes Carter, "[i]nstead she describes herself" (522). According to Carter, the autobiographical nature of Colette's work is underscored when Robert Phelps, author of *Earthly Paradise*, an autobiography taken from the writings of her lifetime, is able to write a "perfectly coherent biography" of Colette by merely assembling extracts from her work (522). Carter notes the objective subjectivity of Colette's work: "The apparent objectivity of her prose is a device to seal these people in her own narrative subjectivity." She describes Colette's prose as "narcissistic"—we admire Sido, but also the narrator's love for her (523).

Celebrating Colette's feminism, Carter suggests that while Beauvoir's memoirs are almost entirely about Sartre, even though she is conspicuously absent from his, Colette, by comparison, "simply did not believe that women *were* the second sex" (525). Colette, she goes on, celebrated the status quo of femininity, its physical glamour and its capacity to subvert and withstand the boredom of patriarchy. Here again Carter distinguishes between different Colettes. She prefers Colette's earlier "fictions," such as the *Claudine* novels. They are "more interesting" than the autobiographical work, which she describes as "obsessive gush" (524). The *Chéri* novels, Carter contends, are about the power politics of love (527). This makes her an ambivalent ally to the women's movement. "She is like certain shop-stewards," suggests Carter, "who devote so much time to getting up management's nose that they lose sight of the great goals of socialism" (526). Carter concludes by affirming that Colette's contribution lay outside the realm of the literary: "Apart from the *Chéri* novels and one or two others, [Colette's] achievement as a whole *was* extraordinary though not in a literary sense; she forged a career out of the kind of self-obsession which is supposed, in a woman, to lead only to tears before bed-time, in a man to lead to the peaks" (528).

Carter found Woolf somewhat less inspiring. Comments like this one, made in response to an article on bread (and specifically on British food writer Elizabeth David's book on bread), demonstrate the nature of Carter's problems with Woolf:

> Virginia Woolf? Yes. Although otherwise an indifferent cook, Virginia could knock you up a lovely cottage loaf. You bet. This strikes me as just the sort of pretentious frivolous and dilettantish thing a Bloomsbury *would* be good at—knowing how to do one, just one, fatuously complicated kitchen thing and doing that one thing well enough to put the cook's nose out of joint. "I will come into the kitchen, Louie," she said to this young employee of hers, "and show you how to do it." (*Shaking a Leg* 95)[50]

Despite this hostility to Woolf the woman, Carter admired Woolf's work. However, like Beauvoir and others, she distinguished between the accessible Woolf (for Carter, *Orlando*) and the inaccessible Woolf. The picaresque nature of many of Carter's characters, such as the gender-bending Eve of *A Passion for New Eve* and the flamboyant and elusive circus performer Fevvers of *Nights at the Circus*, highlight Carter's debt to the Woolf of *Orlando*.[51]

Thus the French rejection of Colette is matched by the English rejection of Woolf. Many of the same criticisms are leveled at the foremother by her successor in both cases: she does not speak for women; her work is out of date; she represents the old order, not the new. In this way, in each case the foremother represents a kind of Woolfian "Angel in the House," as Elaine Showalter suggests (1 n. 1), who embodies convention and submission to a set of values unacceptable to the later writer. But the reader from abroad sees things differently. As do Colette's French successors, Woolf's English successors celebrate the foreign voice. Geographically, socially, and politically freer, the foreign writer is less clearly defined as one thing or another, less predictable, and more mysterious than one's own foremother. The particulars of her life, her class, her friends, and her affiliation with one group of writers as opposed to another hold less importance. Considered an insider at home, she remains an outsider for those reading from abroad.

In conclusion, I want to look at two recent works that initially complicate but ultimately confirm the pattern explored here. Jeanette Winterson's celebration of Woolf (along with Gertrude Stein) as a major influence on her work in her *Art [Objects]: Essays on Ecstasy and Effrontery* and Julia Kristeva's honoring of Colette in her recent third volume of *Le génie féminin* suggest an effort to celebrate the literary foremother on her own ground, Woolf in English, Colette in French.[52] However, Kristeva's acknowledgment of her status as an outsider—she is Bulgarian born—and Winterson's insistence that Woolf's work, her words, be understood independently from Woolf the woman suggest a stepping away from rather than an addressing of the issues raised by the other writers included in this study.

Winterson (1961–), author of the semi-autobiographical *Oranges Are Not the Only Fruit, The Passion,* and *Sexing the Cherry,* is unequivocal about her debt to Woolf, once going so far as to declare herself Woolf's natural heir on a late show television special in Britain.[53] In her *Art [Objects],* a series of essays about writing, Winterson explains in detail the relationship of her work with that of Woolf. In contrast to West, Richardson, and Carter, Winterson looks exclusively to the work and contends that readers are unconcerned with the ways in which a writer's life and a writer's work intersect (27). She dismisses speculation about Woolf's life and its relationship to her art as "bulldust," instead insisting that "the only honest undistorted focus is her work" (63).[54]

> There has been so much concentration on Woolf as a feminist and as a thinker, that the unique power of her language has still not been given the close critical attention it deserves. When Woolf is read and taught, she needs to be read and taught as a poet; she is not a writer who uses words for things, for her, words are things, incantatory, substantial. In her fiction, her polemic is successful because it is subordinated to the right of spells. (70)

Woolf's strength, according to Winterson, is her way with words: "Unlike many novelists, then and now, she loved words. That is she was devoted to words, faithful to words, romantically attached to words, desirous of words. She was territory and words occupied her" (75).

> A work of art is abundant, spills out, gets drunk, sits up with you all night and forgets to close the curtains, dries your tears, is your friend, offers you a disguise, a difference, a pose. Cut and cut through it and there is still a diamond at the core. Skim the top and it is rich. The inexhaustible energy of art is transfusion for a worn-out world. When I read Virginia Woolf she is to my spirit, waterfall and wine. (65)

Allying her own method with that of Woolf and Gertrude Stein, Winterson asserts that all we can be sure of about a writer who emerges from her own work is her fictionality: "Like Stein, I prefer myself as a character in my own fiction, and like Stein and Woolf, what concerns me is language" (53). She adds: "Like *Orlando* and [her own] *Oranges are Not the Only Fruit*, [Stein's] *The Autobiography of Alice B. Toklas* is a fiction masquerading as a memoir"—rather than memoir masquerading as fiction (53).[55] Winterson's comments recall Colette's epigraph to *La naissance du jour*, drawn from the text itself: "Imagine-t-on, à me lire, que je fais mon portrait? Patience, c'est seulement mon modèle" (53) ("Do you imagine when reading me that I am portraying myself? Be patient, it's only my model"). In this way, Winterson sets aside some of the issues that turned Carter, Richardson, and West away from Woolf. Nationality, class, sexuality, and engagement or lack thereof cease to have a bearing on the work of art.

Kristeva makes no such claim with regard to Colette and her work. While she celebrates Colette's love of words and explores in detail her "new alphabet," which, she argues, transcends her presence as a woman of the century, she insists that this alphabet is infused with her French *bourguignon* accent, her peasant's earthiness. Her life and her work, according to Kristeva, are "indissociables," although they are at once "subtilement distinctes" (*Le génie féminin* 19) ("[they] cannot be separated, but are subtly distinct the one from the other"). The two flow inextricably together in her work:

> Colette found a language to name *a strange osmosis between her sensations, her desires and her anxieties, between these "pleasures that one flippantly calls physical" and the infinity of the world*—the rustling of flowers, the undulations of animals, sublime apparitions, contagious

monsters. This language transcends her presence as a woman in the century—vagabond or submissive, free, cruel, or sympathetic. Her style mixes her earthly roots and her burgundy accent while soothing them in an alchemy that remains still a mystery to us. She herself calls it "a new alphabet." What alphabet? (My translation)[56]

Colette represents for Kristeva "un legs très précieux de la tradition, tout particulièrement de la tradition française" (*Le génie féminin* 19) ("a very precious legacy of tradition, very particularly a French tradition"). However, reading against the assessments of Yourcenar and Duras, and perhaps suggesting a new era of Colette criticism, Kristeva asserts that Colette cannot be reduced to her Frenchness. Indeed, Colette struggled, Kristeva argues, against any such efforts to define her as one thing or another, a fact confirmed by Carter's assessment of Colette. Her discomfort with the term "writer" was not simply, according to Kristeva, false modesty but arose from the sense that she had that "langue savoure l'univers pour le refaire" ("her language/her tongue savoured the universe in order to remake it" (*Le génie féminin* 16). Her incursions into the world of French literature, her efforts to impose a sensuality there did not take the familiar forms of a triumphal eroticism or a more conventional painful modesty, according to Kristeva. "Provocative, scandalous as a result of her daring customs and behavior, this lovable woman refuses to be pigeonholed as a militant of any kind and preaches no single transgression" (my translation).[57] This ambiguity, a reaction against the status quo, in a form that does not fall into any neat category, Kristeva suggests, accounts for French reactions to her work.[58]

Is Colette, asks Kristeva, for export only, echoing the statements of Edmund White that head up this chapter? "Fallait-il être l'étrangère que je suis pour se laisser fasciner par sa sorcellerie, qui ne serait donc pas seulement française, mais, peut-être, sait-on jamais, universelle?" (17) ("Is it only foreigners, like myself, who are fascinated by her magic, which may not be uniquely French, but, perhaps, who knows, universal?").[59] Does Winterson's *Art [Objects]* mark a change in the critical reception of Woolf's work by women writers at home? While both Kristeva's and Winterson's writings do suggest a change in the tide in terms of the conception of Woolf and Colette among writers of fiction in both England and France, a tradition of exchange persists.

Conclusion

A Dining Room of One's Own:
Woolf and Colette on Food and Sex

[A] good dinner is of great importance to good talk. One cannot think well, love well, sleep well, if one has not dined well (Virginia Woolf, *A Room of One's Own*, 18)

'I always think of a novel as a finely done soufflé, underdone it is clammy, overdone it is desiccated. I think of *Adolphe*, and *La Princesse de Clèves* . . . ' (Colette, quoted in Prokosch 237)

I love [Colette] for that diversity and energy—as I mistrust those who assert that the artist is not "pure" unless she inhabits the airless attic of her painful shyness or haughty elitism and disdains all the clutter and chatter of the world. Colette believed in clutter and chatter. They nourished her and nourished her writing. She knew that art does not survive long without life—and life is impure. It is bouillabaisse, not distilled water. (Erica Jong, Introduction to Colette's *The Other Woman*, viii)

FOOD, AND ON occasion French food, provides a link between Virginia Woolf and Colette. Colette is renowned for her love of food, her *gourmandise*.[1] Her works are full of sumptuous dinners, orgies of flavor, thrown together at the last minute, replete with "local ham, tomatoes and peaches, cheeses, almond tarts" (116).[2] Much of the work on Woolf and food, by contrast, focuses on her strained relationship with food and her anorexia.[3] Hence, implicit in Erica Jong's comment on Colette cited above is a reference to Woolf: the airless attic (a room of one's own), painful shyness, haughty elitism, the distilled water—all fall into the category of common misreadings of Woolf's life and work. In response, I look at those moments where Woolf appears to enjoy her food and to celebrate eating as a means to tie her closer to Colette.

With this inquiry I draw conclusions about the larger question around which this book is focused: how might reading Woolf's work alongside Colette's make Woolf's work more palatable, more accessible? And further, how might reading Colette alongside Woolf enable us to give Colette her due in terms of the seriousness, the sophisticated nature and innovative quality of her writing?

Food functions as a powerful tool in the works of both Woolf and Colette. In each case food, and its preparation and presentation, often functions as a means of seduction. Food and sex are bound together in the works of both writers. Nationality also informs each writer's relationship to and presentation of food and sex in their work. Stereotypically prudish about sex and inept in the culinary arts, the British are the antithesis of the French, skilled in both the kitchen and the bedroom.

No Good Food, Please: We're British

I must cook dinner—maccaroni [*sic*] cheese with a bacon fry. But, perversely, I long for the Ivy [Restaurant] and champagne. Too many souls and bodies to be satisfied: the Puritan and the Harlot. Mixed marriages result in this mixed Virginia. (Woolf to Ethel Smyth, *Letters* 6: 309)

Despite a problematic relationship with food brought on by bouts of mental illness, Woolf enjoyed eating and drinking, especially French food and wine. Throughout her diaries and letters we find descriptions of what she ate and drank and where. In 1908 Woolf visits Italy and France with Vanessa and Clive Bell: "[W]e drank an immense amount of coffee and sat out under the electric light talking about art. I wish we were 10 years younger, or 20 years older, and could settle to our brandy and cultivate the senses" (*Letters* 1: 369). Again, in 1928, when in Burgundy with Vita Sackville-West, Woolf writes to Leonard Woolf from Saulieu with obvious enjoyment, describing what she and Vita have been eating: "[W]e began with paté of duck, went on to trout, gnocchi, stuffed chicken and spinach made with cream and then sour cream and a delicious cake and then pears ad lib; as the marmots say" (*Letters* 3: 534). And in June 1929, after returning from a visit to France, she notes that she and Leonard almost bought a villa in Cassis and again expresses her love of France and food.[4]

I almost bought La Boudard [a villa near Fontcreuse that Leonard and Virginia began to buy, but the purchase of which was never completed]. [T]his island means heat, silence, complete aloofness from London; the sea; eating cakes in the new hotel at La Ciotat; driving to Aix; sitting on the harbour dining [. . .] a great deal of cheap wine & cigars. (*Diary 3:* 232)[5]

The quality of the food abroad contrasts sharply with that available at home. As the appropriately French critic Claudine Jardin suggests, when exploring the question of Woolf's privilege, the quality of life and liberty afforded the middle-class young woman in turn-of-the-century England was reflected in the poor quality and homogeneity of the food at home. The tyrannous institutions of boiled beef and teatime, suggests Jardin, threatened to stifle and choke Woolf:

> Is it a privilege to be born one January 26, 1882 (*sic*), in London, into a respectable bourgeois family for whom boiled beef, plush furniture, the ceremony of teatime, and polite conversation are still institutions; the family system a tyranny; the taste for solitude a provocative original form of behavior interpreted as a form of rebellion? The family is a circle that protects you and, if you're not of a strong disposition, presents a strong risk of destroying you. (My translation; Jardin 11)[6]

Woolf's ill health certainly affected her relationship with food. In an interview included in Noble's *Recollections,* Barbara Bagenal, an artist and a friend of Vanessa Bell's who worked as a typesetter for Hogarth Press, recounts what Vanessa Bell had told her of Woolf's inability to eat when ill: "Vanessa told me that during one of her earliest illnesses Virginia would not eat anything at all" and had to be spoon-fed. Bagenal herself also witnessed Woolf "flip meat from her plate onto the tablecloth [at lunch] obviously not knowing what she was doing" (150). Leonard Woolf speculated on the symptoms of Woolf's illness in terms that suggest she might have been anorexic: "'It might have been said that she had a (quite unnecessary) fear of becoming fat; but there was something deeper than that, at the back of her mind or in the pit of her stomach a taboo against eating'" (quoted in Showalter 269).[7]

In her interview with Noble, Bagenal laments the fact that except for walking, Woolf had no hobbies, which might have helped her rest from work. She did not sew or knit, and she did not know how to cook, says Bagenal, at least in the first days of her marriage:

One week-end, when Virginia and Leonard were staying at Asheham,
I walked over from Charleston to stay the night with them. When I
arrived, Virginia said that she did not know what we could have for
supper because the woman who came in to cook for them was ill. I
suggested that I made some scrambled eggs. Virginia was amazed and
said, "Can you really cook scrambled eggs?" (152)

Despite her condition (and reports to the contrary), Woolf did in fact
like to cook. However, as Louie Mayer, the Woolfs' cook and housekeeper, remembers, time constraints kept Woolf out of the kitchen:
"[S]he did not want to give time to cooking and preferred to be in her
room working" (Noble 157). In 1914, however, Woolf took cooking
lessons "at an institution in Victoria Street," where she "distinguished
[herself] by cooking [her] wedding ring into a suet pudding (*Letters* 2:
55). In 1929 she wrote to Vita: "I have only one passion in life—cooking. I have just bought a superb oil stove. I can cook anything. I am free
forever of cooks. I cooked veal cutlets and cake today. I assure you it is
better than writing these more than idiotic books" (*Letters* 4: 93). Woolf
appears to have particularly enjoyed baking bread, a task at which she is
said to have excelled.[8]

Woolf's relationship with food is complicated by her attitudes
toward sex. Questions regarding Woolf's sexuality have preoccupied
and divided critics. Woolf's sister, Vanessa Bell (usually considered the
more sensual and sexual of the two sisters), discusses with her husband,
Clive Bell, her sister's inability to enjoy sex, "'the Goat's coldness'"
(quoted in Lee 331). A friend of the Woolfs and a fellow Bloomsbury
person, Gerald Brennan, describes how Leonard's efforts to make love
to Virginia on their honeymoon met with "'such a violent state of
excitement'" that he stopped, fearing she might have an attack of madness (quoted in Lee 331). On her honeymoon Woolf read four or five
novels, including, in just one sitting, Dostoevsky's *Crime and Punish-
ment* (Lee 323). Nigel Nicolson, son of Vita Sackville-West, in his book
about his parents, *Portrait of a Marriage,* writes that "Virginia was sexually frigid" (201). Copulation, suggests Claudine Jardin, did not interest Woolf (95). *To the Lighthouse*'s Lily Briscoe's sense of release at having escaped the "dilution" that marriage entails comes to mind here:
"[S]he need not marry, thank Heaven: she need not undergo that
degradation. She was saved from that dilution" (102).

The sexual nature of Woolf's relationship with Vita Sackville-West is
also unclear (one marked by gaps, literally, where lines in a letter are
scored out). Nigel Nicolson contends that "[Woolf's] friendship was the

most important fact in Vita's life, except Harold [Nicolson's father and
Vita's husband], just as Vita's was the most important in Virginia's,
except Leonard, and perhaps her sister Vanessa" (201). In response to
Woolf's nephew Quentin Bell's suggestion that "'[t]here may have
been—on balance I think there probably was—some caressing, some
bedding together' [on the part of Woolf and Vita]" (quoted in Nicolson 202), Nicolson quotes a series of letters from Vita to Harold that
imply that Vita's relationship with Virginia was more spiritual than physical. While he then goes on to add, "[t]he physical element in their
friendship was tentative and not very successful, lasting only a few
months, a year perhaps," he continues, "[i]t is a travesty of their relationship to call it an affair" (205).

   Woolf's and, more generally, the Bloomsbury group's response to
Radclyffe Hall's lesbian novel, *The Well of Loneliness,* covered here in
chapter 1, throws into question her attitude toward homosexuality. In
her biography Lee suggests that Woolf shied away from identifying herself as a lesbian: "[S]he was the recipient of feelings she did not identify with her own. She played up to these feelings, but played up, at the
same time, her marriedness, her delicate health, and her inviolability"
(49–91). Thus, Lee suggests, women's friendships in Woolf's work are
always situated in a heterosexual context, such as Lily Briscoe and Mrs
Ramsay in *To the Lighthouse* and Sally Seton and Clarissa Dalloway in
Mrs Dalloway (491). Lee takes issue with the characterization of Woolf
as "frigid," calling such an assessment simplistic. She claims rather that

   Virginia Woolf's sexual squeamishness, which plays a part in the indi-
   rections and self-censorship of the novels, is combined with a powerful, intense sensuality, an erotic susceptibility to people and landscape,
   language and atmosphere, and a highly charged physical life. (332)

   In a similar way, in her article "Virginia Woolf's Two Bodies,"
Molly Hite responds to those critics who characterize Woolf's prose
and, she adds, to some degree Woolf the woman, as *disembodied,* as
"preoccupied with transcendent and worldly things [. . .] alienated
from or overtly hostile to everyday social life, especially the sloppy
region of sensual and sexual experience" (17). In response, Hite distinguishes between Woolf's two bodies. The first is the *social body:* "the
body for others, the body cast in social roles and bound by the laws of
social interaction" (1), "a body at risk" (6). This social body, Hite
argues, is often the Victorian/Edwardian maternal body, the body that
Woolf most often ascribed to her female (literary) predecessors (9). The

second, a *visionary body*, "in fundamental respects different from the gendered body," is a body that "enabled Woolf to create passionate and sensuous female characters without embroiling them in the societal consequences of female eroticism that had shaped the romance plot" (1). This
second "female modernist body," Hite suggests, represents "an inspired
solution to the problem of women's culturally sanctioned vulnerability":
[i]t is "the body sealed off from social consequences, secure from interruption or invasion: a corporeal correlative of the room of one's own"
(6). "Woolf's visionary body," argues Hite, "was designed to help evade
the snares that identity set for the middle-class English woman, offering
an inviolable place for momentary but definitive experience" (17).

A key to Woolf's discomfort with sex might be her nationality, that
is, the prudishness stereotypically ascribed to the English. In Woolf's
first novel, *The Voyage Out*, a long discussion between Helen Ambrose
and St John Hirst about differences between the sexes ends with the following exchange, highlighting British prudishness. Hirst exclaims: "'So
there's no reason whatever for all this mystery [about sexual differ-
ence]!'" to which Helen responds "'None, except that we are English
people'" (149). This comment parallels Mrs Malone's lament in *The
Years* over the ineptitude of British cooks. She is in total agreement with
the contents of an article being read aloud by her daughter, Kitty, which
suggests that even if the British had the best ingredients, they would not
know what to do with them: "'With the best flesh, fish and fowl in the
world,' she read, 'we shall not be able to turn them to account because
we have none to cook them' [. . .] Just when one wanted to impress
people, like those Americans, something went wrong. It had been the
fish this time" (78). Kitty continues to read the article aloud: "'' . . . the
children saw a good deal of cooking which, poor as it was, yet gave them
some taste and inkling of knowledge. They now see nothing and they
do nothing but read, write, sum, sew or knit'''" (78).

A Soul Full of Red Beans and Bacon

"Je n'ai l'âme pleine que de haricots rouges et de petits lardons
fumés." (*Claudine en ménage* 83) ("My soul is full of nothing but
haricot beans and little strips of bacon" [415])

Unlike dictators, who are nearly always vegetarians and eat men,
Colette liked good cooking, and her style proves it. Her style is heady,
spares the salt and avoids fat, uses pepper, garlic and various herbs,

and is not afraid of letting you bite a raw little red pimento, one of those little gnome-hats, which burn your mouth . . . (Cocteau, *My Contemporaries* 132)

For Colette, food, sex, and writing are tightly bound together. Claudine's boast to a young man of letters in *Claudine en ménage,* cited above, might well be Colette's. Her friend and contemporary writer Violet Trefusis defines Colette in terms of food. Colette, according to Trefusis, was happier to talk about cooking and gardening than she was about her work (see chapter 2). Abbé Mugnier also remarks on Colette's love of talk about food and wine:

> She talked cooking and Château d'Yquem, and the dishes one could serve with it. She brings everything down to gourmandise: the greed for food, the greed for sensual pleasure. She kept repeating that purity is a temptation like the others, and not a nobler one. (Quoted in Thurman 361)

Claude Chauvière, Colette's secretary for a time, in the opening chapter of her book *Colette,* entitled "Colette est une grande vivante" ("Colette lives large"), pictures Colette at the table and in the kitchen. "'J'ai faim,' cries Colette" (1); "'Pauline, J'ai faim!'" (4) ("'I'm hungry,' shouts Colette"; "'Pauline, I'm hungry!'").

> Overflowing with life, with activity, she is radiant with physical joy, clutching tight to her strong heart everything that breathes in order to blow it out, to crush it, to express the substantial marrow of which it is made up. Then with her hands out in front of her, she goes toward the universe in order to seize more and taste everything. Meanwhile, passive, idle, greedy, she munches apples and eats the filling out of chocolate éclairs. (My translation)[9]

Colette, Chauvière writes, did not throw big dinner parties but preferred intimate feasts with a few carefully chosen friends (2). Does Colette have domestic skills, queries Chauvière? She creates disorder around her, suggests Chauvière, but she knows the value of things. If her cook tries to cheat on the bill, Colette lets it pass, simply because "'elle fait si bien le chou farci'" (3) ("'she makes stuffed cabbage so well'"). Colette knows how to eat, says Chauvière, and, even rarer in a woman, she knows about wines (5). Chauvière quotes Colette's musing over the origin of her *gourmandise,* which she characterizes as a religion of sorts:

Figure 14
Colette at her table. Roger Schall.

Which ancestor left me, despite such frugal parents, this sort of religion of sautéed rabbit, garlic leg of lamb, soft-boiled egg with red
wine, all served up between walls of a barn coated with natural-col-
ored curtains where the red rose of June, pinned up, shines? (My
translation; quoted in Chauvière)[10]

Food and friendship are inextricable in her life and her work. The
bond between Colette and her friend Annie de Pène (Thurman 275) and
that with Winnie de Polignac were formed around food. In her memoir,
Mes apprentissages, Colette is impressed by the appetite of actress Caroline Otero [Lina], wondering if it can possibly exceed her own. She
admires Otero's ability to gorge herself without appearing greedy.

I have always enjoyed good food, but what was my appetite compared
with Lina's? Her queenliness melted, and a gentle bliss, an air of

happy innocence took its place. Her teeth, her eyes, her glossy lips
shone like a girl's. There are few beautiful women who can guzzle
without loss of prestige. Lina did not push away her plate until she
had emptied it four, five times. (14)[11]

Colette was upset by women who did not eat. A gymnast and a leader
in technologies of the body, one of the first to experiment with face-lifts,
perms, blood transfusions, and exercise, she seems, however, never to
have fallen victim to the rage to stay thin (Thurman 366). In part due
to the crippling arthritis from which she suffered, along with her love of
good food, she became quite heavy later in life. She was disturbed by the
eating habits of the half American, half English poet and writer Renée
Vivien. In *Le pur et l'impur* (1932), she describes her relationship with
Vivien, whom she calls first by her real name, Pauline Tarn (88–108).[12]
Like Colette herself, Renée was reticent about her work, concealing the
books she gave to Colette in a bouquet of violets, a basket of fruit,
under a length of Chinese silk. "Nos rapports amicaux n'eurent [. . .]
rien de littéraire" (89) ("Our relationship was [. . .] in no way literary"
[81]) suggests Colette.[13] Central to Colette's description of Vivien are
several dinner parties at the poet's apartment. Claustrophobic and
oppressive, her dining room is lit by three brown candles, her dining
table, low, in the style of the Far East, is strewn "pêle-mêle" with sweet
and spicy offerings: "strips of raw fish rolled up on glass wands, *foie gras,*
shrimps, salads seasoned with sugar and pepper—and there was a well-
chosen Piper-Heidsieck champagne *brut,* and very strong cocktails—
Renée Vivien was ahead of her time" (82).[14] Colette describes Vivien's
manner of ingesting without flinching these potent cocktails of her own
making, which Colette herself deemed undrinkable. Colette learns that
this woman, "with the neck of a victim," subsists on "une cuillerée de
riz, d'un fruit, surtout d'alcool" (92) ("a few spoonfuls of rice, some
fruit or other, and alcohol—especially alcohol" [83]). Vivien died at 30.
When another friend, Annie de Pène, died, Colette blamed her anorexia for her death. Thurman contends that

> Colette blamed Annie's dieting for her death to convince herself that
> her own accumulated flesh was a kind of life insurance. She had been
> gaining weight steadily since she had stopped exercising profession-
> ally, and she had lost her figure. "Colette paid for her greed," writes
> Dormann, "with liver trouble . . . violent indigestion, and kidney
> problems." (Thurman 275)

Oddly enough, it appears that Colette showed more restraint with sex than with food—more restraint with sex than her celebrity would have us believe. Indeed, in *Mes apprentissages,* she declares: "What is known as the Bohemian life has always suited me about as badly as a hat trimmed with ostrich feathers or a pair of earrings" (44).[15] The blood that runs in her veins, she asserts in the same text, is "inconveniently" "[le] sang monogame" (1065) ("monogamous blood" [119]). Colette was married three times. In the first two cases, her first marriage to Henry Gauthiers Villars (Willy) and her second to Henri de Jouvenel, the husbands' infidelities upset the marriages. Like Renée of her early novel *La vagabonde* (1914), who, upon being badly emotionally damaged by the philandering of her first husband, the portrait painter Adolphe Taillandy (modeled on Willy), renounces love, Colette suffered considerably as a result of her husbands' disloyalties. Despite her reputation as a promiscuous woman, toward the end of her life, "[Colette] would tell a friend that, apart from three husbands, she had taken only three lovers" (Thurman 84). Indeed, Maurice Goudeket claims, to the surprise, he writes, of many people, that there was no one more modest than his wife. To their assertion: "'Vous oubliez qu'elle a été danseuse nue'" ("you forget that she was a nude dancer"), he points to the limited extent of her nudity, "un seul sein" ("just one breast"), and the comparative isolation from the audience of the performer, behind the footlights, on stage (31). Colette, he continues, took her work seriously and refused to let what was a natural tendency, rather than a learned behavior (modesty), prevent her from doing the job properly.

Like Woolf, Colette had both male and female partners. One of the more settled lesbian relationships was that which Colette shared with la Marquise de Morny (Missy), with whom she lived at Rozven, an estate between St. Malo and Cancale in Brittany bought by Missy for Colette in 1910, between her first and second marriages.

Colette's attitude toward homosexuality, like Woolf's, was contradictory. While she made no secret of her lesbian liaisons, she responded to her daughter's revelation of her lesbianism with disapproval (Thurman 136). The lesbian relationship of Claudine and Rézi in *Claudine en ménage* is set in a heterosexual context. Claudine's husband Renaud licenses the relationship and provides an apartment where the two women can meet privately. Claudine subsequently realizes that her husband's involvement is greater than she had first thought when she discovers that he is also using the apartment for his own liaisons with Rézi. By the beginning of the fourth novel in the series, *Claudine s'en va,* however, relations with Renaud have been reestablished, Rézi is out of the picture, and heterosexual order is reestablished.

A Dining Room of One's Own

Why did men drink wine and women water? Why was one sex so prosperous and the other so poor? What effect has poverty on fiction? What conditions are necessary for the creation of works of art? (*A Room of One's Own* 25)

I think housekeeping is what I do best, and I mean to run our house on very remarkable lines. Does housekeeping interest you at all? I think that it really ought to be just as good as writing, and I never see—as I argued the other day with Nessa—where the separation between the two comes in. At least if you must put books on one side and life on t'other, each is a poor and bloodless thing. But my theory is that they mix indistinguishably. (Woolf to Violet Dickinson, *Letters* 1: 272)

I can housekeep [. . .] O my eye—why should it be confined to the drawing room, or style to the study? (Woolf to Violet Dickinson, *Letters* 1: 261)

Woolf understood the importance of food to the literary work. As E. M. Forster suggests, in Noble's *Recollections,* food is central to Woolf's work:

It is always helpful, when reading her, to look out for the passages which describe eating. They are invariably good. They are a sharp reminder that here is a woman who is alert sensuously. She had an enlightened greediness which gentlemen themselves might envy, and which few masculine writers have expressed. There is a little too much lamp oil in Charles Meredith's wine, a little too much paper crackling on Charles Lamb's pork, and no savor whatever in any dish of Henry James's, but when Virginia Woolf mentions nice things they get right into our mouths, so far as the edibility of print permits. (193)

Thus, in *A Room of One's Own,* Woolf notes the failure on the part of novelists to tell the reader what is being eaten (10). To write about food, she suggests, is to defy convention:

[I]t is part of the novelist's convention not to mention soup and salmon and ducklings, as if soup and salmon and ducklings were of no importance whatsoever, as if nobody ever smoked a cigar or drank a glass of wine. Here, however *I shall take the liberty to defy that convention* and to tell you that the lunch on this occasion began with soles, sunk in a deep dish, over which the college cook had spread a counterpane of the whitest cream, save that it was branded here and there with brown spots like the spots on the flanks of a doe. After that came the partridges, but if this suggests a couple of bald, brown birds on a plate you are mistaken. Partridges, many and various, came with all their retinue of sauces and salads, the sharp and the sweet, each in its order; their potatoes, thin as coins but not so hard; their sprouts, foliated as rosebuds but more succulent. And no sooner had the roast and retinue been done with than the silent serving-man, the Beadle himself perhaps in a milder manifestation, set before us, wreathed in napkins, a confection which rose all sugar from the waves. To call it pudding and in so relate it to rice and tapioca would be an insult. Meanwhile the wineglasses had flushed yellow and flushed crimson; had been emptied; had been filled. (My emphasis; 10–11)

Food gives color and shape to the work, according to Woolf—"potatoes, thin as coins," "sprouts, foliated as rosebuds," "a confection which rose all sugar from the waves." Food nourishes body and soul, she adds. It draws company together:

And thus by degrees was lit, halfway down the spine, which is the seat of the soul, not that hard little electric light which we call brilliance, as it pops in and out upon our lips, but the more profound, subtle and subterranean glow, which is the rich yellow flame of rational intercourse. No need to hurry. No need to sparkle. No need to be anybody but oneself. We are all going to heaven and Vandyck is of the company—in other words how good life seemed, how sweet its rewards, how trivial this grudge or that grievance, how admirable friendship and the society of one's kind, as, lighting a good cigarette, one sunk among the cushions in the window-seat. (11)

In *A Room of One's Own* food is used to contrast the opulence of the men's college and the comparative poverty of the women's:

Dinner was ready. Here was the soup. It was a plain gravy soup. There was nothing to stir the fancy in that. One could have seen through the transparent liquid any pattern that there might have been on the plate itself. But there was no pattern. The plate was plain. Next came beef with its attendant greens and potatoes—a homely trinity, suggesting the rumps of cattle in a muddy market, and sprouts curled and yellowed at the edge, and bargaining and cheapening, and women with string bags on Monday morning. There was no reason to complain of human nature's daily food, seeing that the supply was sufficient and coal miners doubtless were sitting down to less. Prunes and custard followed. And if anyone complains that prunes, even when mitigated by custard, are an uncharitable vegetable (fruit they are not), stringy as a miser's heart and exuding a fluid such as might run in misers' veins who have denied themselves wine and warmth for eighty years and yet not given to the poor, he should reflect that there are people whose charity embraces even the prune. Biscuits and cheese came next, and here the water-jug was liberally passed round, for it is the nature of biscuits to be dry, and these were biscuits to the core. That was all. The meal was over. (17)

A good meal, Woolf argues, is necessary for good thinking, sleeping, and loving. She is particular about what makes a good meal: "The lamp in the spine does not light on beef and prunes" (18). The narrator's friend, fortunately, has a drop of something in "a squat bottle and little glasses," which enables them to "repair some of the damages of the day's living" (18–19).

Woolf frequently folds food and eating into her work. Food often serves to make a comment about social inequality, as it does here in *A Room of One's Own*. We see this, for example, at several moments in *The Years*. After the unexpected death of both of their parents, Digby and Eugénie Pargiter, Magdalena (Maggie) and Sara (Sally) Pargiter "cooked their own food" (169); in the "Present Day" section of the novel, Sara and North content themselves with an underdone, stringy leg of mutton, a "slabbed-down mass of cabbage [. . .] oozing green water [and] yellow potatoes that looked hard," followed by "an ornate pudding, semi-transparent, pink, ornamented with blobs of cream" (319, 321).

In this chapter, however, I focus on those moments where food functions as a tool of seduction, where food and sex are tied together in the text. These moments echo Woolf's suggestion about the sensuality of food and dining in *A Room of One's Own* and run counter to conceptions of the woman and her work as somehow disembodied, disconnected from the physical.

Woolf incorporates at least one French dish into her work. In *To the Lighthouse*, Mrs Ramsay serves up *bœuf en daube* (beef stew).[16] The dish and the meal at which it is consumed sit at the center of *To the Lighthouse*. The meal of *bœuf en daube* is a means, on the part of Mrs Ramsay, to seduce William Bankes, to bring him to her table and into the family fold. Like Mr Pepper of Woolf's first novel, *The Voyage Out*, Bankes disdains British food and British cooks, just as he is suspicious of Mrs Ramsay's beauty and charity: "[He] would prose for hours (until Mr Ramsay slammed out of the room) about salt in vegetables and the iniquity of English cooks" (24).[17] Bankes hates the interruptions that meals en masse entail: "Mrs Ramsay had to break off here to tell the maid something about keeping food hot. That was why [Bankes] preferred dining alone. All those interruptions annoyed him" (88).

Mrs Ramsay succeeds in her conquest of William Bankes with the French dish.

> "It is a French recipe of my grandmother's," said Mrs Ramsay, speaking with a ring of great pleasure in her voice. Of course it was French. What passes for cooking in England is an abomination (they agreed). It is putting cabbages in water. It is roasting meat till it is like leather. It is cutting off the delicious skins of vegetables. "In which," said Mr Bankes, "all the virtue of the vegetable is contained." And the waste, said Mrs Ramsay. A whole French family could live on what an English cook throws away. (100–101)[18]

Bankes approves of the *bœuf en daube:* "It was rich; it was tender. It was perfectly cooked. How did she manage these things in the depths of the country? he asked her. She was a wonderful woman" (100). The meal, in its capacity as a scene of seduction, is preceded by nervous apprehension on the part of the seducer: "There was a smell of burning. Could they have let the Boeuf en Daube overboil?" (82). Its successful execution is accompanied by thoughts of marital union: Mrs Ramsay is thinking of love and marriage, of Paul Rayley and Minta Doyle, when the completed dish arrives:

> [A]n exquisite scent of olives and oil and juice rose from the great brown dish as Marthe, with a little flourish, took the cover off. The cook had spent three days over that dish. And she must take great care, Mrs Ramsay thought, diving into the soft mass, to choose a specially tender piece for William Bankes. And she peered into the dish with its shiny walls and its confusion of savoury brown and yellow

meats and its bay leaf and its wine, and thought. This will celebrate
the occasion—a curious sense rising in her, at once freakish and tender, of celebrating a festival, as if two emotions were called up in her,
one profound—for what could be more serious than the love of man
for woman [. . .] (100)

The sensual, almost sexual nature of the description of the dish, the
exquisite scent, the tenderness of the meat, the shine and the color, and
Mrs Ramsay's selection of the tenderest piece for William Bankes
underscore the sense in which this meal is a means to seduce Bankes.

The beef dish in *To the Lighthouse* is followed by fruit. Rose Ramsay's
fruit arrangement—"the grapes and pears, [. . .] the horny pink-lined
shell, [. . .] the bananas"—make Mrs Ramsay think of a trophy salvaged
from the bottom of the sea, Neptune's banquet, the grapes held over
Bacchus's shoulder "(in some picture) among the leopard skins and the
torches lolloping red and gold. . . ." (97).[19] Like the meat, the fruit has
a sexual quality. Another of the Ramseys' guests, Augustus Carmichael
"feasts" his eyes on the plate (97). However, rather than attempt to
please, as she does with Bankes, Mrs Ramsay tries to keep the presentation intact; she "[keeps] guard over the dish of fruit (without realising
it) jealously, hoping that nobody would touch it," perhaps suggesting an
attempt on her part to protect her daughter's virginity (108). Adding to
the sense of Mrs Ramsay's orchestration of the dish, she toys with the
fruit display in a way similar to Lily Briscoe's play with light and shadow in her portrait in the same novel: "Her eyes had been going in and
out among the curves and shadows of the fruit, among the rich purples
of the lowland grapes, then over the horny ridge of the shell, putting a
yellow against a purple, a curved shape against a round shape, without
knowing why she did it, or why, every time she did it, she felt more and
more serene" (109).

The relationship between food and sex is also highlighted by Charles
Tansley's comments about women in *To the Lighthouse:* "They did nothing but talk, talk, talk, eat, eat, eat" (85), he thinks to himself. This reads
as an accompaniment (the logical second half) to Tansley's negative
appraisal of women: "'can't write; can't paint'" (91). Tansley's attitude
anticipates that of his mentor, Mr Ramsay, who is upset when Augustus
Carmichael asks for more soup at dinner, a request met conversely with
pleasure by Mrs Ramsay in her capacity as hostess: "He loathed people
eating when he had finished [. . .] He hated people wallowing in food,
Mr Ramsay frowned at her" (95–96).

Food also functions as a tool of seduction in *Mrs Dalloway.* Food creates bonds and cements rivalries (it is no coincidence, perhaps, that the plane flying overhead in the early pages of *Mrs Dalloway* spells out the word "toffee" [21]). Thus, Lady Bruton, whose condescension upsets Clarissa, discreetly woos Hugh Whitbread and Richard Dalloway with crisp white linen, red fruit, and turbot in a cream sauce, and Miss Kilman, Clarissa's rival for the affections of her daughter, attempts to seduce Elizabeth with chocolate éclairs at the Army and Navy stores. A third meal, that of Peter Walsh, among the middle class in a restaurant, stands in opposition, along with these last two scenes, to the main meal and climax of the book, Mrs Dalloway's dinner party for the prime minister.

Milicent Bruton is famous for her lunch parties, which, we learn from Clarissa, "were said to be extraordinarily amusing" (30).[20] When Hugh Whitbread and Richard Dalloway lunch with Lady Bruton ("[s]he had got them there on false pretences, to help her out with a difficulty," she tells them [104]), they are lulled into a sense of security, "at peace with the entire universe," by the colors and smells of the spread:

> And so there began a soundless and exquisite passing to and fro through swing doors of aproned white-capped maids, handmaidens not of necessity, but adept in a mystery or grand deception practised by hostesses in Mayfair from one-thirty or two, when, with a wave of the hand, the traffic ceases, and there rises instead this profound illusion in the first place about food—how it is not paid for; and then that the table spreads itself voluntarily with glass and silver, little mats, saucers of red fruit; films of brown cream mask turbot; in casseroles severed chickens swim; coloured, undomestic, the fire burns; and with the wine and the coffee (not paid for) rise jocund visions before musing eyes; gently speculative eyes; eyes to whom life appears musical, mysterious; eyes now kindled to observe genially the beauty of the red carnations which Lady Bruton (whose movements were always angular) had laid beside her plate, so that Hugh Whitbread feeling at peace with the entire universe, and at the same time completely sure of his standing [. . .] (104–5)

The food reflects Lady Bruton's double purpose: its slippery sauces cover the turbot (aptly chosen for its one-sidedness—both of this flat fish's eyes are normally on the left), just as her hospitality masks a lower purpose—she intends to use Hugh and Richard to write a letter to the newspaper. The swimming severed chickens, which hint at a violence at odds with the calm of Lady Bruton's dining room, suggest a disjunction between appearance and reality. "Coloured, undomestic, the fire burns," the meal has the bacchanalian quality of Rose's fruit plate in *To the Lighthouse*. The solemnity and gravity of the event is undercut when Hugh "dives" into the casserole and, while Lady Bruton and Richard Dalloway talk, thinks only of his chicken (106–7). Lady Bruton's musing over the greatness of men is deflated by its juxtaposition with Hugh's finishing up his soufflé (109).

Lady Bruton's failure to include Clarissa at these lunches suggests that an implicit rivalry exists between the two women. Lady Bruton cannot understand why men like Richard marry women like Clarissa (106). Clarissa, for her part, however, is not jealous of Lady Bruton. Rather, she sees her future in the older woman, whose face, "a dial cut in impassive stone," manifests "the dwindling of life" (30). Clarissa's efforts to seduce the prime minister in *Mrs Dalloway* echo those of Lady Bruton and bring the two women closer together.

In a scene that counterbalances the superficial sumptuousness of Lady Bruton's lunch, Miss Kilman eats lunch with Elizabeth Dalloway at the Army and Navy stores. Elizabeth's history tutor and companion has a fraught relationship with food; she fills the emptiness in her life, the sexlessness, the meanness (which Clarissa sees as an extension of her religious zeal) with food. In the absence of other comforts, food remains her sole source of pleasure: "Sometimes lately it had seemed to her that, except for Elizabeth, her food was all that she lived for; her comforts; her dinner, her tea; her hot-water bottle at night" (129).

> Elizabeth rather wondered whether Miss Kilman could be hungry. It was her way of eating, eating with intensity, then looking, again and again, at a plate of sugared cakes on the table next them; then, when a lady and a child sat down and the child took the cake, could Miss Kilman really mind it? Yes, Miss Kilman did mind it. She had wanted that cake—the pink one. The pleasure of eating was almost the only pure pleasure left her, and then to be baffled even in that! (130)

At the Army and Navy stores, Elizabeth's surprise at Miss Kilman's voraciousness and her refusal to eat cake with her history tutor suggest a rejection of Miss Kilman's advances. "Elizabeth, with her oriental bearing, her inscrutable mystery, sat perfectly upright; no, she did not want anything more" (131). Miss Kilman fingers "the last two inches of a chocolate éclair" as she questions Elizabeth jealously as to whether or not she will attend her mother's party. The pathetic quality of Miss Kilman's loss of Elizabeth to Mrs Dalloway as the young woman abandons her in the store is enhanced by Woolf's description of Miss Kilman stranded "among the éclairs" (133). "She was about to be split asunder, she felt. The agony was so terrific. If she could grasp her, if she could clasp her, if she could make her hers absolutely and forever and then die; that was all she wanted" (132). Miss Kilman has "large gooseberry-coloured eyes" (125)—suggesting the bitterness that consumes her as well as her redundant third-party status in the mother-daughter relationship.

As Clarissa prepares her dinner party for the prime minister, her former love, Peter Walsh, eats alone in a restaurant. His manner of ordering and eating earns him the respect of the other diners:

> It was not that he said anything, for being solitary he could only address himself to the waiter; it was his way of looking at the menu, of pointing his forefinger to a particular wine, of hitching himself up to the table, of addressing himself seriously, not gluttonously to dinner, that won him their respect; which, having to remain unexpressed for the greater part of the meal, flared up at the table where the Morrises sat when Mr Walsh was heard to say at the end of the meal, "Bartlett pears." (159–60)

Peter's uttering of the ordinary words "Bartlett pears" suggests his connection to the world at large—those excluded from Clarissa's dinner party, from her world—represented by his fellow diners, the nouveau riche, middle-class Morrises (Mr Morris prefers Liverpool to London, has two cars, but still mends his boots on Sunday; Miss Elaine Morris is training for the family business; her brother has a scholarship to go to Leeds [160]).

In preparation for the prime minister, Clarissa dispatches the servant girl Lucy to bring up the Imperial Tokay—"the tokay, from the Emperor's cellars"—for the prime minister (166). Clarissa is the least successful in her handling of food. She serves salmon at her party; however, it is underdone, the cook's perennial problem. This culinary faux pas figures in the text as just one more example of Clarissa's failure to get things quite right. The superficiality of Clarissa's effort is highlighted by the lack of concern downstairs, in the kitchen.

> It made no difference at this hour of the night to Mrs Walker among the plates, saucepans, cullenders, frying-pans, chicken in aspic, ice-cream freezers, pared crusts of bread, lemons, soup tureens, and pudding basins which, however hard they washed up in the scullery seemed to be all on top of her, on the kitchen table, on chairs, while

the fire blared and roared, the electric lights glared, and still supper had to be laid. All she felt was, one Prime Minister more or less made not a scrap of difference to Mrs Walker. (165)

This division between Clarissa's place in the house and that of the servants is underscored when Clarissa enters the hall of the house: "she [Clarissa] felt like a nun who has left the world and feels fold round her the familiar veils and the response to old devotions. The cook whistled in the kitchen" (29).

Food and sex also feature together in Woolf's first novel, *The Voyage Out*. A storm early in the novel upsets the stomachs of many of the passengers aboard the *Euphrosyne*, Willoughby Vinrace's ship bound for the Amazon. Willoughby describes the three stages of seasickness convalescence as "the milk stage, the bread-and-butter stage and the roast-beef stage" (64). The third beef stage significantly follows one of the passenger's, Richard Dalloway's, fumbled kiss and embrace of Willoughby's daughter Rachel, the central character in the novel (66–67). At the table, Rachel's father, perhaps implying his complicity with his daughter's seducer, shouts "'Beef for Mr Dalloway!'" (67).

Woolf's comments in *A Room of One's Own* about the unconventional nature of works that contain descriptions of food point to the innovative quality of Colette's novels and find the two writers at the same table. Colette's books are full of food. Examples include Colette's *Journal à rebours* and *De ma fenêtre,* the latter of which documents the efforts of occupied Parisians to improvise in the kitchen in the face of shortages. As Mona Ozouf suggests: "The first thing that grabs you, when you begin reading Colette's work, is the smell: it gives off a delicious smell of chocolate, wax, ripe peaches, toast" (my translation).[21] Colette is, as Elaine Marks has suggested in her 1960 book *Colette,* "[a] psychologist of the senses, a poet of the sensuous" (5). According to Christiane Milner, Colette's work functions like an analyst: she listens to and detects the movements of her own orality so thoroughly that she quickly provides a hook for the buried or undeciphered orality of her readers: "Her texts are like invitations to indulge in fantasies of orality [. . .] Words must take the form of sensation, good form, just as Pâti-Pâti opens his mouth to eat a plump strawberry" (my translation).[22]

While food is mediated in Woolf's work, Woolf's characters plan and present, they handle cooked food, Colette's characters work with raw food. The meals of Colette's novels, Colette's fictional feasts, are impromptu and seasonal, using freshly grown and picked ingredients. Food for Colette seduces both creator and consumer, whereas in

Woolf's work food is more of an offering for the guest. The role of food in Woolf's work reflects the urban/Victorian nature of her prose; in Colette's it emphasizes the predominantly rural, provincial nature of Colette's subjects.

In the second novel in the *Claudine* series, *Claudine à Paris*, a novel that sees the young protagonist move from her father's Parisian apartment to her lover's, food consoles and distracts her from her recent move from the provinces to Paris (which occurs at the end of *Claudine à l'école*). Further, the role of food in this second novel in the series anticipates its later function as a vehicle for the young woman's sexual initiation. In *Claudine à Paris*, Claudine's signature food, with all its phallic overtones, is the luxuriantly overripe banana: "By buying them ripe and letting them rot just a little, bananas are sheer heaven, like eating Liberty velvet!" (*CC* 227).[23]

She eats bananas in order to gain strength after her illness, during which she did not eat, on first arriving in Paris (where she agrees to be sensible, although the Parisian fresh eggs taste like printed paper [18/217]), and she shares "overripe bananas, cold drinks and salty biscuits" (290) with her nephew Marcel.[24] Food compensates Claudine for her discomfort at the house of her Tante Cœur: "I was eating a little patty of truffles that would have consoled a widow the day after her bereavement" (*CC* 240).[25] She follows the truffles with "a delicious tangerine ice [that] detached me from all other preoccupations" (241).[26]

Claudine's early attraction for her cousin Uncle Renaud in *Claudine à Paris* involves food: "My cousin Uncle [. . .] asked me for some tea. He demanded cream and, furthermore, two lumps of sugar, also a sandwich, not the top one because it must have got dry, and various other things. But he had the same type of greediness as I had and I didn't get impatient" (*CC* 262).[27] A shared *gourmandise*, love of food, cements sexual relationships in Colette's work. As Gaston Lachaille sends sweets to Gilberte in *Gigi*, so Renaud courts Claudine with chocolates (90, 142). Renaud takes notes on Claudine's favorite things: rotten bananas, chocolates, lime buds, the inside of the tails of artichokes, the gum on fruit trees, new books, and penknifes with lots of blades (90/263). Luce, Claudine's school friend, like Claudine, is seduced by the foodstuffs provided by her uncle/seducer: "'sweets and pastries and little birds to eat. And even better than that, champagne at dinner'" (*CC* 308).[28] In the same way, Renaud seduces the young boarders Hélène, Pomme, and the others with candies, at Claudine's old school in Montigny in the opening pages of the third *Claudine* novel, *Claudine en ménage*. Later in this same novel, Claudine, now married to Renaud, embarks on a lesbian relationship with Rézi—a relationship first sanctioned and then enjoyed by Renaud himself. Food also plays a role in this love affair: Claudine catches Rézi biting into her sandwich, planting her teeth where Claudine's teeth had recently been (135).

In the fourth *Claudine* novel, *Claudine s'en va,* Claudine, the stability of her relationship with her husband reestablished (having left Renaud on discovering he, too, is sleeping with Rézi, Claudine and Renaud are now "married lovers" [523]), puts away six lobster sandwiches at a party before attacking a plate of cream cakes topped with praline. When another female guest suggests she be careful lest she get fat with such a diet (Claudine's arms, she suggests, "'are filling out into a charming, but dangerous roundness'" [523]) Claudine responds by suggesting the other woman might improve her looks if her thighs were only as fat as Claudine's arms.

In *Claudine s'en va* the mature Claudine portrays herself as an innovator in cooking technology. She claims to have invented a chocolate toaster, a flea comb for Fanchette (her cat), the stove without holes for roasting winter chestnuts, pineapples in absinthe, and spinach tart and also to have originated the idea of a drawing room-cum-kitchen (529). Food and its preparation for Claudine and Colette are not relegated to the kitchen but spill out into the drawing room. Her tastes are both high and low. Claudine shocks the straitlaced Annie by making a point of ordering cheap wine, "the twelve sous a litre" kind (540).

Food is tied up with etiquette and love in Colette's *Gigi.* Gigi's Aunt Alicia, who is training Gigi in the art of being a marriageable woman, teaches Gigi "the three great difficulties in a girl's education": how to eat *homard à l'américaine,* boiled eggs, and asparagus, claiming that lack of elegance while eating these three foods has upset many a marriage (16–17). Gigi, according to her aunt Alicia, "is so greedy! If only her brain worked as well as her jaws" (20).[29] Alicia gives Gigi precise instructions about how to eat ortolans, break bread, and cut meat—"[O]rtolans should be cut in two, with one quick stroke of the knife, and no grating of the blade on the plate. Bite up each half" (43);[30] "She would remember what she had been taught, break her bread up quickly, eat with her mouth shut and take care, when cutting her meat, not to let her fore-finger reach the blade of her knife" (42)[31]—and how to choose cigars (48). It is, in part, the camomile tea of Inez, Gigi's grandmother, that brings Gigi's millionaire suitor, Gaston, heir to a sugar fortune, to the house—their home cooking, a simple cassoulet, appears to inspire in Gaston a nostalgia for life in the bosom of the family, out of the public eye, among women who do not ask for precious stones or furs and can talk about scandalous things in a decent way (E25/13). Gaston, like his predecessor, Renaud, courts Gigi with candies—licorice and caramels.

In Colette's *Chéri* the maturity of Chéri's older lover, the forty-nine-year-old former courtesan Léa de Lonval, is reflected in her attitudes toward food. Her tastes contrast markedly with those of Claudine and Gigi. Léa, who has reached an age where she feels she can afford herself "quelques petites douceurs" ("some small treats"), "aimait l'ordre, le beau linge, les vins mûris, la cuisine réfléchie" (9) ("liked order, fine linen, wines in their prime, and carefully planned meals at home" [7]). Early in the novel, having sent her young lover home to his mother for the day, she dines alone: "[She] lunched in solitary bliss, with a smile for the dry Vouvray and for the June strawberries, served with their stalks, on a plate of Rubelles enamel as green as a tree-frog after rain" (12).[32] Whereas Léa's tastes are light and refined, the title character Chéri (whose real name is Fred Peloux), by contrast, enjoys rich, creamy dishes, such as *cœurs à la crème* (62) [cream cheese (50)] and "le chocolat crémeux et le beurre glacé" (173) ("cream-frothed chocolate and butter off the ice" [140]). Léa knows about cooking: the *cœurs à la crème* are made at her house, and she has the recipe for the *langoustines avec une sauce crémeuse* that Chéri also enjoys (33). Léa lures Chéri into the countryside with the promise of "[r]ipe strawberries, fresh cream, cakes, grilled spring chicken" (27).[33] On learning of Chéri's imminent marriage to Edmée, Léa continues her habit of mothering Chéri over dinner: "'Take the brownest crusts. Don't eat so much new bread . . . You've never learnt how to choose a fruit . . . 'All the time, secretly disgruntled, she was reproaching herself" (50).[34] Léa's decline, following Chéri's marriage, is mapped on her body. By the end of the novel, "[h]er cheeks and chin were pulled down by an invisible weight, and this added a look of sadness to the trembling corners of her mouth. Chéri found intact amidst this wreckage of beauty the lovely commanding nose and the eyes as blue as a blue flower" (150).[35]

Food creates bonds among women in Colette's *Duo*. In *Duo*, in the absence of her jealous, overbearing husband, Michel, Alice enjoys a meal of the servant Maria's leftovers, minced meat and rice, rolled in lettuce leaves, browned from a long cooking, followed by melon jelly (74–75). Alice "mangeait en gourmande" (75) ("ate heartily"). The strained meals à deux in *Duo* give way to impromptu meals alone or with sisters in *Le toutounier.* Like Léa in *Chéri*, Alice celebrates her newfound freedom with a simple meal of her own design.

She remembered that she was lunching alone and felt no desire for any restaurant [. . .] she bought some fresh fennel, a tin of tuna fish, new-laid eggs, cream cheese and a quarter bottle of champagne. But the imperious hunger that gnawed at the pit of her stomach disorganized her snack. While one egg was dancing about in the boiling water, Alice ate the tuna fish without bread, sprinkled pepper on the cheese, and chewed the fennel as dessert without realizing that she had not opened the little bottle of champagne. She put it away in cupboard No. 2, which was in the kitchen. On the sink, a pair of silk stockings was soaking in an enamel basin. (179)[36]

As in the semi-autobiographical *La naissance du jour,* the single plate on the table signals the independence of the mature woman, here the narrator Madame Colette, rather than her abandonment:

A second place doesn't take much room now: a green plate, a thick antique glass, slightly cloudy. If I say that it is to be taken away for good, no pernicious blast will blow suddenly from the horizon to make my hair stand on end and alter the direction of my life as it once did. If that place is removed from the table I shall still eat with appetite. There is no longer any mystery, no longer a serpent coiled under the napkin ringed, to distinguish it from mine, with a brass lyre which once held in place, at the top of the music-stand of the last century, the loose papers of a score where only the down-beats were marked, spaced at intervals as regular as tears. This place belongs to the friend who comes and goes, and no longer to the master of the house given to treading the resounding boards of a bedroom up above during the night. On days when the plate, the glass and the lyre are not in front of me, I am merely alone, and not abandoned. (*Break of Day* 10)[37]

Dinners in *La naissance du jour* (Colette's tribute to her mother, Sido) are impromptu affairs ("les dîners impromptus" [137/115]), undertaken on a whim, not dictated by any predetermined timetable so as not to violate the peace and privacy of each diner's summer retreat. Madame Colette and her neighbors dine on local ham, tomatoes, peaches, cheese, almond tarts, sausages, and baguettes at the top of a hill (137/115–16). From here the diners proceed to the jetty bar for drinking and dancing. Winemaking and love, and food and love, the heart and the stomach, are closely linked in *La naissance du jour:* "'Autumn is the only vintage time, perhaps that is true in love too'" (30);[38] "Any love, no matter what, if one lets it have its way, tends to turn itself into a sort of alimentary canal" (30).[39]

Men, claims Colette's narrator, regard housework, especially the preparation of a meal, with a combination of religious awe, boredom, and fear (55/36). Madame Colette prepares for her neighbors "a southern luncheon [. . .]: salads, stuffed *rascasse* and aubergine fritters, an everyday meal which I usually enriched with a roast bird" (36).[40] She describes a recipe to Vial: "Four little chickens split in half, beaten with the flat of the chopper, salted, peppered, and anointed with pure oil brushed on with a sprig of *pebreda*? The little leaves of the *pebreda*, and the taste of it, cling to the grilled flesh" (36).[41] Contemplating the chicken, Madame Colette contemplates vegetarianism. "I think I may soon give up eating the flesh of animals; but not to-day" (37).[42] The explanation she offers Vial for this change in diet suggests that she ties a renunciation of meat eating with a renunciation of love relationships: "When one stops liking a certain kind of cannibalism, all the other kinds leave of their own accord, like fleas from a dead hedgehog" (37).[43] This food scene serves as a prelude to a sensual moment between Colette and her younger admirer Vial. Colette asks Vial to pour some oil for her:

> He bent his bare body, polished by the sun and salt. His skin caught the light, so that he was green round the loins and blue on the shoulders, according as he moved, like the dyers of Fez. When I said "Stop!" he cut short the thread of golden oil and straightened himself, and I laid my hand caressingly for a moment on his chest, as one does with a horse. He looked at my hand, which proclaims my age—in fact it looks several years older—but I did not withdraw it. (37)[44]

Food has many places in Colette's work—it infiltrates the drawing room, the bedroom, the study. This pervasiveness is reflected in Claudine's conceptualization of the drawing room-cum-kitchen in *Claudine s'en va*. Just as Claudine takes food out of the kitchen and into the drawing room, so Colette, like Woolf, mixes food and fiction, work and pleasure.

The Last Course

Habit has made English—the ordinary English of which most books are made—as colorless, as tasteless as water. French, even the daily

use, has wine in it; it sparkles; it tingles; it has its savor. (Woolf, "On
Not Knowing French," 348)

Food seduces in the works of both writers. Woolf, like Colette, as the
above quote suggests, understands the intersection of food and wine,
sex and writing and the capacity of the work of art, like food and wine,
to give pleasure and to delight the senses. The more overt sensual nature
of Colette's work—her French, which "sparkles [. . .] tingles [and] has
its savor"—when laid alongside Woolf's writing, highlights the sensu-
ousness, the Frenchness, of the work of her English contemporary, one
she achieves despite the paucity of the British palate and pantry.

In a broader sense, the intersection of Woolf's and Colette's treatment of and attitudes toward food and sex supports the potential of
comparative analysis of their work. Along with the social networks the
two women shared, their writer's visions, and their influence at home
and abroad, their folding of food into their work suggests that fruitful
conversation might have been had if Woolf and Colette had found
themselves at the same table.

Appendix

(1) A Comparative Chronology of the Works of Woolf and Colette

Figure A.1

YEAR	COLETTE	WOOLF	OTHER RELEVANT EVENTS AND PUBLICATIONS
1900	*Claudine à l'école*		Freud's *On Psychoanalysis*
1901	*Claudine à Paris*		
1902	*Claudine en ménage*		Conrad's *Heart of Darkness*
1903	*Claudine s'en va*		
1904	*Minne, Dialogues de bêtes*		Blanche paints Colette
1905	*Les égarement de Minne, Sept dialogues de bêtes*		Willy's *Maugis amoureux*
1906			
1907	*La retraite sentimentale*		
1908	*Les vrilles de la vigne*		
1909	*L'ingénue libertine*		
1910			
1911	*La vagabonde*		Willy's *Lélie fumeuse d'opium*
1912			
1913	*L'envers du music hall, L'entrave, Prrou, Poucette et quelques autres*		
1914			
1915		*The Voyage Out*	

Figure A.1 (continued)

YEAR	COLETTE	WOOLF	OTHER RELEVANT EVENTS AND PUBLICATIONS
1916	*La paix chez les bêtes*		
1917	*Les heures longues, Les enfants dans les ruines*		
1918	*Dans la foule*		
1919	*Mitsou*	*Night and Day*	
1920	*Chéri, La chambre éclairée*		
1921		*Monday or Tuesday*	
1922	*La maison de Claudine, Le voyage égoïste*	*Jacob's Room*	Woolf is reading Proust; Joyce's *Ulysses;* West's *The Judge*
1923	*Le blé en herbe*		Vita Sackville-West's *Challenge* appears
1924	*La femme cachée, Aventures quotidiennes*		
1925	*Enfants et les sortilèges*	*The Common Reader, Mrs Dalloway*	
1926	*La fin de Chéri*		
1927		*To the Lighthouse*	Blanche paints Woolf; publishes article in *Nouvelles littéraires* on Woolf; Jean Larnac publishes *Colette*
1928	*La naissance du jour*	*Orlando: A Biography*	Hall's *Well of Loneliness* trial; West's "The Strange Necessity"; Woolf visits Burgundy with Vita; Woolf is awarded the Prix Femina Vie Heureuse-Bookman prize for *To the Lighthouse*
1929	*La seconde, Sido*	*A Room of One's Own;* "On Not Knowing French"	*A Room* on sale at Sylvia Beach's Shakespeare and Company; West's "Virginia Woolf and Autumn"; Yourcenar's *Alexis*

Figure A.1 (continued)

YEAR	COLETTE	WOOLF	OTHER RELEVANT EVENTS AND PUBLICATIONS
1930	Histoires pour Bel-Gazou, Douze dialogues des bêtes		Smyth first contacts Woolf; Hamwood Papers published
1931		The Waves	
1932	Paradis terrestres, La treille muscate, Prisons et paradis, Ces plaisirs (Le pur et l'impur)	The Common Reader II	Colette reads D. H. Lawrence's Lady Chatterley's Lover
1933	La chatte	Flush: A Biography	Trefusis's Tandem; White's Frost in May
1934	Duo, La jumelle noire		
1935	Cahier de Colette		Trefusis's Broderie anglaise
1936	Mes apprentissages, Chats		Mary Gordon's Chase of the Wild Goose (published by Hogarth)
1937	Bella-Vista	The Years	Woolf is reading Mes apprentissages sent to her the year before by Janie Bussy; appearance of Les vagues, Yourcenar's translation of The Waves
1938		Three Guineas	Woolf is reading Sido.
1939	Le Toutounier		Woolf is reading Duo in France; Freund photographs both Woolf and Colette; Sarraute's Tropisme
1940	Chambre d'hôtel	Roger Fry: A Biography	
1941	Journal à rebours, Julie de Carneilhan	Between the Acts	Woolf commits suicide
1942	De ma fenêtre		
1943	Le Képi, Flore et Pomone		
1944	Gigi, Trois . . . Six . . . Neuf		
1945	Belles saisons		
1946	L'étoile vesper		
1948	Pour un herbier		
1949	Trait pour trait, Journal intermittent, Le fanal bleu, En pays connu		Beauvoir's Le deuxième sexe

(2) Publication Dates of Translations

Figure A.2 shows the dates of the first publications of the works of Woolf and Colette in French and English, respectively. Works appearing at the same time, such as *Mrs Dalloway* and *La promenade au phare*, which both appeared in French in 1929, are placed on separate lines for clarity. The precise dates of publication are given in Figure A.1.

Figure A.2

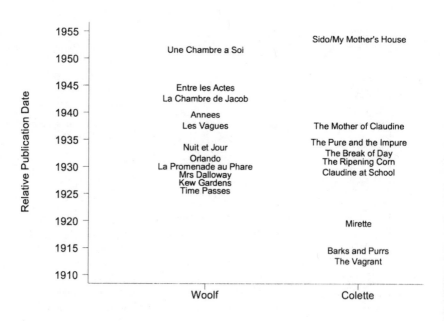

Notes

Author's note: Translations from the French are the author's unless otherwise noted.

Notes to Introduction

1. In *La pêche aux souvenirs* Blanche writes: "Ma bonne, très fidèle amie Colette, j'avais connu la misérable créature que vous étiez, quand vous sautiez du banc où vous posiez, pour voir si le coupé du Jockey-Club arrivait. Willy serait-il avec la comtesse de Guimont Fautru? S'embrasseraient-ils? / Suffocante, baignée de larmes comme un bébé, vous alliez vous étendre sur le canapé de chinz. Ma femme entrait à l'atelier. Elle vous emmenait en bas, boire de l'eau de mélisse des Carmes, tamponner votre front d'ouate trempée dans du vinaigre de Bully. Rose délaçait votre corset, puis vous calait sur son lit avec une boule chaude et des oreillers" (289–90) ("My good, very faithful friend Colette, I knew you as the unhappy creature that you were, when you jumped up from the bench where you were posing, to see if the Jockey Club coupe was pulling up. Would Willy be with the Countess Guimont Fautru? Would they be in an embrace? Suffocating, your face bathed in tears like a baby, you threw yourself down on the chintz divan. My wife came into the studio. She took you downstairs to drink tonic water from Carmes, to mop your forehead with cotton wool soaked in Bully vinegar. Rose loosened your corset, and then tucked you up in her bed with a hot water bottle and pillows"). Colette also provides an account of her sittings for Blanche. While drawn to his portrait of Proust, Colette felt that Blanche never achieved the tone of abandonment, the familiarity of model and painter, painter and model. "Je crois qu'il n'aima ni ma jeunesse, ni la tristesse qu'il y pressentait et que peut-être il lui est advenu de plaindre" ("I believe that he liked neither my youth nor the sadness that he detected there and that he perhaps came to pity it"; quoted in Pichois and Brunet 81).

2. Reviewing an exhibition of Blanche's work at the Hôtel Charpentier in Paris, American journalist Janet Flanner (also known as Genêt) makes reference to this painting. She says that Blanche "[comes] a cropper only in 'An Imaginary Portrait of Virginia Woolf'—whom his imagination led him to believe looked like Queen Mary" (54). The title Flanner gives the portrait appears to be her own.

3. Other artists and photographers of the period created ties between Woolf

and Colette. German photographer Gisèle Freund photographed both writers in 1939. Cecil Beaton took Colette's photograph (see Mitchell's *Colette: A Taste for Life*). Woolf refused him. However, Beaton went ahead and, much to Woolf's consternation, included her in his book, *The Book of Beauty* (see 566–67), along with two sketches taken from other people's photographs of Woolf. American photographer Man Ray photographed Woolf for *Vogue* magazine in 1934 (Hermione Lee writes that "the photographs he took of Virginia Woolf, made up, hair shining and smoothly centre-parted, elegantly dressed, have become part of her legend. American photographer Man Ray placed her in cool, contained attitudes, in one with her right hand raised, looking aside, and in another with hands loosely crossed in front of her, looking up quizzically at the lens. If you didn't know who she was, you would see, from these pictures, a woman of great powers, formidable intelligence and humour, and a daunting social presence" [659]); American photographer Lee Miller, Man Ray's lover and student, photographed Colette, also for *Vogue,* in 1944.

4. For connections between Bloomsbury artists and their French contemporaries, see Caws and Wright's *Bloomsbury and France.*

5. Woolf was a great admirer of Marcel Proust, a portion of whose work at least she read in translation (by C. K. Scott-Moncrieff). In a 1922 letter to Roger Fry, she describes the intense pleasure she experiences reading Proust's work: "But Proust so titillates my own desire for expression that I can hardly set out the sentence. Oh if I could write like that! I cry. And at the moment such is the astonishing vibration and saturation and intensification that he procures—theres something sexual in it—that I feel I *can* write like that, and seize my pen and then *I can't* write like that. Scarcely anyone so stimulates the nerves of language in me" (*Letters* 2: 525). And, again to Fry: "[M]y great adventure is really Proust. Well— what remains to be written after that? I'm only in the first volume, and there are, I suppose, faults to be found, but I am in a state of amazement; as if a miracle were being done before my eyes. How, at last, has someone solidified what has always escaped—and made it into this beautiful and perfectly enduring substance? One has to put the book down and gasp. The pleasure becomes physical—like sun and wine and grapes and perfect serenity and intense vitality combined" (*Letters* 2: 565–66). Colette refers to Blanche's portrait of Proust in her description of the writer in *Mes cahiers:* "Quand j'étais une très jeune femme, il était un bien joli jeune homme. Fiez-vous au portrait que peignit de lui Jacques-Émile Blanche. Cette étroite bouche, cette brume autour des yeux, cette fraîcheur fatiguée, les traits et l'expression appartiennent vraiment à Marcel Proust jeune. [. . .] Sur la toile de Jacques Blanche et dans mon souvenir, les yeux de Marcel Proust sont bien pareils, ouverts en hauteur, plus anxieux qu'étonnés, et d'une naïveté trompeuse" (*Œuvres complètes* [hereafter *OC*] *14:* 144) ("When I was a very young woman, he was a very pretty young man. Look at Jacques-Émile Blanche's portrait of Proust. That narrow mouth, that shadow around the eyes, that wearied freshness, the traits and expressions really belong to the young Marcel Proust. [. . .] On the canvas of Jacques Blanche and in my memory, the eyes of Marcel Proust are the same, open looking upwards, more anxious than astonished, and possessing a feigned naivete").

6. Reinforcing the contemporaneity of Woolf and Colette, the *To the Lighthouse* article is, interestingly, flanked by a news item about Colette and contemporary

writer Francis Carco. An interview with Colette by Francis Ambrière, entitled "Chez Colette," appeared in *Les nouvelles littéraires* on November 16, 1929.

7. Blanche had used an old canvas for the painting of Willy and Colette, and, rather symbolically, as the summer wore on the old portrait (of Mlle Marie de Heredia in a white dress) appeared through the as yet incomplete new one, like "Ophélie immergée et visible" (*Œuvres* 3:1025) ("a pale Ophelia submerged but visible" [62]). Blanche painted Colette's portrait in 1902 and also provided a frontispiece of Colette for her *Sept dialogues de bêtes*, which was published in 1905.

8. "French literature," Woolf wrote in a letter to Gerald Brennan, "falls like a blue tint over the landscape" (*Letters* 2: 599). In "On Not Knowing French," Woolf writes: "It is a delight, after mumbling over the old stories of our old memoirs in the familiar English atmosphere of joints and butlers and port and Parliament and Queen Victoria on the throne, to flash instantly into the brilliance of Mérimée and the court of Napoleon and the Empress Eugénie. After trudging through muddy lanes and damp shrubberies we seem to tiptoe a little self-consciously upon polished floors under crystal chandeliers. And all our ramblings round and about this figure and that, as we pick our way through the ramifications of French memoirs, are full of surprises and excitements—of terrifying encounters with great ladies more severe than our own, of interviews with dukes and diplomats who seem (such is the prestige of the French) more pompous, more polite than our local nobility" (348).

9. For example: "When [Colette] is working she does not see people. When people are there she likes to make them talk or else talk to them about something more interesting than work, and for her everything is interesting. The story has been told about an earnest girl undergraduate who went to see Virginia Woolf with the hope, of course, of talking about books. But Virginia Woolf, perversely enough, wanted to talk about gas ovens instead, whether they were worth while, would the price come down, and wasn't a coal range perhaps better? *Colette would have understood*" (my emphasis; Crosland, *Colette* 210).

10. Rose compares Jean Rhys and Colette: "The young Jean Rhys was a chorus girl in London and a demimondaine in 1920s Paris. The story of her life in her twenties and thirties as revealed in the autobiographical novels bears a remote resemblance to Colette's. The locales were similar. Rhys, too, lived on the other side of respectability, and she struggled, less successfully than Colette, for independence from men" (104–5).

11. Critics have also noted similarities in the lives of the two writers: "[B]oth came from large families, both loved the capital cities where they lived for part of their lives, both had a circle of friends that included the gifted writers and artists of their time, and each, in her own way, rejected conventional standards of behavior. Both were married to Jewish husbands [Leonard Woolf and Maurice Goudeket] during World War II" (Bonne 23). I would add a few other details: both recognized the value of work to the emancipation of women. Both worked in a professional capacity as a writer. Both loved France and French literature.

12. "Colette est plus attentive au présent qu'au passé, aux lettres françaises qu'aux lettres étrangères; l'homme l'intéresse autant, sinon plus, que l'œuvre, ou même que l'écrivain; elle se fait souvent de la chose littéraire une vision concrète, et elle n'a guère souci de se piquer d'érudition" (24). In terms of Colette's knowledge of English literature, we know that she read Shakespeare. A copy of D. H.

Lawrence's *Lady Chatterley's Lover* was provided by Una Troubridge. In *Mes apprentissages,* Marcel Schwob reads to the ailing Colette, "Mark Twain, Jerome K. Jerome, Dickens or Moll Flanders—which he had not translated at the time" (38). Colette's admission that she read the diaries of the Ladies of Llangollen in the original in *Le pur et l'impur* suggests she at least had a reading knowledge of English.

13. When asked in an interview by French writer Maurice Dekobra if she was a feminist, shortly after having written *La vagabonde* (1910)—a novel about an independent and powerful woman, a novel that I believe falls quite squarely into the category of feminist novels—Colette responded with an emphatic no: "Ah non!" Suffragettes, she told Dekobra, disgusted her, and if any of her compatriots were to try to imitate them, she would be made to understand that her behavior was not acceptable in France. "Savez-vous ce qu'elles méritent, les suffragettes?" she asked Dekobra. "Le fouet et le harem . . ." (quoted in Pichois and Brunet 188) ("Do you know what they deserve, the suffragettes? [. . .] The whip and the harem"). While Colette's comments were undoubtedly deliberately inflammatory, as Pichois and Brunet suggest (188), they did not lack conviction. Colette did not concern herself in any direct way with the improvement of the condition of women. However, as biographer Michèle Sarde points out, this does not mean that Colette was not concerned with the fate of women. Citing Karl Marx's preference for the works of Honoré de Balzac, monarchist and reactionary, over those of Émile Zola, a socialist, for the reason that in Balzac he found material that fed, without dogmatic distortion, his reflection on French history, she suggests that "L'œuvre de Colette, qui n'a jamais eu de préoccupation idéologique, passe incomparablement mieux la rampe que les écrits féministes de son époque, et prête à une méditation sur la femme et son histoire" (464) ("Colette's work, devoid of any ideological slant, comes across to the audience with far greater clarity than does the feminist writing of her day, and it is an invaluable aid in the consideration of women and history" [8]), a view with which Colette biographer Judith Thurman concurs: "[S]he defines the second sex as the strong one; she challenges the received ideas about the incapacity of females for work, pleasure, autonomy, and aggression; she rises to the challenge of becoming both a person and a woman" (251). While neither Sido, Colette's real and fictional mother, nor Colette considered themselves feminists, according to Sarde, both asserted their independence as women: Sido, within her own domestic domain, and Colette, within the parameters of the written text.

14. I borrow terms here from Ottavi. She footnotes a reference to J. J. Mayoux, who, she notes, in his *Vivants piliers* (213) "signale [. . .] une parenté entre 'l'intellectuelle mondaine' et la 'sensuelle' (181 n.) ("signals [. . .] a relationship between 'the worldly intellectual' and the 'sensual'").

Notes to Chapter 1

1. As I note in the introduction and chap. 3, Woolf makes numerous references to her reading of Colette in her letters: "Ethel [Smyth] had sent Virginia an article on Anna de Noailles by the French fiction writer Sidonie-Gabrielle Colette (1873–1954). Virginia read at least three of Colette's books, two of autobiography (*Mes apprentissages,* 1934, *Sido,* 1929) and one of fiction (*Duo,* 1934), and the

two writers sent each other messages through mutual friends" (*Congenial Spirits* n. 375).

2. I will refer to all of these women by their last names, with the exception of Vita and Violet. The two writers shared other friends and acquaintances; however, for the purpose of this chapter, I have limited my focus. Other shared female acquaintances include Rebecca West, Katherine Mansfield, and Victoria Ocampo.

3. This type of biographical project falls in line with a number of other studies undertaken by Modernist scholars, for example Shari Benstock's *Women of the Left Bank* (1986), Bonnie Kime Scott's *The Gender of Modernism* (1990) and *Refiguring Modernism* (1995), and, most recently, Caws and Wright's *Bloomsbury and France* (2000). While the last of these does not focus specifically on women, the prevalence of women-centered collective biography, especially covering the Modernist period, is worth noting. This results in part from feminist critics' efforts to promote the work of women writers and artists who have not received the recognition accorded to their male counterparts. These studies draw on previously unpublished archival material only recently available, following the deaths of many figures of this generation. These women-centered biographical studies grow out of the work of early feminist critics, more general in terms of period, such as Gilbert and Gubar's *Madwoman in the Attic* (1979) and Louise Bernikow's *Among Women* (1980), which attempted a recuperation of women's voices. They in turn took their cue from pivotal texts such as Harold Bloom's *Anxiety of Influence*. Scott diagrammatically maps connections among writers in a fashion similar to that undertaken here.

4. In 1939 Colette and Maurice Goudeket spent part of the summer in Dieppe. It appears, however, that they arrived after Woolf had already returned home. Goudeket references Bloomsbury: "[L]e mois d'août 1939 nous trouva pour la première fois hésitants sur le lieu de nos vacances. Nos amis Léopold Marchand nous persuadèrent de les passer avec eux à Dieppe. Climat frais, lumière pâle, mer grise, le contraste avec nos heures méridionales était complet. Mais Dieppe et son air vieillot, son bord de la mer conventionnel, ses villas dont certaines datent de Charles X, ne manquait pas de charme. La duchesse de Berry, Madame Récamier, les Anglais de l'époque victorienne, les blondes misses à crinoline, *la bohème de Bloomsbury* la hantaient encore un peu" (my emphasis; 173) ("In August 1939 we hesitated for the first time on our holiday destination. The Marchands persuaded us to stay with them in Dieppe. The moderate climate, the pale light, the grey sea, the contrast with our time in the South was complete. But Dieppe with its quaintness, its typical seaside, its houses, some of which date from the time of Charles X, had a certain charm. The duchess of Berry, Madame Récamier, the Victorian-era English people, the blond ladies in crinolines, the Bloomsbury bohemians could still sometimes be found there"). American artist Ethel Sands lived in Dieppe.

5. The ice metaphor recalls the "nice names" Ethel Smyth had for Woolf, among them the "frozen falcon," a name used by "someone at a concert [who] said she looked like that—so still, so alert," and "'4d. for 9d.' because," writes Ethel, "she asks a lot, and gives little—in quantity at least" (quoted in St John 223–24). It echoes Gisèle Freund's description of Woolf as "frail and luminous, [. . .] the embodiment of her prose" (*The World* 130). The bicolored ice metaphor also resonates with Maurice Goudeket's description of his wife, Colette, as "[u]n produit de la plus pure terre française, française jusqu'au bout des ongles" (17) ("a

product of the most pure French earth, French to very the tips of her fingernails").
According to Noailles, Colette has a "beau visage aigu de renard" (97) ("a beautiful face sharp as a fox"); Trefusis describes how her "foxy face looked up at me
through a fuzz of hair that might have been undergrowth" (*Don't Look Round*
90); and according to Rebecca West, Colette has the air of a Spanish fighting bull:
" [West] first saw Colette at the railway station at St.-Raphaël, waiting 'with the
stance of a Spanish fighting bull' and holding her bulldog by a wine-coloured
crepe de Chine scarf twisted through its lead. She admired Colette as a writer for
putting 'into infallible artistic form her gross, wise, limited, eternal views about
life'" (Glendinning 151–52). Here Glendinning quotes from West's *Ending in
Earnest* (see chapter 4).

6. While Woolf envied Colette's writing style and that of Proust, Phyllis Rose
contends that she really felt no threat: "Contemporaries, moreover, provoked an
unhealthy sort of rivalry. They were doing the same things she was, but—as she
put it—on a different railway track. It was distracting. She had to remind herself
that 'East Coker' could be good and her own work, different as it was, could also
be good. With French writers, she was on safer ground. They were from a different country, wrote in a different tradition. So she could read Colette and Proust
with pleasure, while Mansfield and Joyce produced anxiety and irritation" (*Woman
of Letters* 262).

7. Woolf loved France. In 1923 she wrote to her friend the French painter
Jacques Raverat, "I felt a kind of levity and civility and frivolity and congeniality
upon me with the first sight of Dieppe [cf. Colette and Dieppe]. How much more
enjoyable in some queer way France is than England" (quoted in Caws and Wright
3). Caws and Wright contend that what attracted Woolf to France was "the inten-
sity and kind of thought she believed was, in some sense, dependent on the language" (14). In her diary on October 30, 1930, Woolf writes: "I say 'I will cut
adrift—I will go to Roger in France—I will sit on pavements and drink coffee—I
will see the Southern hills [. . .] I need solitude. I need space. I need air. I need
the empty fields round me; & my legs pounding along roads; & sleep; & animal
existence" (*Diary* 3 323). Colette is also known for her passion for travel literature:
"Voyages, ah! voyages! Les soixante-huit volumes de la collection du *Tour du
Monde,* lus d'un bout à l'autre plusieurs fois. Livingstone, Stanley, Huc, Landon,
Arago, Comte de Beauvoir, Schweinfurth, Madame Ida Pfeifer, tant d'autres . . ."
(Goudeket 149) ("Travel, ah! Travel! The sixty-eight volumes of the Around the
World collection, read from cover to cover several times. Livingstone, Stanley,
Huc, Landon, Arago, Comte de Beauvoir, Schweinfurth, Madame Ida Pfeifer, and
so many others").

8. For a discussion of Freund's photographic methodology, see Nicola Luckhurst's "Photoportraits: Gisèle Freund and Virginia Woolf." Luckhurst is current-
ly at work on a biography of Freund.

9. "The umbilical cord which had bound *Roger Fry: A Biography* to Virginia's
brain for two years was, as I said, finally cut when she returned the proofs to the
printer on May 13, 1940; 319 days later on March 28, 1941, she committed suicide by drowning herself in the River Ouse" (L. Woolf, *The Journey* 44).

10. "[J]e n'aurais jamais cru que le genre humain en viendrait là encore une
fois." Colette writes from Dieppe (where she has been staying August 12–28) to
Mme Léopold Marchand, "Maurice a vu une arrivée de train, bondé d'Anglais qui

quittaient la Côte, qui n'est plus d'Azur, mais de m . . . , et regagnaient leur Angleterre" (*Lettres de la vagabonde,* 265) ("Maurice saw the arrival of a train, packed full of English people who were leaving the coast, which is no longer of Azure, but sh . . , in order to get back to their England").

11. See Freund's *Three Days with Joyce,* originally published as *Trois jours avec Joyce* (1982). The photographs were taken in the late 1930s.

12. Ocampo authored a number of pieces about Woolf, including *Virginia Woolf en su diario* (1954), and did much to promote her work in the Spanish-speaking world. She arranged for Jorge Luis Borges to translate *Orlando* and *A Room of One's Own* into Spanish and published both at *Sur.*

13. Indeed, in 1939 Woolf wrote to Vita that she was in a rage over Freund's plan to show the photographs she had taken of Woolf: "That devil woman Giselle [*sic*] Freund calmly tells me she's showing those d__d photographs—and I made it a condition she shouldn't. Don't you think it damnable?—considering how they [Ocampo and Freund] filched and pilfered and gate crashed—the treacherous vermin. Do give her a piece of my mind if you see her. I loathe being hoisted about on top of a stick for any one to stare at" (*Letters* 6: 351). In 1946, when she returned to London, Freund showed the photographs she had taken to Leonard Woolf. On subsequent visits Freund returned to see Leonard, who helped her select other writers for her collection. She photographed Leonard: "He himself visibly enjoyed posing. I could not help but think that his wife's death had freed him of the dreadful apprehensions that had weighed on his life for so many years" (*The World* 137).

14. See Adrienne Monnier's "The Country of Faces" on Freund (in *The Very Rich Hours* 231–33).

15. Leonard Woolf makes reference to the proposed publication of *Ulysses* in his letters. In 1957 he thanks John McCallum of Harcourt, Brace and Company for a copy of Beach's *Ulysses in Paris.* "It recalls the moment," he writes, "when Miss Harriet Weaver brought us the MS of *Ulysses* and we tried without success to get an English printer to print it" (501).

16. See Wickes's *The Amazon of Letters* and Beach's *Shakespeare and Company* for more on Beach and Monnier's relationship with Natalie Barney. Wickes suggests that Barney did not know Woolf, although she did correspond with Vita Sackville-West (177). Barney read Woolf's work and discussed it with, among others, Dolly Wilde (Wickes 185). Radclyffe Hall, Wickes hypothesizes, associated Barney and Woolf, and he cites as evidence Hall's description in *The Well of Loneliness* of Valérie Seymour (based on Barney), which reminds him of passages from *Mrs Dalloway* (177–78).

17. Monnier published Valery Larbaud's French translation of *Ulysses.*

18. Vita's account of her affair with Violet appears in *Portrait of a Marriage,* published posthumously by her son Nigel Nicolson, and in her novel *Challenge,* the publication of which was delayed at the request of Vita's mother until 1923, when it appeared in the United States. In *Challenge* Vita is "the erotic Julian" and Violet, his cousin, the "erratic Eve" (*Violet to Vita* 21).

19. In her letters Violet called herself Lushka (Alyosha) (perhaps explaining Woolf's choice of Russian as a nationality; Violet is Sasha in *Orlando*), and Vita either Mitya (Dmitri) or Julian (*Violet to Vita* 21). In *Portrait of a Marriage,* Nicolson writes that "their very names must be changed to something more suited to their rebellion" (149).

20. "I have seen [Violet] and Colette together and one can hardly imagine two more different women—one of them earthy, always in direct contact with everything; the other ethereal, seeing everything as if through a prism. Yet they understood each other in certain deep-seated essentials of which they alone were conscious" (Goudeket quoted in *Violet to Vita*, n. 255).

21. "Vita Sackville-West was also in Florence in 1950, where she met Philippe Jullian to discuss a biography of Violet Trefusis, but it seems unlikely that Una met her other than by accident, as they had never been in the same 'set,' despite Vita's willingness to speak on behalf of *The Well* at its trial twenty-two years earlier. Vita, Violet and Virginia Woolf had all been 'closet' inverts, lacking the courage and honesty of Una and John [Radclyffe Hall]" (Ormrod 297).

22. "Although Hall and the Bloomsbury writers believed in many of the same principles, their methods of dealing with them, even of thinking about them, were diametrically opposed. Bloomsbury's writers and philosophers held most things at bay with an amused and abstract detachment. They liked spinning ideas, juggling truths, catching evasions, netting improprieties, ridiculing the establishment. Hall, though a complex creature herself, was by comparison simplistic and straightforward. The notion of overlapping truths did not interest her. The barbarity of suppressing 'the Truth' did. [. . .] Hall's unambiguous stance on lesbianism, both in personal terms and as a literary theme, conflicted with the intellectual complexity of Bloomsbury's multi-layered sexualities. Secondly, Hall's openness rattled both Forster and Woolf. Forster was a discreet homosexual and an indiscreet misogynist, while Virginia Woolf was a 'married lesbian' whose marriage protected her public image, despite the important love affair she was conducting at that very time with Vita Sackville-West, also married" (Cline 250).

23. In a letter to Woolf, Vita writes: "I feel very violently about The Well of Loneliness. Not on account of what you call my proclivities; not because I think it is a good book; but really on principle [. . .]. Because, you see, even if the W. of L. had been a good book,—even if it had been a great book, a real masterpiece,— the result would have been the same. And that is intolerable. I really have no words to say how indignant I am" (*Letters of Vita Sackville-West and Virginia Woolf*, 279–80).

24. "'Mais il y a un point où je suis anti-John, parce que, sans doute, je suis une créature assez grossière: c'est l'impression chez Stephen [c'est le nom pris par l'héroïne] d'anormalité. Or, je dis que, si un 'anormal' se sent anormal, il n'est pas anormal. Attendez, je vais dire mieux: un ou une anormal ne doit jamais avoir une sensation d'anormalité, au contraire, une femme aimant une femme (ou un homme aimant un homme), pense: 'Qu'est-ce qu'un univers rempli de cochons monstrueux qui sont différents de moi?' Voilà une partie de ce que je souhaite tant vous dire au sujet du livre'" (quoted in Pichois and Brunet 384).

25. "'Elle est un constructeur paisible de grands édifices, et moi je ne bâtis jamais que des bungalows'" (quoted in Pichois and Brunet 385).

26. "'Son souvenir m'est vif, et très physique, la belle forme de sa tête, l'argent doré de ses cheveux, et ses beaux traits, et ce sombrero espagnol qu'elle portait volontiers . . . Certains êtres ne devraient pas mourir'" (quoted in Pichois and Brunet 385).

27. In *Shakespeare and Company* Sylvia Beach expresses regret that she did not have an opportunity to meet Hall at Barney's salon: "Unfortunately, I missed the

chance to make the acquaintance at [Barney's] *salon* of the authoress of *The Well of Loneliness,* in which she concluded that if inverted couples could be united at the altar, all their problems would be solved" (115).

28. "Most of our visits to Paris were punctuated by the gift of another of [Colette's] books. I have them all with those witty dedications for which she seemed never to lack inspiration . . . Yes; Paris was always beloved and always new, always a signal for carefree enjoyment. It became 'ours' and until the summer of 1926, when she was actually beginning to write the book, nobody was less aware than John that she was absorbing copy for *The Well of Loneliness*" (Troubridge 83–84).

29. For more information about Hall's relationship with Souline, see Glasgow (1997).

30. "Colette rapproche le couple Una-John de celui que formaient les dames de Llangollen, qu'on rencontre dans *Le Pur et l'impur*" ["Colette compares the couple Una and John with that of the Ladies of Llangollen, whom one encounters in *Le pur et l'impur*"]. This quotation comes from a letter at the Bibliothèque Nationale that was part of a Colette exhibition (catalogue no. 561) (quoted in Pichois and Brunet 385 and n. 544).

31. At Polignac's house, British novelist and Bloomsbury associate Rosamund Lehmann met not only Colette but also, among others, Jean Cocteau and dramatist Edouard Bourdet (de Cossart 202–3). Conspicuous absences from Polignac's salon are American writer Gertrude Stein and her lover Alice Toklas. Claude Francis and Fernande Gontier note that despite Cocteau's pleas, Stein was never invited to Polignac's salon. While the majority of Polignac's guests were homosexual, Stein was considered, according to Francis and Gontier, too bohemian, too grotesquely masculine (*Colette* 329). Stein did belong to Natalie Barney's Académie des Femmes, as did Colette. Her work, pieces of which were translated by Barney, was presented at one of Barney's Fridays (Wickes 167).

32. "She also found Winnaretta fascinating because of her association with Proust, although there was no secret about how strained their relations had been at times. Virginia was far from discouraged. She pressed Winnaretta to tell her more about him and was delighted when Winnaretta sent her one of Proust's letters, which she recently rediscovered among her papers. A present of gramophone records of Beethoven's Quartet opus 130, accompanied it. At first sight, the friendship of these two women was surprising: they were both quite dominating characters but, on the other hand, they both had very gentle, shy sides to their natures, which they seemed to bring out in each other" (de Cossart 201–2).

33. When Colette traveled to Belgium to deliver an address in honor of Anna de Noailles and to accept her own nomination to the Académie royale belge de langue et de littérature française, Polignac accompanied her (Cossart 196). Smyth corresponded with Noailles and her sister Hélène. Her letters were mainly concerned with her infatuation with Polignac.

34. "Je distribuerai le rôle du soleil à Madame Colette et à Madame de Noailles le rôle de la lune qui est le soleil des statues et, en quelque sorte, ce pâle et froid soleil des morts dont La Rochefoucauld nous affirme qu'il est la gloire" (46–47) ("I will give the role of the sun to Madame Colette and to Madame de Noailles the role of the moon, which is the sun of statues, in a way, this pale and cold sun of the dead, the glory of which La Rochefoucauld affirms for us."

35. "lasse de dissimulation, provocante, effrontée, sûre de soi, paisible aussi comme Cybèle, énigmatique comme la déesse africaine, chatte et tigre" (Noailles 97).

36. "Je ne décrirai pas ici le génie de Colette; autorisez-la à faire usage d'un dictionnaire entier, elle y creusera son gîte, produira par jaillissement et avec labeur, dit-elle, une œuvre succulente, sanguine, végétale, où tous les vocables sembleront avoir été raflés et distribués sans pourtant que nulle adjonction vienne alourdir un récit qui se réclame de la vie et de la nécessité" (Noailles 98).

37. Woolf received the prize at the Institut Français in South Kensington. The award was founded in 1904 by twenty-two female collaborators on a magazine called *Vie heureuse* as an alternative to the Académie Goncourt, where all the judges were men. Ironically, two thirds of the recipients were men. Radclyffe Hall won the Prix Femina Vie Heureuse–Bookman Prize for her novel *Adam's Breed* in 1927 (Cline 218).

38. Woolf would also have been familiar with Noailles via Polignac, and from reading Colette's speech honoring Noailles, which was sent to her by Smyth. A further link exists as a result of Noailles's friendship with Ocampo, the editor of *Sur,* who also corresponded regularly with Woolf.

39. Woolf appears to be recounting what Victoria Ocampo had told her at the Man Ray photography exhibition where they first met in November 1934: "And so to Me de Noailles, dying of extinguished vanity in a small flat. She lay in bed, bedizened, covered with dozens & dozens of veils &c: began plucking them off; was never still a moment, lighting lamps & putting them out; demanded worship; was not old, but had outlived her fame. Nothing wrong with her but the death of her great fame. And she left letters to Barrès wh. his widow holds; & the doctor is piecing the story together" (*Diary* 4: 263–64).

40. The passages from *A Room of One's Own* are the following: "The woman composer stands where the actress stood in the time of Shakespeare" and "One can only repeat Dr. Johnson's dictum concerning a woman preacher, transposed into terms of music. 'Sir, a woman's composing is like a dog's walking on his hind legs. It is not well done, but you are surprised to find it done at all'" (*A Room,* quoted in Collis 175).

41. Woolf's letters reveal her ambivalent feelings about Ethel. She writes to Quentin Bell: "The reason why Ethel Smyth is so repulsive, tell Nessa, is her table manners. She oozes; she chortles; and she half blew her rather red nose on her table napkin. Then she poured the cream—oh the blackberries were divine—into her beer; and I had rather dine with a dog [. . .]. She was however full—after dinner—of vigorous charm; she walked four miles; she sang Brahms; the sheep looked up and were not fed. And we packed her off before midnight" (*Letters* 5: 226–27).

Notes to Chapter 2

1. Dusinberre goes on to suggest that Woolf did, however, maintain her interest in the topic, citing comments made to Ethel Smyth in 1941 about her plans to write an autobiography: "there's never been a womans [*sic*] autobiography. Nothing to compare with Rousseau. Chastity and modesty I suppose have been the

reason [. . .] I should like an analysis of your sex life. As Rousseau did his" (*Letters* 6: 453, quoted in Dusinberre 203).

2. In this essay, based on a lecture given to the London/National Society for Women's Service on January 21, 1931, Woolf loosely recounts her trajectory as a writer, then describes the angel in the house and her killing of the angel. She somewhat comically suggests that having earned enough money to buy a Persian cat with her first writer's revenue, she then, desiring a motorcar, writes a novel in order to secure one. The last segment of the essay and perhaps the one that takes us most closely to the question of the sexual life of women involves a description of a man writing and a woman writing in a trance of sorts, unconsciously. She asks her audience to imagine her as a fisherman engrossed in thought, a fishing rod in her hand. Her mind sweeps freely back and forth across the water, "round every rock and cranny of the world that lies submerged in the depths of our unconscious being" until suddenly the line "raced through her fingers" (61). "Her imagination had rushed away" (61). There is a smash, and confusion ensues. "To speak without figure," writes Woolf, "she had thought of something, something about the body, about the passions which it was unfitting for her as a woman to say. Men, her reason told her, would be shocked" (61). In summing up, she writes that while the first experience involving the angel in the house was one she could deal with, the second, "telling the truth about my own experiences as a body," is not something she feels she has solved (62). This question is also raised in *A Room*.

3. In *The Years* the subject of sex—for example, the rumor of Eugénie Pargiter's infidelity, and the extramarital affair of the patriarch Abel Pargiter with his mistress Mira (one thinks particularly of the interrupted neck-touching scene early in the novel)—is broached but again in a veiled fashion.

4. For a discussion of the ellipses in Woolf's *Three Guineas*, see Shari Benstock's "Ellipses: Figuring Feminisms in *Three Guineas*" in *Textualizing the Feminine*.

5. Adrienne Monnier, proprietor of a bookstore called La Maison des Amies des Livres, which sat opposite Beach's on the rue de l'Odéon, confirms that Woolf's work was available in Beach's bookstore (6).

6. See my chapter 1 and Jones (1993) on Woolf's knowledge and use of the Ladies of Llangollen for *Orlando*. Woolf's failure to use the story in an explicit way perhaps also results from the reticence about sex that in part prevented the writing of a sequel to *A Room*.

7. George Borrow, author of *Lavrengo* and *The Bible in Spain*, figures in the relationship of Vita Sackville-West and Violet Trefusis. Critics suggest that Vita based aspects of her novel *Challenge* on Borrow's work. Vita and Violet also adopted Romany phrases from Borrow's work in their correspondence.

8. "Une bibliothèque nombreuse et bien fournie, une vue et une situation délicieuse . . . Une vie égale, paisible, une parfaite amitié" (126). In some senses, *Le pur* is Colette's most English book, in part perhaps because of her collaboration with Hall and Troubridge. Thus, in the first part of the book, a young man smiles with "une bouche anglaise" (9); here also English people frequent the opium den (21/16). In the third section of *Le pur*, a curtain is fastened with "une épingle anglaise" ("a safety pin") (36); when Colette's narrator leaves Boldini's studio, she adjusts "le nœud d'une régate qui venait de Londres" (74) ("the knot of a mannish necktie that had been imported from London" [67]); Colette paints a portrait

of the half British and half American Renée Vivien ("so typically English" [80]), using her British name Pauline Tarn first; and Vivien wants to go to a fancy-dress ball as Jane Grey, who became Queen of England for nine days in 1553 before being executed. In the seventh part, Colette describes the English couple, the Ladies of Llangollen. In the eighth part, the workers in Willy's "'atelier de littérature'" whom Colette befriends are for the most part English (145/133); one among them receives a long letter from London and they curse in English (153/141); another speaks to Colette in "his French, which was correct but accented" (150). Finally, in the ninth part, Colette's friend "appuyait sa tête au dossier d'un gros fauteuil imité de l'anglais, affreux et vert" (169) ("sink[s] into a deep English armchair, green and hideous" [156]).

9. For the judgment against *The Well*, and contemporary and recent commentary on the text, see Doan and Prosser's *Palatable Poison*.

10. Like the Ladies, Hall and Troubridge were exiles of sorts, preferring the openness of France and Italy to the restrictedness of their home country. Hall's link to the two works is significant in the sense that it reminds the reader of the differences in attitudes toward issues such as homosexuality, or Sapphism, an issue treated in both *A Room* and *Le pur*, in Paris and London, in France and England at this period. Hall's portrayal of a liberal France, where her work and her lifestyle were better received, and a more repressed England (in *The Well*, for example) anticipates the focus of the two works under analysis here. While questions of homosexuality and female sexuality are buried or veiled in Woolf's *A Room*, in Colette's *Le pur* these same issues take center stage.

11. This lapse in time merits questions—in part because Woolf's novels were translated very quickly after their initial appearance in English. *Le pur* was first translated into English in 1966. It appears that Colette read *The Well of Loneliness* in English.

12. "Ce qui me manque, c'est le 'Journal' où se fût révélée la cadette, Sarah Ponsonby, la proie [. . .] La secrète, c'est cette Sarah qui se tait et qui brode. Un Journal de Sarah Ponsonby, quelle lumière!" (137).

13. It is important to note that the part of *Le pur* that deals with Don Juan began as a contribution to a series of supplements to great works.

14. "[A]tteignent le refuge du sommeil à deux, de la veille à deux, de la nocturne angoisse à deux" (139). These everyday things include: "Amour, travaux ménagers, soins du jardin, lectures à la veillée, visites reçues, rendues, longue, mondaine et minutieuse correspondance; gourmandise anglaise, répartie tant sur le mouton froid que sur le 'fruit de la Passiflore accommodé au sucre et au vin de Madère'" (139) ("Love, housework, gardening; in the evening, reading; visits received and paid back; long, worldly and detailed correspondence; English gourmandizing—cold mutton being favored equally with 'the fruit of the Passiflora served with sugar and Madeira wine'" [127]).

15. When the appearance of the work was broken off abruptly just weeks after it began—in mid-sentence, according to Janet Flanner (*The Pure and the Impure*, "Translator's Introduction")—the editor wrote to Colette that protests from all sides had forced him to stop publishing her work. The serialization of Colette's *Le blé en herbe*, this time in *Le matin* in 1922, was also suspended midstream due to its portrayal of a fifteen-year-old boy's sexual initiation at the hands of an older woman (Sarde 404–5).

16. "'Il agite de vieilles choses d'amour, se mêle des amours unisexuelles—enfin il fait ce qu'il peut'" (quoted in Pichois and Brunet 322).

17. "[C]e livre qui n'est qu'une galerie de vieux péchés" (to Hélène Picard, quoted in *Œuvres* 3: 1514).

18. Marcus argues that "The brilliance of *A Room of One's Own* lies in its invention of a female language to subvert the languages of the patriarchy. Like her novels, it is about reading and it trains us to read as women. Its tropes figure new reading and writing strategies, enlisting punctuation in the service of feminism with the use of ellipses for encoding female desire, the use of initials and dashes to make absent figures more present and transforming interruption, the condition of the woman writer's oppression [. . .] into a deliberate strategy as a sign of woman's writing." She adds that Woolf renders interruption "a positive female form" (*Languages* 187). In *Œuvres* 3, Jacques Dupont suggests that the apparent diversity of *Le pur* has an aesthetic function, at the same time as and because it involves a reflexive process. By juxtaposing diverse episodes, he suggests, one is able to draw through the work "the red thread of a continuous and intense meditation, which adds another layer to these anecdotes and portraits that sparkle in their own right. The discontinuity of the episodes, their frequently dramatic alternation [. . .], is the premium of pleasure offered to the reader so he or she can follow without reticence the meanderings of an inquiry—a quest—that proceeds oftentimes obliquely and in a biased fashion" (my translation 1508).

19. In *Le pur* characters from different episodes in the book are brought together, such as Charlotte and Damien. Colette returns to the Ladies of Llangollen in the closing pages of the work. In *A Room* Woolf returns to Judith Shakespeare at the end of her text; she also makes a second reference to the *Well of Loneliness* trial (mentioning Bodkin). The name of Mary Carmichael is one among possible identities for herself as narrator early on in the text (5); the name reappears later as that of the fictional novelist whose work Woolf examines.

20. "Bannie et présente, témoin translucide, [le narrateur] goûtai[t] une paix indéfinissable, qui n'allait pas sans une certaine vanité d'affiliée" (151).

21. "La figure voilée d'une femme fine, désabusée, savante en tromperie, en délicatesse, convient au seuil de ce livre qui tristement parlera du plaisir" (31).

22. "[C]otonneuse, rêche et douce comme sont les pêches dures à gros velours" (10).

23. "Mais du sein de ce silence même un son naquit imperceptiblement dans une gorge de femme, un son qui s'essaya rauque, s'éclaircit, prit sa fermeté et son ampleur en se répétant, comme les notes pleines que le rossignol redit et accumule jusqu'à ce qu'elles s'écroulent en roulade . . ." (12).

24. "Le son charmant de sa voix, l'attaque râpeuse de certaines syllabes, une manière vaincue et suave de laisser tomber dans le registre grave la fin des phrases . . . Quelle séduction" (15).

25. "[L]'idée de mystère que nous attachons aux êtres dont nous ne connaissons que la simplicité" (19–20).

26. "Tête nue, bien prise et un peu ronde dans sa robe noire, elle n'avait pas endossé le kimono rituel" (21).

27. "[N]otes pleines, réitérées, identiques, l'une par l'autre prolongées, précipitées jusqu'à la rupture de leur tremblant équilibre au sommet d'un sanglot torrentiel" (23).

28. "Un génie femelle, occupé de tendre imposture, de ménagement, d'abné-gation, habitait donc cette tangible Charlotte, rassurante amie des hommes . . . Assise et les jambes étendues, elle attendait oisive, à mon coté, de reprendre la tâche dévolue à celui qui aime le mieux: la fourberie quotidienne" (23).

29. "'Le seul bruit de maître qu'un homme fasse dans une maison, c'est, quand il est encore sur le palier, le tâtonnement de sa clef à l'entrée de la serrure'" (31).

30. "Je m'embarque, quand je pense à Charlotte, sur un voguant souvenir de nuits que ni le sommeil, ni la certitude n'ont couronnées" (31).

31. "Me verrais-je amenée, aux premières pages d'un livre, à déclarer que l'homme est moins destiné à la femme que la femme n'est faite pour l'homme? Nous verrons bien" (33).

32. "[U]n lé de Paris mouvant et silencieux, un vol de mouches de feu sur un lac d'asphalte. Une facile illusion, de nuit dangereuse, au dehors, de sécurité sous des vieux murs, chauds de secrets, m'enveloppe" (34). In her biography, Lee asserts that *A Room* "was as much about London as about the history, education and writing of women" (553). In the same way, Colette's *Le pur* might be read as a book about Paris.

33. "Je n'ai pas à savoir [. . .] s'il comporte un boudoir à glaces, et des appareils de lupanar . . ." (42).

34. "Je me plaisais à sa présence, comme je me plais à celle des animaux vélo-ces qui, dans le repos, sont immobiles. Il parlait peu, et je crois qu'il était médiocre en tout, sauf en sa mission" (50).

35. "L'obsession de la puissance égalerait-elle, pour un amant, l'obsession de l'impuissance?" (65).

36. "C'est entre nous un usage nonchalant que de suspendre la phrase en son beau milieu, dès que celle qui écoute a compris celle qui parle [. . .] On n'imag-ine pas le nombre de sujets et de mots que bannissent de leur conversation deux femmes qui peuvent se dire tout. Elle s'offrent le luxe de choisir [. . .] J'éclatai de rire,—il fait bon mesurer et narguer, d'un peu loin, les griffes des vieux dangers aussi grimaçants et vifs . . ." (68–70).

37. "Elle ressemblait, en dormant, un peu au Dante, un peu à un hidalgo fin, un peu au saint Jean-Baptiste vu par Léonardo de Vinci" (71).

38. "Puis j'allai reprendre mon poste au bord d'une table-bureau, d'où mes yeux de femme suivirent, sur le vélin turquoise, une courte et dure main de jar-dinier, qui écrivait" (72).

39. It is thought that Woolf borrowed her fictional author's name and book title from Mary Stopes, who wrote a novel called *Love's Creation* using the pen name Mary Carmichael in 1928.

40. Woolf's question recalls Colette's narrator's conversation with Marguerite Moreno in *Le pur:* "We had the comfortable habit of leaving a sentence hanging midway as soon as one of us had grasped the point" (68).

41. Woolf uses the same words, "new combination," several years later to describe Colette's work, specifically her novel *Sido* (*Letters* 6: 301). See chapter 3.

42. "[U]ne compagnie étrange, qui ne vivait plus que d'un reste de vie crain-tive et de son snobisme épuisé" (74–75).

43. "Anxieux et voilé, jamais nu, l'androgyne erre, s'étonne, mendie tout bas . . ." (84).

44. "[Her sensibility] feasted like a plant newly stood in the air on every sight

and sound that came its way. It ranged, too, very subtly and curiously, among almost unknown or unrecorded things; it lighted on small things and showed that perhaps they were not small after all" (92–93).

45. "On sent qu'une imagination féminine, captive sous le front découvert du faux homme, regrette de n'avoir pu se dépenser en jabots, en rubans, en étoffe soyeuse . . ." (110).

46. "'Une femme qui reste une femme, c'est un être complet'" (112).

47. "La pudeur qui sépare deux amants, pendant des heures de repos, d'ablutions, de maladie, ne se glisse guère entre deux corps jumeaux, pareillement affligés, voués aux mêmes soins, aux mêmes chastetés fatidiques" (120–21).

48. "J'étais fidèle à mon rôle de meuble agréable, et je les écoutais d'un air expert" (151).

49. "Une espèce d'austérité la couvrait, austérité nécessaire et que, pourtant, je ne puis comparer à nulle autre, car elle n'était pas de parade ni de précaution, ni engendrée par la peur morbide qui galvanise, plus souvent qu'elle ne les bride, tant de pourchassés" (160).

50. "Personne ne m'a parlé comme lui de la couleur bleue, ni du copeau de cheveux d'or tourné autour d'une oreille sanguine" (163).

51. The ambiguity of this reference is captured in French in the opening sentence, which is cleverly without gender: "Auprès de leur art de feindre, tout semble imparfait" (168).

52. "Ménagez, dans le dernier tiers de ma vie, une place nette, pour que j'y pose ma crudité de prédilection, l'amour. Rien que de la tenir devant moi et de sagement la respirer, la tâter de la main et de la dent, elle me garde le teint frais" (177).

53. "Une sorte de purgatoire gymnique, où s'entraînent tour à tour tous les sens" (180).

54. "Inévitable, mais élastiquement retenu, puis lâché un moment, repris encore, il a presque les vertus de l'*exerciser*" (181).

55. "J'ai cessé d'échanger, je n'échangerai plus jamais, par-dessus un homme, à travers un homme, cette vive menace [. . .]" (185).

Notes to Chapter 3

1. Studies of space and gender in Woolf's work include Abel (1989), Beer (1990), Benstock (1991), Bowlby (1988), Kamuf (1988), Smith (1993), and Solomon (1989).

2. One of a number of grammatical figures adopted by Woolf to create an impression of temporal simultaneity was the parenthesis. Thus, in 1926, again in relation to the "Time Passes" section of *To the Lighthouse*, Woolf writes: "Could I do it in parenthesis? so that one had the sense of reading the two things at the same time?" (*Diary* 3: 106). Rather than fulfilling its common function of con noting an interval or interlude or simply containing a passage that is grammatically inessential to the sentence, the parenthesis serves for Woolf as a method of juxtaposing two events, thoughts, or ideas taking place at the same moment, while retaining their separateness, the one laid alongside, superimposed on, or overlapping with the other.

3. Mrs Ramsay redefines space as she crosses from one room to another: "It was necessary now to carry everything a step further. With her foot on the threshold she waited a moment longer in a scene which was vanishing even as she looked, and then, as she moved and took Minta's arm and left the room, it changed, it shaped itself differently; it had become, she knew, giving one last glance over her shoulder, already the past" (*To the Lighthouse* 111).

4. Studies of space in Colette's work include Resch's discussion of rooms and windows in *Corps féminin, corps textuel* (1973) and Berthu-Courtivron's analysis of the childhood home in *Espace, demeure, écriture* (1992).

5. This was an ease to which Colette aspired throughout her career but which, to her own mind, she was never able to attain. She was "the only [girl] brought into the world not to write" (*Looking Backwards* 16). See chapter 4.

6. Anna de Noailles (a lesser-known French poet, whose place Colette would take at the Académie royale de langue et de littérature française in 1936 at her death) describes Colette's relationship to the dictionary in terms that are remarkably similar to those of Woolf. "Je ne décrirai pas ici le génie de Colette; autorisez-la à faire usage d'un dictionnaire entier, elle y creusera son gîte, produira par jaillissement et avec labeur, dit-elle, une œuvre succulente, sanguine, végétale, où tous les vocables sembleront avoir été raflés et distribués sans pourtant que nulle adjonction vienne alourdir un récit qui se réclame de la vie et de la nécessité. Ne lui accordez plus que l'emploi des adjectifs, Colette les disposera d'une main si habile à construire, que le monde viendra se refléter en eux, y installer avec une loyale astuce ses opulents bagages immenses et réduits. Colette, dès qu'elle écrit, penchant sur son travail [. . .] sait fonder une contrée, élever des villes, susciter la mer et le ciel variés. A l'égal du Nil deifié, elle rend fertile et vivace le feuillet aride, fait croître des récits envahissants, tentateurs et redoutables par leur active présence" (Noailles, *Le livre de ma vie,* quoted in Colette, *Lettres à ses pairs* 60) ("I will not describe Colette's genius here; let her use an entire dictionary, she will hollow out a home for herself there; she will produce in spurts and with labor, she says, a succulent, fiery, organic work, in which all the terms will appear to have been rifled and distributed without, however, any addition that might weigh down a story that takes as its authority life and necessity. Don't let her use anything but a few adjectives, Colette will dispose of them with a hand so skilled at building that the world will come to be reflected in them and will install there with a loyal astuteness its opulent possessions immense and reduced. Colette, as soon as she starts writing, bent over her work [. . .] knows how to found a country, raise up towns, bring to life the sea and the varied sky. Like the deified Nile, she gives life and fertility to the dry leaf, cultivates stories that insinuate themselves, their presence tempting and frightening"). For Noailles's relationship with Woolf and Colette, see chapter 1.

7. "Je me logeais en boule entre deux tomes du Larousse comme un chien dans sa niche" (32).

8. "Musset, Voltaire, et Les Quatre Évangiles brillaient sous la basane feuille-morte. Littré, Larousse et Becquerel bombaient des dos de tortues noires [. . .] D'Orbigny [. . .] Camille Flammarion [. . .] Élisée Reclus, Voltaire jaspés, Balzac noir et Shakespeare olive" (31).

9. "Beaux livres que je lisais, beaux livres que je ne lisais pas, chaud revêtement des murs du logis natal, tapisserie dont mes yeux initiés flattaient la bigarrure cachée . . ." (33).

10. " . . . Les plus hermétiques ne m'étaient-ils pas les plus chers? Voilà longtemps que j'ai oublié l'auteur d'une Encyclopédie habillée de rouge, mais les références alphabétiques indiquées sur chaque tome composent indélébilement un mot magique: Aphbicécladiggalhymaroidphorebstevanzy" (32–33).

11. "Je ne prenais pas de lampe pour choisir l'un d'eux, le soir, il me suffisait de pianoter le long des rayons" (31).

12. Jane Marcus describes Colette's creation of a "'new female alphabet'" in *Virginia Woolf and the Language of Patriarchy* (5–17). See chapter 5 for a discussion of Julia Kristeva's discussion of Colette's "alphabet of feminine pleasure" (24).

13. "A son âge—pas tout à fait huit ans—j'étais curé sur le mur. Le mur, épais et haut, qui séparait le jardin de la basse-cour, et dont le faîte, large comme un trottoir, dallé à plat, me servait de piste et de terrasse, inaccessible au commun des mortels. Eh oui, curé sur un mur. Qu'y a-t-il d'incroyable? J'étais curé sans oblig-ation liturgique ni prêche, sans travestissement irrévérencieux, mais, à l'insu de tous, curé. Curé comme vous êtes chauve, monsieur, ou vous, madame, arthri-tique" (29).

14. "Loin de moi l'idée de demander à l'un de mes parents: 'Qu'est-ce que c'est, un presbytère?' J'avais recueilli en moi le mot mystérieux, comme brodé d'un relief rêche en son commencement, achevé en une longue et rêveuse syllabe . . . Enrichie d'un secret et d'un doute, je dormais avec le *mot* et je l'emportais sur mon mur" (29).

15. "'Presbytère!' Je le jetais, par-dessus le toit du poulailler et le jardin de Miton, vers l'horizon toujours brumeux de Moutiers. Du haut de mon mur, le mot sonnait en anathème: 'Allez! vous êtes tous des presbytères!' criais-je à des bannis invisibles. Un peu plus tard, le mot perdit de son venin, et je m'avisai que 'presbytère' pouvait bien être le nom scientifique du petit escargot rayé jaune et noir . . ." (29).

16. "Elle admire les pétales de nacre, puis les laisse tomber et les écrase sous son espadrille" (157).

17. "Où s'en vont, plus tard, cette volonté énorme d'ignorer, cette force tran-quille employée à bannir et à s'écarter?" (32).

18. "J'essayai encore de réagir . . . Je luttai contre l'effraction, je serrai contre moi les lambeaux de mon extravagance, je voulus obliger M. Millot à habiter, le temps qu'il me plairait, dans la coquille vide du petit escargot nommé 'presbytère' . . ." (30).

19. "Colette wrote *My Mother's House* because Bertrand had asked her to show him the house and the village of Saint-Sauveur, because she kept telling him sto-ries about her childhood [. . .] It is as if Bertrand had given Colette the imagi-natively satisfying motherhood that she wanted [. . .] She had become the moth-er, where it mattered, for her, as a writer" (Jouve, *Colette* 114–15).

20. "Une femme de lettres qui a mal tourné: voilà ce que je dois, pour tous, demeurer, moi qui n'écris plus, moi qui me refuse le plaisir, le luxe d'écrire . . ." (15).

21. "Vous voulez que je fasse comme tout le monde? que je me décide? Celui-là ou un autre, après tout! . . . Vous voulez troubler ma paix reconquise, orienter ma vie vers un autre souci que celui, âpre, fortifiant, naturel, d'assurer moi-même ma subsistance? Ou bien vous me conseillez un amant, par hygiène, comme un

dépuratif? Pour quoi faire? je me porte bien, et, Dieu merci! je n'aime pas, je n'aime pas, je n'aimerai plus personne, personne, personne!" (97).

22. "Je pars, chaque tour de roue m'éloigne de Paris, je pars, un printemps glacé perle en durs bourgeons à la pointe des chênes, tout est froid, humide d'un brouillard qui sent encore l'hiver, je pars, quand je pourrais, à cette heure, m'épanouir de plaisir encore contre le flanc chaud d'un amant!" (196).

23. "Ecrire! plaisir et souffrance d'oisifs! Ecrire! . . . J'éprouve bien, de loin en loin, le besoin, vif comme la soif en été, de noter, de peindre . . . Je prends encore la plume, pour commencer le jeu périlleux et décevant, pour saisir et fixer, sous la pointe double et ployante, le chatoyant, le fugace, le passionnant adjectif . . . Ce n'est qu'une courte crise,—la démangeaison d'une cicatrice . . . Il faut trop de temps pour écrire! Et puis je ne suis pas Balzac, moi . . . Le conte fragile que j'édifie s'émiette quand le fournisseur sonne, quand le bottier présente sa facture, quand l'avoué téléphone, et l'avocat, quand l'agent théâtral me mande à son bureau [. . .]" (16).

24. "[C]ette conseillère maquillée qui me regarde, de l'autre coté de la glace [. . .] Elle me regarde longtemps, et je sais qu'elle va me parler . . . Elle va me dire:—Est-ce toi qui est là? . . . [. . .] Pourquoi es-tu là, toute seule? et pourquoi pas ailleurs? . . ." (5–6).

25. "Décide-toi ou ne te décide pas, voyons. Ça te va ou ça ne te va pas?" (107).

26. "'Vous partez, chérie? Qui donc a décidé ça? [. . .] Mais je n'ai pas encore donné mon consentement'" (158).

27. "J'ai l'air de réfléchir, mais je ne réfléchis pas. Hésiter, ce n'est pas réfléchir . . ." (107).

28. "Pouah! tout ce manège, cette cuisine autour de l'amour,—autour d'un but qu'on ne peut même pas nommer l'amour,—je les favoriserais, je les imiterais, moi? Pauvre Dufferein-Chautel! Il me semble parfois que c'est vous qu'on trompe, ici, et je devrais vous dire . . . vous dire quoi? Que je suis redevenue une vieille fille, sans tentation, et cloitrée, à ma manière, entre les quatre murs d'une loge de music-hall? Non, je ne vous le dirai pas, car nous ne savons échanger, comme à la dixième leçon de la Berlitz School, que des phrases élémentaires, où les mots pain, sel, fenêtre, température, théâtre, famille, tiennent beaucoup de place . . . Vous êtes *un homme,* tant pis pour vous! Chacun dans ma maison semble s'en souvenir, non comme moi, mais pour vous féliciter, depuis Blandine, qui vous contemple avec une satisfaction jamais lassée, jusqu'à Fossette, dont le large sourire canin dit pareillement: 'Enfin! voilà dans la maison *un homme*—voilà L'HOMME!' Je ne sais pas vous parler, pauvre Dufferein-Chautel. J'hésite entre mon langage à *moi,* un peu brusque, qui ne daigne pas toujours finir les phrases, mais chérit la précision d'un terme technique,—mon langage d'ex-bas-bleu,—et l'idiome veule et vif, grossier, imagé, qu'on apprend au music-hall, émaillé de 'Tu parles!' de 'Ta gueule!' . . . 'J'les mets!' . . . 'Très peu pour moi!' . . . A force d'hésiter, je choisis le silence . . ." (92–93).

29. "Laissez-moi attendre, parée, oisive, seule dans ma chambre close, la venue de celui qui m'a choisie pour harem" (167).

30. "le couple amoureux, prisonnier d'une chambre tiède, isolé par quatre murs du reste de la terre . . . c'est le rêve familier d'une jeune fille très ignorante de la vie" (168).

31. "L'avenir, pour moi, ici ou là . . . Mon goût tardif,—acquis, un peu artificiel,—des déplacements et du voyage fait bon ménage avec un fatalisme foncier et paisible de petite bourgeoise. Bohème désormais, oui, et que les tournées ont menée de ville en ville, mais bohême ordonnée, attentive à recoudre elle-même ses nippes bien brossées; bohême qui porte presque toujours sur elle [sa mince fortune, mais dans] le petit sac en peau de daim, les sous sont d'un côté, l'argent blanc de l'autre, l'or caché précieusement dans une pochette à secret . . . Vagabonde, soit, mais qui se résigne à tourner en rond, sur place, comme ceux-ci, mes compagnons, mes frères . . . Les départs m'attristent et m'enivrent, c'est vrai, et quelque chose de moi se suspend à tout ce que je traverse,—pays nouveaux, ciels purs ou nuageux, mers sous la pluie couleur de perle grise,—s'y accroche si passionnément qu'il me semble laisser derrière moi mille et mille petits fantômes à ma ressemblance, roulés dans le flot, bercés sur la feuille, dispersés dans le nuage . . . Mais un dernier petit fantôme, le plus pareil de tous à moi-même, ne demeure-t-il pas assis au coin de ma cheminée, rêveur et sage, penché sur un livre qu'il oublie de lire? . . ." (83–84).

32. "Non, rien ne me retient ici, ni ailleurs. Aucun cher visage ne surgira du brouillard, comme une fleur claire émerge de l'eau obscure, pour crier tendrement 'Ne t'en va pas!' [. . .] c'est comme si j'étais déjà partie" (112).

33. "Mon rire brusque, au lieu de le détromper, l'égare davantage, mais je me sens, ce soir, si taquine et si gaie, légère, déjà presque en voyage . . . Oh! oui, partir, repartir, oublier qui je suis et le nom de la ville qui m'abrita hier, penser à peine, ne refléter et retenir que le beau paysage qui tourne et change au flanc du train, l'étang plombé où le ciel bleu se mire vert, la flèche ajourée d'un clocher cerné d'hirondelles . . ." (102).

34. "Comme je suis loin! déjà partie, dispersée, réfugiée, dans le voyage . . . Leurs voix s'étouffent, s'éloignent, mêlées à des grondements de trains, des sifflements, à la houle berceuse d'un orchestre imaginaire . . . Ah! le doux départ, le doux sommeil, qui m'emporte vers un rive qu'on ne revoit pas! . . ." (115).

35. "Vous avez l'air d'avoir fermé les yeux pour cacher une joie plus forte que vous! Parfaitement! vous n'avez pas un visage de femme endormie . . ." (117).

36. "[M]on langage à moi, un peu brusque, qui ne daigne pas toujours finir les phrases" (93).

37. "A quoi bon écrire, et plaider, et discuter? . . . Mon voluptueux ami ne comprend que l'amour . . ." (212).

38. "[I]l écrit simplement, mais, cela se devine, sans facilité. Sa belle écriture fleurie retarde l'élan de sa main" (202).

39. "Pense-t-il? lit-il? travaille-t-il? [. . .] Point d'esprit, une certaine rapidité de compréhension, un vocabulaire très suffisant que rehausse une belle voix étoffée, cette facilité au rire, à la gaieté enfantine qu'on peut remarquer chez tant d'hommes, voilà mon amoureux. [. . .] un regard parfois absent, chercheur [. . .] Il a voyagé, mais comme tout le monde: pas très loin, pas souvent. Il a lu ce que tout le monde lit, il connaît 'pas mal de gens' et n'arrive pas à nommer, en dehors de son frère ainé, trois amis intimes" (88–89).

40. "Ecrire, écrire, lancer à travers des pages blanches l'écriture rapide, inégale, qu'il compare à mon visage mobile, surmené par l'excès d'expression. Ecrire sincèrement, presque sincèrement" (222).

41. "Cela sent l'indifférence, l'abandon, l' 'à quoi bon?', presque le départ . . ." (86).

42. "Je soigne seulement, pour moi plus que pour eux, le décor menteur et sommaire où je vis si peu" (87).

43. "Un abri, et non un *home,* c'est tout ce que je laisse derrière moi"; hotels are "plus familiers, plus tutélaires" (193).

44. "[J]e viens de traverser, sans m'y arrêter, un pays qui est le mien, celui de mon enfance [. . .] Peut-être n'est-il beau que parce que je l'ai perdu . . ." (199–200).

45. "Sans défense, perméable à cet excès, pourtant prévu, de parfums, de couleur, de chaleur, je me laisse surprendre, emporter, convaincre" (211).

46. "D'où vient que je me balance ce soir sur une houle invisible, comme un navire que renfloue la mer? C'est un soir à voguer jusqu'à l'autre côté du monde" (207–8).

47. "Je me suspends, encore un instant, encore un instant, à la plus grande folie, à l'irrémédiable malheur du reste de mon existence. Accrochée et penchante comme l'arbre qui a grandi au-dessus du gouffre, et que son épanouissement incline vers sa perte, je résiste encore, et qui peut dire si je réussirai? . . ." (221).

48. "'Vous êtes le meilleur des hommes, et vous méritiez la meilleure des femmes. Ne regretterez-vous pas d'avoir choisi seulement [. . .]'" (219).

49. "Mais, signée, datée, et close enfin, c'est quand-même une lettre inachevée . . . La rouvrirai-je? . . ." (246).

50. This refusal is temporary: "At the end of *The Vagabond,* Renée chooses freedom, an unmediated relation to the world. She renounces the man she loves not to lose that freedom. But in the sequel, *The Shackle,* she falls a fascinated prey to powerful and wayward Jean, ends the novel trapped, waiting, indoors . . ." (Jouve, *Colette* 99).

51. "[L]es plus beaux pays de la terre, je refuse de les contempler, tout petits, au miroir amoureux de ton regard . . ." (247).

52. "Tu me voulais illuminer de cette banale aurore, car tu me plaignais obscure. Obscure, si tu veux: comme une chambre vue du dehors. Sombre, et non obscure. Sombre, et parée par les soins d'une vigilante tristesse, argentée et cré-pusculaire comme l'effraie, comme la souris soyeuse, comme l'aile de la mite" (248).

53. "'Quelle vie,' pensa-t-il, vindicatif, 's'il faut toujours buter à toute parole, à tout geste contre quelque chose de caché, de vibrant, de saignant'" (50).

54. "Les mots feu, fin, flammes, riaient à son imagination, avec leurs *f* qui souf-flaient l'incendie et sa fumée . . ." (106).

55. "Il lui lança, à travers ses lunettes, un regard si vif et si illisible qu'elle s'in-terrompit" (105).

56. "[L]e bloc-notes qu'Alice couvrait de son écriture élastique et variable, fine dans les marges, grosse en tête des pages vierges" (58).

57. "'Mon courrier est en panne, et le geste d'écrire, que je déteste, va me remettre les nerfs en place, et me donner sommeil'" (105).

58. "Les éléments épars d'un rêve mêlant l'image des tours basses de Cransac, la silhouette de Chevestre haut et noir—'comme un curé, comme un curé,' chan-tonnait-elle—un essaim de papiers multicolores, et diluant le tout dans l'ombre massive qui stagnait entre deux bibliothèques escarpées et impassibles, elle crut en songe qu'elle se levait, rassemblait les papiers et fuyait" (91).

59. "Le toutounier . . . La gîte, la caverne, ses marques humaines, ses traces

humbles contre les murs, son incurie qui n'est pas sale . . . Personne n'y a été heureux, mais personne ne veut le quitter . . ." (150).

60. "[L]a convention de légèreté, de silence et d'ironie qui régissait leurs rapports" (124).

61. "Elle s'abandonna enfin au 'toutounier natal,' vaste canapé d'origine anglaise, indestructible, défoncé autant qu'une route forestière dans la saison des pluies. Un coussin vint à la rencontre de la nuque d'Alice. Son cuir était froid et doux comme une joue. Elle flaira le vieux maroquin tout imprégné de tabac et d'un parfum de chevelures et lui donne un petit baiser" (117).

62. "[E]lle fit 'ventre creux' pour passer entre la demi-queue du piano et le mur, et elle reprit contact d'une manière originelle avec le grand canapé, c'est à dire qu'elle s'assit en amazone sur le dossier capitonné, bascula et se laissa rouler sur le siège" (115).

63. "'Paragraphe VII du code toutounier . . . '—'ce qui est à toi est à moi, ce qui est à moi est à toi'" (176).

Notes to Chapter 4

1. Colette biographer Michèle Sarde writes that "the only thing—in the arts at any rate—(in France) that enabled [women] to overcome the blemish of being women were either nobility or social status, and this is why, in France, the gallery of women writers extends from Marie de France to Simone de Beauvoir, and includes Marguerite de Navarre, Mme de Lafayette, Mlle de Scudéry, Mme de Sévigné, Mme de Staël, George Sand, who was the Baronne Dudevant, and all of Colette's contemporaries, from Anna de Noailles to the Princesse Bibesco. Colette does not fall into this tradition. She is neither what a mot vaguely reminiscent of Restif de la Bretonne has called her, a 'perverted peasant,' nor was she a noble: she is a pure product of the middle class" (66–67). George Sand, in many senses an early Colette, was writing novels in nineteenth-century France. However, Sand's transgressions (her love affairs, her cross-dressing), unlike Colette's, were authorized by her affiliation with the aristocracy, a privilege not available to Colette (Crosland, *Colette* 171).

2. Like Woolf, these eighteenth- and nineteenth-century women writers were part of middle-class families, many the children of clergymen. They were preceded by Aphra Behn, Dorothy Osborne, and Lady Winchilsea (see *A Room* 58–78).

3. Much of the scholarship on fathers and mothers in the writings of Woolf and Colette has focused on the semi-autobiographical works, such as *To the Lighthouse* (1929) in Woolf's case and *La maison de Claudine* (1922), *Sido* (1928), and *La naissance du jour* (1929) in Colette's. See Flieger (1992), Ottavi (1974), Marcus (1987), Bowlby (1992), and Bonne (1978). Readers of the father figure in Woolf's work have tended to paint him as a one-dimensional figure. Woolf's fathers are generally considered to be "oppressive or ineffectual," managing, in either case, "to burden, demean or disappoint their women" ("Fathers in General," Schlack 53). Lisa Tyler contends that "all of the fathers represented in *The Voyage Out* are either negligent or abusive" (27). Further casting fathers (and some mothers) in an aggressive role, Louise DeSalvo argues: "Every one of [Woolf's] novels describes a child abandoned, a child ignored, a child at risk, a child abused,

a child betrayed" (14). Readings of fathers in Colette's work are overshadowed by readings of the part real, part fictional mother, Sido. The importance of the father in the daughter's achievements has been "underestimated," as Nicole Ward Jouve contends (*Colette* 52). The father in Colette's work is read as "hardly a father-fig-ure, [. . .] a mere *figurant* in the tales of childhood [. . .] relegated to the side-lines, glimpsed only in fleeting asides to the mother-daughter love story" (*Colette and the Fantom Subject,* Flieger 67). Flieger uses psychoanalysis to read what she terms "the paternal intertext in Colette's writing. "When considered in oedipal terms, to be sure, the familial nest is not a haven, an 'Earthly Paradise' (to cite Richard Phelps's collection of Colette's autobiographical writings): it is rather a ménage à trois, an arena of competition, staging a struggle for independence and for access to subjectivity" ("Colette and the Captain" 23).

4. Countering Colette's take on her own work, Joan Hinde Stewart suggests that the *Claudines* represent a "a unique response to an extraordinary demand [. . .] What is extraordinary is not that [Colette] should have so easily acceded to [Willy's] requiring her to write, but that she should have created an enduring comic heroine and at the same time turned out so original and so sustained a por-trait of female strength, sexuality and lust" (23).

5. Both novels base characters on real-life writers. St John Hirst of *The Voyage Out* is Lytton Strachey. A young writer whom Colette encounters in *Claudine en ménage* is Marcel Proust, and Flossie of *Claudine s'en va* is Natalie Barney.

6. "Many have noted that [*The Voyage Out*] is 'an unusual bildungsroman' (Susan Dick, "Tunneling")" (quoted in Hussey 341). "Reversing the usual format of the *Bildungsroman,* Woolf offers a heroine who will not grow into the world as it is constituted. If Rachel learns anything in the course of a short life-time, it is the art of disengagement" (Ruotolo 21).

7. This is more so the case with Mr Ramsay of *To the Lighthouse,* of whom Woolf wrote: "I suppose that I did for myself what psychoanalysts do for their patients. I expressed some very long felt and very deeply felt emotion. And in expressing it I explained it and then laid it to rest" (*Moments of Being* 81). In a let-ter to Jacques-Émile Blanche, Woolf insists that she did not mean to create an exact portrait of her father in Mr Ramsay—but that "a book makes everything into itself, and the portrait became changed to fit as I wrote" (*Letters* 6: 517).

8. "Mon père, né pour écrire, laissa peu de pages. Au moment d'écrire, il émi-ettait son envie en soins matériels, disposait autour de lui le nécessaire et le super-flu de l'écrivain" (*Le Képi, OC* 9: 433).

9. Nancy K. Miller refers to Colette as "the daughter of the mother—and mother of a daughter—[who] chooses to write of and from the garden rather than the library" ("The Anamnesis of a Female 'I'"173), and Jane Marcus, refer-encing Colette's semi-autobiographical *La naissance du jour,* suggests that Colette "is content to write the mother's body, the arrows, rays, 'yes, yeses,' strokes, and 'plant-like convolutions' in her female alphabet" (*Languages* 13). Michèle Sarde calls Sido a "beneficent goddess" (22), and Judith Thurman adds that "the flash of defiance Colette saw in Sido's garden face became the light she wrote by" (26).

10. "La trentaine, donc, et une exceptionelle disette d'amitiés féminines, de complicités, d'appuis féminins. La complice idéale, l'appui véritable, je les avais tous deux dans Sido, lointaine et proche, Sido à qui j'écrivais chaque semaine deux

NOTES 197

lettres, trois lettres, bourrées de nouvelles vraies et fausses, de descriptions, de van-
tardises, de riens, de moi, d'elle . . . Elle est morte en 1912. Après vingt-trois ans,
un réflexe, qui ne veut pas mourir, m'attable à mon bureau, ou à un guéridon
d'hôtel si je voyage, et je jette mes gants, et je demande 'des cartes postales avec
des vues du pays,' comme elle les aimait . . . Et pourquoi cesser de lui écrire? M'arrêter à un obstacle aussi futile, aussi vainement interrogé que la mort?" (*Mes
apprentissages, Œuvres* 3: 1054).

11. "Vocation, signes sacrés, poésie enfantine, prédestination? . . . Je ne retrou-
ve rien de tel dans ma mémoire. [. . .] Non, je ne voulais pas écrire. Quand on
peut pénétrer dans la royaume enchantée de la lecture, pourquoi écrire? [. . .]
Mais dans ma jeunesse, je n'ai jamais, *jamais* désiré écrire. Non, je ne me suis pas
levée la nuit en cachette pour écrire des vers au crayon sur le couvercle d'une boîte
à chaussures! Non, je n'ai pas jeté au vent d'ouest et au clair de lune des paroles
inspirées! Non, je n'ai pas eu de 19 ou 20 pour un devoir de style, entre douze et
quinze ans! Car je sentais, chaque jour mieux, je sentais que j'étais justement faite
pour ne *pas* écrire" ("La Chaufferette," *Journal à rebours, OC* 9: 311–13). Other
comments include: "Quelle douceur j'ai pu goûter à une telle absence de vocation
littéraire! Mon enfance, ma libre et solitaire adolescence, toutes deux préservées du
souci de m'exprimer, furent toutes deux occupées uniquement de diriger leurs
subtiles antennes vers ce qui contemple, s'écoute, se palpe et se respire" (*Journal
à rebours:* 313) ("What calm I tasted in the absence of literary vocation! My childhood, my free and solitary adolescence, both free from the concern of expressing
myself, were both occupied uniquely in directing their subtle antennae toward
what one sees, hears, feels and breathes").

12. "Je suis devenue écrivain sans m'en apercevoir, et sans que personne s'en
doutât. Sortie d'une ombre anonyme, auteur de plusieurs livres dont quelques-uns
étaient signés de mon nom, je m'étonnais encore que l'on m'appelât écrivain [. . .]
et j'attribuais ces coïncidences renouvelées à un hasard complaisant, hasard qui de
palier en palier, de rencontre en prodige, m'a amenée jusqu'ici" ("Discours de
réception," *OC* 14: 69).

13. See *Letters* (1: 123–24, 133–34) on Leslie Stephen's death.

14. Balzac's novel is also about broken families. In the novel there is a regret
for loss of social order (at the dissolution of the Empire in 1839). Characters
include the father, Hulot, a slave to his sexual appetite, and his wife's cousin Bette,
"Lisbeth Fischer, whose physical and moral ugliness is the antithesis to the saintly
grace and beauty of her cousin Adeline, [and who] concentrates all her talents and
energies onto the secret vengeance of the Hulot family" (introduction to the Penguin Classics edition). French novels recur in *To the Lighthouse*.

15. For example, Edward Pargiter has translated Sophocles' *Antigone* for his
cousin Sara in *The Years* (51, 135). For further references see Hussey (1995) and
Schlack (1979).

16. "There are however these two marriages; and they show that she was capa-
ble of falling in love with two very different men, one, to put it in a nutshell, the
pink of propriety; the other, the pink of intellectuality. She could span them both"
("Sketch of the Past" 85).

17. A later version of Lytton Strachey is Neville in *The Waves* (Lee 256–58).

18. Schlack remarks that "on the matter of Rachel's death, critics have generally been in a quandary. 'It is typical of Mrs Woolf's indifference to plot that the

reason Rachel fell victim to the fever . . . is never made clear,' says one. In their search for clear reasons, itself an unproductive approach to Woolf's characteristic evasion of clear reasons, critics are likely to complain of the suddenness of Rachel's death, calling it a failure of aesthetic vision and design that leads to an improbable, arbitrary, unmotivated death" (*Continuing Presences* 19).

19. According to Lee, Woolf played the Lady Sabrina in Milton's *Comus* as part of Clive Bell's play-reading society, which he began at the end of 1907: "(the song summoning 'Sabrina fair' would haunt her, and she would put it into *The Voyage Out*)" (252).

20. See Schlack (*Continuing Presences,* 19–27) for a detailed, alternative reading of the significance of *Comus.*

21. These words also tie Rachel to another literary forefather, Shakespeare. *The Tragedy of Locrine* was a play attributed to Shakespeare. Furthermore, in *The Merchant of Venice,* where Portia is tied to her father's will via the three caskets between which potential suitors must choose in order to win her hand, the words "Brutus" and "curb" appear within a few pages of each other in the opening act: "Her name is Portia, nothing undervalued To Cato's daughter, Brutus' Portia" (74), and "I may neither choose who I would nor refuse who I dislike, so is the will of a living daughter curbed by the will of a dead father" (76).

22. Lisa Low reevaluates Woolf's choice of *Comus* for *The Voyage Out* in her essay "'Listen and Save.'" While Milton is conventionally cast in the role of "father of modern female doom" (117), Low highlights the fact that *Comus,* unlike *Paradise Lost,* is empowering for women. The heroine of *Comus,* Low argues, is "no shrinking violet [. . .]. On the contrary, she is a powerful and speaking heroine who resists her suitor and slays her enemies single-handedly" (119).

23. This follows on after a mention of a man with mules and has been read as a reference to Richard Dalloway. Early in the novel we learn that "In Spain he and Mrs. Dalloway had mounted mules, for they wished to understand how the peasants live" (31). Hewet misses this reference and is appalled to think that Rachel is referring to "the little dirty man downstairs" and that he might have some connection to her illness.

24. Ruotolo suggests that Rachel's death came as a relief to Terence Hewet. During her confinement he suffers as much as Rachel does (45). "Only through dying does she sustain the illusion he requires. No longer free to question— Rachel's final 'perplexity' dissolves once her eyes close for the last time—she affords in death a foundation for Hewet's peace of mind that she could not give him so long as he lived" (46).

25. In her book *Their Fathers' Daughters,* Elizabeth Kowaleski-Wallace uses a mixture of fictional, biographical, and autobiographical writing to explore the contradictions inherent in the identification of two lesser-known nineteenth-century writers, Hannah More and Maria Edgeworth, with their fathers. In their work she detects anger against patriarchy, coupled with a simultaneous desire for that which patriarchy provides. Identification with the father often figures in the works of nineteenth-century women writers, contends Kowaleski-Wallace (and she cites Frances Burney's *Evelina* [9]), as an essential step in the process of differentiation from the mother and from the negatives associated with her role. Further, identification with the father, she suggests, provides access to a literary tradition not available via the mother.

26. I do not include a discussion of the fifth book in the series, entitled *La retraite sentimentale,* here. A gap of several years separates *Claudine s'en va* from *La retraite sentimentale,* published in 1907, following *Minne, Les égarements de Minne,* and *Dialogues de bêtes.* In *La retraite* Renaud is exiled to a sanitorium, where he is recovering from neurasthenia. His jealousy at having to leave Claudine in Paris has sent her, ever devoted to her "invalid" husband—although now wielding the upper hand in the marriage—to Casamène, to the house of Annie. Here they are joined, against Claudine's will, by Marcel, Renaud's son. Across the length of the work, Annie, who has now taken the young Claudine's place in a number of ways—a development anticipated by *Claudine s'en va*—makes a series of confessions regarding her sexual exploits to a somewhat shocked Claudine. Claudine's brief attempt to console Annie for her solitude by asking Marcel, who likes men, not women, to sleep with Annie backfires on Claudine. Renaud, whose return is anticipated throughout the novel by a devoted Claudine, does make it back to Casamène; however, he is now an old man, more like a grandfather than a father (in this way Claudine retains his influence—he is a forebear but at an even greater distance), and no longer at ease with Claudine. We see no interaction between Renaud and Claudine in the book. When Renaud's death is announced to the reader, almost eighteen months after it occurred, when Annie, her sister-in-law and brother, Marthe and Léon, and Maugis, the theatre critic who appeared in earlier *Claudines,* come to pay their condolences, Claudine does not mourn. Preferring her memories to the slab of white stone that marks his grave, Claudine continues to sleep in the same bed where Renaud died. As Margaret Crosland suggests in the introduction to her English translation of this book, we find in this work (the burgeoning of) Colette's fascination with the natural world. The novel ends with Claudine in the provinces among the flora and fauna that are so prominent in her later work, contemplating a new turn in her physical and emotional life, one anticipated by Annie, that is, desire without love.

27. In September 1897 Willy, tidying his desk, comes across Colette's manuscript. He starts reading: "'Nice . . . ' He opened a second notebook, said not another word, a third, a fourth . . . 'Christ,' he grumbled. 'I'm an ass . . . ' He shuffled the notebooks together, threw on his top hat, and ran to a publisher . . . And that is how I became a writer" (*Mes apprentissages,* quoted in Thurman 106).

28. Colette's fellow writer Rachilde, the author of *Monsieur Vénus,* attributed the *Claudines* to Willy: "*Claudine à l'école* n'est ni un roman, ni une thèse, ni un manuscrit, ni quoi que ce soit de convenu ou d'attendu, c'est une personne vivante et debout, terrible [. . .] De Willy le livre est un chef-d'œuvre. De Claudine, le même livre est l'œuvre la plus extraordinaire qui puisse éclore sous la plume d'une débutante, elle promet un peu plus que la gloire à l'auteur: le martyre, car il n'y aura jamais assez de pierres et de couronnes de ronces à lui jeter" (quoted in *Œuvres* 3: 1249). ("*Claudine at School* is neither a novel, nor a thesis, nor a journal, nor a manuscript, nor is it anything conventional or expected, it is a living, upright, formidable person [. . .] By Willy, the book is a masterpiece. By Claudine, the same book is the most extraordinary work to flourish under the pen of a novice, and it promises a little more than glory to its author: martyrdom, for there will never be enough stones or crowns of thorns to throw at her" [partial translation and longer extract in Thurman 115–16].)

29. See D'Hollander. In her short story "Le Miroir" (*Les vrilles de la vigne*), Colette suggests that Claudine is her double.

30. "Captain Jules Colette, dreamer and author of unwritten books, has merged with [Colette's] scientific elder brother Achille to become a distracted father, preoccupied with his experiments in malacology and composing a treatise on slugs" (Stewart 15). "Le père de Claudine, rêveur tout occupé de 'malacologie' fait songer au capitaine Colette. On a dit aussi que c'était le docteur Robineau-Desvoidy, pittoresque figure de Saint-Sauveur, 'le dernier des diptéristes.' En fait, le personnage doit être un amalgame: aux manies du savant s'ajoutent des traits de caractère du capitaine, tel du moins que sa fille le voyait en 1900" (Abastado 31).

31. "Si j'avais une maman, je sais bien qu'elle ne me laisserait pas vingt-quatre heures ici, mais papa, lui, ne voit rien, ne s'occupe pas de moi, tout à ses travaux, et ne s'imagine pas que je pourrais être plus convenablement élevée dans un couvent ou dans un lycée quelconque. Pas de danger que je lui ouvre les yeux!" (*Claudine à l'école* 8–9).

32. "Je suis souris dans la bibliothèque de papa" (*Claudine à l'école* 182).

33. "Cette pièce [the father's library] apparaît donc d'emblée comme l'espace privilégié de toutes les transgressions" (27). Berthu-Courtivron suggests that the father's library is a temporary refuge. She detects a shift from the daughter's initial association of books with the father's library to one linking them to the maternal house: "En effet, dans le premier roman (*Claudine à l'école*) les livres appartiennent explicitement à la bibliothèque paternelle, alors que vingt ans plus tard, ils font partie intégrante de la maison maternelle recréée (la nouvelle elle-même s'intitule: 'Ma mère et les livres') et forment le 'chaud revêtement des murs du logis natal' (MCl, Pl II 989 [*Maison de Claudine* in the Pléiade edition, Volume II, of Colette's work]). A leur chaleur toute imaginaire s'ajoute une ascendance maternelle, autre produit de l'écriture: 'Presque tous m'avaient vue naître,' (MCl, Pl II 988), comme dans les premiers romans les bois avaient vu naître Claudine. C'est aussi au milieu des livres que Minet-Chéri se niche. C'est enfin par rapport au jugement critique de la mère qu'ils sont évoqués dans le reste de la nouvelle. Cette deuxième version donne l'image d'une maison une et indivisible, sous l'égide de la mère" (Berthu-Courtivron 28) ("In effect, in the first novel (*Claudine at School*), books belong explicitly to the paternal library, although twenty years later, they form an integral part of the recreated maternal house (the short story itself is called 'My Mother and Books') and constitute the 'warm covering of the walls of the house where I was born.' To their imaginary warmth is added a maternal ascendance, another product of writing: "Almost all of them witnessed my birth," like in the first novels the woods saw Claudine being born. It is also in the midst of the books that Minet-Chéri curls up. It is then in terms of the mother's critical judgment that they are mentioned in the rest of the short story. This second image gives the impression of a singular and unified house, under the aegis of the mother").

34. "Je lis, je lis, je lis. Tout. N'importe quoi" (*Claudine à Paris* 180).

35. "Qu'est-ce que tu lis? Tout ce que tu trouves? Toute la bibliothèque de ton père?" (*Claudine à l'école* 25).

36. Daudet was an associate of Willy. Louÿs was a friend of both Willy and Colette. Colette frequented the salon of Lucien and Jeanne Muhlfeld. Lucien was

a fellow writer of Willy's at *L'Écho de Paris* (Thurman 125).

37. In his preface to *Aphrodite,* Louÿs, who says he wishes to exalt love (not condemn it), writes of his Egyptian heroine Chrysis: "As courtesan, she will play her part with the frankness, the ardour, and also the pride of every being who had a vocation and occupies a freely elected place in society. She will possess the ambition to rise to the highest seat of honour; and it will not even occur to her that her life might have need of excuse or dissimulation" (ix). This description highlights the similarities between Chrysis and Claudine. One critic, François Coppée, describes *Aphrodite* as "un beau livre, mais un livre très impur" (Clive 220) ("a beautiful but very impure book"). In a 1914 review of the play based on the novel, Alphonse Brisson wrote that *Aphrodite* had replaced the work of Longus and Boccaccio in the high school student's desk (Clive 131).

38. For a discussion of Adam's works, see J. An Duncan's "The Early Novels of Paul Adam."

39. "'I was born in Balzac,' [Colette] told an interviewer as an old lady. 'He was my cradle, my forest, my travels.' And she called herself 'one of those people who, from childhood, devote themselves to a single author.' But she also reads Alphonse Daudet, Hugo, Merimée, Labiche, Zola, Taine, Voltaire, the tales of H. C. Andersen—and Shakespeare in translation" (Thurman 41).

40. "Votre Zola n'y entend rien de rien, à la campagne. Je n'aime pas beaucoup ce qu'il fait, en général . . ." (*Claudine à Paris* 64).

41. Régnier was an associate of Pierre Louÿs. The two men are linked via their relationships with the same woman. Régnier and Louÿs both loved Marie de Heredia, who became Régnier's wife in the early 1890s and Louÿs's lover in the late 1890s.

42. "Ah! voilà . . . vous n'avez pas lu, parce qu'il ne sera jamais terminé, son grand travail sur la *Malacologie de Fresnois*" (*Claudine à l'école* 28).

43. "Comment voulez-vous que l'espoir naissant de pareilles constatations laisse à un passionné malacologiste le sentiment de la paternité, de sept heures du matin à neuf heures du soir? C'est le meilleur homme et le plus tendre, entre deux repas de limaces" (*Claudine à l'école* 29).

44. "Papa est une force de la Nature; il sert l'obscur Destin. Sans le savoir, il est venu ici, pour que je pusse rencontrer Renaud; il s'en va, ayant rempli sa mission de père irresponsable . . ." (*Claudine en ménage* 79).

45. "C'est un père comme lui [Renaud] qui me manque. Oh! Je ne veux pas dire du mal du mien; ce n'est pas de sa faute s'il est un peu spécial" (*Claudine à Paris* 123).

46. "À cause de ce noble père, plutôt lunatique, qui est le mien, j'ai besoin d'un papa, j'ai besoin d'un ami, d'un amant . . ." (*Claudine à Paris* 227).

47. "Mais c'est rasant comme tout! [. . .] je veux dire que ce sont des articles très sérieux . . ." (*Claudine à Paris* 122)

48. "Ma liberté me pèse, mon indépendance m'excède; ce que je cherche depuis des mois—depuis plus longtemps—c'était, sans m'en douter, un maître. Les femmes libres ne sont pas des femmes" (*Claudine à Paris* 229–30).

49. "Mon journal est sans avenir. Je l'ai quitté voilà cinq mois sur une impression triste, et je lui en veux. D'ailleurs je n'ai pas le temps de le tenir au courant" (*Claudine en ménage* 71).

Notes to Chapter 5

1. Showalter asserts that "The harsh criticism of Bloomsbury, of female aestheticism, and especially of Virginia Woolf by writers for *Scrutiny* in the 1930s had pointed out the problems of disengagement. In her late writings, *The Years* (1937) and *Three Guineas* (1938), Woolf herself had tried to move in the direction of social realism. During the 1940s and 1950s, however, women writers, many of an older generation, continued to work in conservative modes untouched by either modernism or a sense of personal experience" (34).

2. We might add to this list another one compiled by Isobel Armstrong: Elizabeth Taylor, Elizabeth Bowen, Rosamund Lehmann, and Rose Macaulay. According to Armstrong, "Virginia Woolf did not immediately become a model for subsequent women writers. Elizabeth Taylor, Elizabeth Bowen, Rosamund Lehmann and Rose Macaulay, for instance—to name a few of the novelists writing between the wars who would have certainly been able to read Virginia Woolf's texts—appear to be almost impervious to the experimental aspects of her work. And certainly, for whatever reasons, it is later feminist theorists rather than women writers who have taken her work up" ("Woolf by the Lake" 259).

3. In *Près de Colette,* Maurice Goudeket explains the initially negative reception of Colette's work in France in this way: the war, he suggests, had set the stage for "a literature of despair": "Une sorte de nihilisme prévalait dans les idées et les attitudes, un réalisme noir qui tournait le dos à la réalité, faite d'un jeu d'ombre et de lumière" ("A sort of nihilism prevailed in ideas and attitudes, a black realism that turned its back on reality, made up of a game of shadow and light"). But a climate in which nihilism reigns, Goudeket adds, is not easy to maintain among the young. Young people, he says, soon discovered Colette's work "comme un appel d'air frais" ("like a breath of fresh air"). "Par elle ils retrouvaient des sources profondes qu'on leur avait dit taries, une représentation du monde qui n'en cachait ni les déficiences ni les beautés, une quête de l'authentique qui est en soi une raison de vivre" (246–47) ("Via her work they rediscovered profound sources that people said had dried up, a representation of the world that hid neither its beauties nor its deficiencies, a search for the authentic, which is in itself a reason for living"). In her biography of Colette, Margaret Crosland cites Louis Bromfield's exploration of Colette's popularity in the United States and England (originally cited in Chauvière's *Colette*). Bromfield and Crosland agree that the fact that Colette was a personality meant that she prospered in the United States and France, where "writers are allowed and are encouraged to be personalities, even though the type of appreciation given them is different. England," Crosland suggests, "has always been suspicious of writers, artists and musicians" (134).

4. In *The Anxiety of Influence* Bloom argues that the successor's reaction to his precursor is, at least at first, an act of rebellion. "Strong poets make [poetic] history by misreading one another, so as to clear imaginative space for themselves" (5).

5. For a thorough overview of the way in which Woolf's work has been read by French critics, see Pierre-Eric Villeneuve's "Virginia Woolf and the French Reader." Caws and Luckhurst's book *The Reception of Virginia Woolf in Europe* includes four chapters on the reception of Woolf's work in France.

6. Joyce Carol Oates writes that English women writers *were encouraged* to be

Woolfian (Showalter 265): "For the past fifty years, Virginia Woolf has dominated
the imaginative territory of the English woman novelist, just as George Eliot dominated it the century before. 'The woman writer is urged to be as Woolfian as possible,' according to Joyce Carol Oates [*New York Times Book Review,* April 15,
1973]—that is, to be subjective, and yet to transcend her femaleness, to write
exquisitely about inner space and leave the big messy brawling novels to her men"
(Showalter 265).

7. "Si l'on s'arrête à considérer la profondeur scintillante de l'œuvre de Mrs.
Woolf, sa légèreté, sa densité claire, et jusqu'aux pulsations irisées d'un style qui fait
penser tour à tour à ce qui traverse et à ce qui est traversé, à la lumière et au cristal,
on en vient à se dire que cette femme si subtilement singulière naquit peut-être à
la minute précise où une étoile se prenait à penser."

8. A link between Colette, Woolf, and Yourcenar is provided by the American
poet Frederic Prokosch, some of whose work Yourcenar also translated (although
her translations were lost when the Germans invaded Paris). In his *Voices: A Memoir* he describes encounters with both Colette and Woolf. His responses to the two
already well-known writers are very similar. Of Colette (234–38) he writes, "And
there she was herself, strangely solemn among her cushions, not in the least what
I expected: sad and lean and very wrinkled, with bags under eyes that were the
color of violets." Colette wears a maroon silk scarf thrown over what appear to
Prokosch to be bony shoulders, and a grey blanket covers her "wasted knees." She
mocks Prokosch for his Americanness ("I'm convinced there is nothing truly deca-
dent in the Americans," she tells him) and talks to him about food, suggesting, "I
always think of a novel as a finely done soufflé, underdone it is clammy, overdone
it is desiccated. I think of Adolphe and La Princesse de Clèves . . ." (quoted in
Prokosch 237). Of Woolf (87–90), whom a friend had described to him as looking like "an exposed nerve," he writes, "she looked profoundly vulnerable and
painfully frail, but also rather dowdy and faded and foxy," untidy but heartbreak-
ingly beautiful. She, too, muses over the nature of the novel; "what is a novel, my
dear boy?" she asks him.

9. "[I]l ne reste plus 'dans ce pâle visage de jeune Parque à peine vieilli mais
délicatement marqué des signes de la pensée et de la lassitude' qu'une bouche qui
ne semble n'avoir jamais su sourire et un regard désolé."

10. "'L'idéal du traducteur' tel qu'elle l'affirmera plus tard à sa traductrice ital-
ienne dans une lettre de 1962, est de donner 'l'impression que l'ouvrage a été
composé dans la langue dans laquelle on le traduit.'"

11. Woolf boasts of her descent from a suitor of Marie Antoinette. Lee explains
the link: "James Pattle of Calcutta made a romantic marriage to a French aristo-
crat, Adeline de L'Etang, the daughter of the Chevalier del'Etang, who had been
a page—possibly a lover—to Marie-Antoinette and an officer of the Garde du
Corps of Louis XVI, and had married the Indian-born Thérèse Blin de Grincourt
(not, as the family legend had it, one of the Queen's maids of honour)" (88). See
my conclusion for more on Woolf's love of France.

12. "[C]herche à créer pour le lecteur cible un nouveau poème qui rentre dans
le système littéraire de ce lecteur." This conforms with Woolf's ideas about translation. In a letter she advises Roger Fry, who has been translating Pierre-Jean
Jouve's poems from French into English, "you might perhaps get greater richness
of language if you were less literal." She praises Fry's talent and laments that so

often "translators are apt to be so entirely wrong in feeling" (*Letters* 2: 73). Fry's translation of several of Jouve's poems from *Vous êtes hommes* appeared under the title *Men of Europe* in 1916. Woolf remarks on translations in letters to Jacques-Émile Blanche (December 1927, *Letters* 6: 519).

13. Somewhat ironically (and at odds with these last comments about Colette), on the first page of his biography of Colette, *L'éternelle apprentie*, Jean Chalon quotes Yourcenar's praise of Natalie Barney, suggesting that it applies equally to Colette: "[Colette] aurait pu faire sien l'hommage que Marguerite Yourcenar avait addressé à Natalie Barney. 'Je vous ai particulièrement su gré d'avoir échappé aux grippes intellectuelles de ce demi-siècle, d'en avoir été ni psychanalysée, ni existentialiste, ni occupée d'accomplir des actes gratuits, mais d'être au contraire restée fidèle à l'évidence de votre esprit, de vos sens, voire de votre bon sens'" (13). ("[Colette] could have made her own the homage that Marguerite Yourcenar had addressed to Natalie Barney. 'I was particularly grateful to you for having escaped from the intellectual grips of this half century, for having been neither psychoanalyst, nor existentialist, nor occupied with accomplishing gratuitous acts, but for remaining, on the contrary, faithful to the evidence of your spirit, of your sense, yes and even your good sense'").

14. "[L]a troupe invisible de femmes qui auraient dû, peut-être, recevoir beaucoup plus tôt cet honneur."

15. "Mme de Staël eût été inéligible de par son ascendance suisse et son marriage suédois: elle se contentait d'être un des meilleurs esprits du siècle. George Sand eût fait scandale par la turbulence de sa vie, par la générosité même de ses émotions qui font d'elle une femme si admirablement femme; la personne encore plus que l'écrivain devançait son temps. Colette elle-même pensait qu'une femme ne rend pas visite à des hommes pour solliciter leur voix, et je ne puis qu'être de son avis, ne l'ayant pas fait moi-même."

16. The text to which Yourcenar refers is unclear. The recording perhaps included both Colette's novel *Gigi* and her novel *Chéri*.

17. Elsewhere, Sarraute repeats this same response to Joyce and Woolf: "Une voie nouvelle s'est alors ouverte pour moi. Il me semblait qu'à partir de ce moment, l'on ne pouvait plus écrire comme on avait écrit auparavant" (quoted in Rykner 164). ("A new channel thus opened up for me. It seemed as if from this moment on, one could no longer work as one had before.")

18. These comments led to some confusion, expressed in a *Times Literary Supplement* article, over the relationship of her work to that of Woolf, Joyce, and Proust. In an attempt to rectify the misunderstanding, she responded to the *Times Literary Supplement* article by affirming her tie and her commitment to the work of these same writers: "Il s'agit donc pour moi non d'attaquer les auteurs que j'ai cités, mais de suivre leur voie et de m'éfforcer de faire après eux ne serait-ce qu'un pas de plus dans la recherche" (quoted in Minogue 193) ("It's a matter then for me not to attack the authors that I cited, but to follow their lead and to force myself to do after them what might very well be nothing more than one more step into the unknown"). Indeed, Sarraute names Woolf, along with Joyce, Proust, and Flaubert, as "precursors." Other influences cited by Sarraute include British Modernists Ivy Compton Burnett and Henry Green. Villeneuve (2002) opens his section on Sarraute in his essay on the reception of Woolf in France with Sarraute's disavowal of Woolf: "'I believe that our sensibilities are very much opposed. For

Virginia Woolf, her entire universe, stirred up by time, rolls along through the consciousness of her characters, who are passive by nature, carried from side to side by
the uninterrupted currents of moments. With me, characters are always in a state
of hyperactivity: a dramatic action plays itself out at the level of their 'tropisms,'
these movements being very quick at the edges of consciousness. This is where our
different styles come from" (quoted in Villeneuve 29).

19. "Des romanciers comme Henry James, Proust, Virginia Woolf n'ont pas
craint—conforme en cela à l'esprit de l'art moderne—de faire un effort d'élucida-
tion, d'essayer d'éclairer certains aspects de leur travail" (*OC* 1661) ("Novelists
such as Henry James, Proust, Virginia Woolf were not afraid—conforming in this
to the spirit of modern art—to attempt to elucidate, to try to shed light on certain
aspects of their work").

20. Sarraute was also involved in a staging of Woolf's play *Freshwater*.

21. Beauvoir's childhood reading of Colette would have a profound impact on
the rest of her life, according to Claude Francis and Fernand Gontier, biographers
of both Beauvoir and Colette: "On the sly she secretly read Paul Bourget,
Alphonse Daudet, Marcel Prévost, Maupassant, and Pierre Loti. She hid *Les Demi-
Vierges* and *La Femme et le Pantin* under her mattress and was thrilled by the
homosexual characters of Colette's "Claudine" books and Claude Farrère's *Made-
moiselle Dax*. This violent sensuality sent prohibitions, proprieties, and soon religion itself flying to pieces in her head" (*Simone de Beauvoir* 43). Francis and Gontier also liken Beauvoir's father, George, to Colette's father, Jules Colette, another
auteur manqué: "[George de Beauvoir] had brought back from the front a number of interesting stories but, using his distaste for malicious and imbecilic critics
as a pretext, never did anything with them—and thereby took after another would-
be author, Colette's father, who had lined his library with blank notebooks des-
tined to receive future works that never existed beyond their titles" (25).

22. "A Colette si semblable à ses livres que j'aime tant avec l'admiration et si je
puis me le permettre l'amitié de J.-P. Sartre" (quoted in Pichois and Brunet 475).

23. Berriau, the hostess, described the meeting of this mismatched crowd as a
success: "On ne pouvait imaginer personnages plus dissemblables, mais ils ont
interminablement parlé du théâtre, de ce qu'ils aimaient, et se sont visiblement plu
mutuellement. Cocteau, il faut le dire, menait la conversation avec tout son charme
et tout son lyrisme, jonglant avec les mots et les images; Colette, toujours vive et
savoureuse, était subjuguée par l'intelligence et la passion froide de Sartre. Le déjeuner a duré jusqu'à sept heures du soir" (quoted in Pichois and Brunet 475) ("One
could not imagine people more dissimilar, but they talked interminably about the
theatre, what they liked, and really appeared to enjoy each other's company.
Cocteau, it has to be said, led the conversation with all of his usual charm and lyricism, juggling with words and images; Colette, still lively and spicy, was transfixed
by Sartre's intelligence and his cold passion. The lunch lasted until seven o'clock in
the evening"). British writer Angela Carter explains Colette's failure to acknowl-
edge Beauvoir at a dinner party she attended with Sartre (recounted in Beauvoir's
memoirs) by suggesting that Colette was busy wondering what on earth Beauvoir
was doing with "a boring old fart like J. P." (*Shaking a Leg* 525).

24. In *The Second Sex* Beauvoir says that there have been no great women
thinkers, writers, or other artists (306–14)—a comment somewhat at odds with
the space she accords Colette in *The Second Sex*. Neither of two recent compara-

tive studies involving Colette and Beauvoir, Bethany Ladimer's book on aging in the works of Colette, Beauvoir, and Duras (1999), or Laurie Corbin's *The Mother Mirror* (1996) on the same trio, comments on Beauvoir's reading of Colette in *Le deuxième sexe*.

25. In another work, *La vieillesse* (*The Coming of Age*), Beauvoir refers to both Woolf and Colette. She mentions the crippling rheumatism that stalked Colette in her later years. She also refers to Woolf's suicide and the role the outbreak of war played in it (*Coming of Age* 16). She cites Woolf quoting Matthew Arnold's comments on old age: "'I loathe the hardness of old age. I feel it coming. I creak. I am embittered. 'The foot less quick to tread the dew, The heart less feeling to emotions now, Crushed hope less quick to rise again' I have just opened Matthew Arnold and I have copied out these lines'" (quoted in *Coming of Age* 688).

26. "La chambre," says Beauvoir, "est en même temps une réalité et un symbole. Pour pouvoir écrire, pour pouvoir accomplir quelque chose, il faut d'abord s'appartenir."

27. "Elle serait restée à la maison, elle aurait fait de la cuisine, de la couture."

28. "J'ai tenté moi-même dans *Le Deuxième Sexe* une analyse analogue à propos de Van Gogh. J'ai essayé de montrer qu'une fille née à la place de Van Gogh n'aurait pas eu les chances qu'il a eues." The passage in *Le deuxième sexe* to which Beauvoir refers is the following: "How could Van Gogh have been born a woman? A woman would not have been sent on a mission to the Belgian coal mines in Borinage, she would not have felt the misery of the miners as her own crime, she would have not have sought redemption; she would not have painted Van Gogh's sunflowers. Not to mention that the mode of life of the painter—his solitude at Arles, his frequentation of cafés and brothels, all that nourished Van Gogh's art in nourishing his sensitivity—would have been forbidden her. A woman could never have become Kafka: in her doubts and her anxiety she would never have recognized the anguish of Man driven from paradise" (793–94).

29. According to Francis and Gontier, between 1929 and 1931 Beauvoir worked on a novel "inspired by Alain Fournier, Virginia Woolf and Rosamund Lehmann" (*Simone de Beauvoir* 118). They suggest that "Virginia Woolf, in her reflections on language and the novel, paralleled de Beauvoir's occupations. Like Woolf, de Beauvoir sought a way to reduce the distance between words and reality" (113). Colette's work is also compared on occasion to Beauvoir's. Elaine Marks cites Jean Cocteau's "amusing" remark from his *Colette: Discours de réception* (quoted in Dupont 184) that Beauvoir's novel *L'invitée* is a "kind of existentialist paraphrase of *Claudine en Ménage*." Marks adds that another of Colette's novels, *Minne*, written subsequently to the first four *Claudines*, is even closer to *L'invitée* (243 n. 10).

30. "For if Chloe likes Olivia and Mary Carmichael knows how to express it she will light a torch in that vast chamber where no one has yet been. It is all half lights and profound shadows like those serpentine caves where one goes with a candle peering up and down, not knowing where one is stepping" (*A Room of One's Own* 84).

31. This is an extract from an interview with Susan Husserl-Kapit in *Signs*, Winter 1975. This distinction made by Duras is picked up by a critic, who sends the reader who cannot stomach the violence of Duras's work to Colette or Simone de Beauvoir: "Plusieurs scènes illustrent ce qu'Isabelle lit dans les yeux de Nathalie

Granger: 'Tous les possibles futurs de la violence, tous ses modes' (p. 74). Que ces modes outrepassent largement ceux de la sensualité pacifique ne devrait pas surprendre. Et s'ils surprennent, autant rêver à d'autres fêtes, autant lire Colette ou Simone de Beauvoir, autant refermer les livres de Marguerite Duras où, explicitement, la violence du désir appelle la seule violence et la mort" (Blot-Labarrère 104) ("Several scenes illustrate what Isabelle reads in the eyes of Nathalie Granger: 'All the possible futures of violence, all its modes' (p. 74). The fact that these modes largely surpass those of peaceful sensuality should not be a surprise. And if they do surprise, better to dream of other festivals, better to read Colette or Simone de Beauvoir, better to shut Marguerite Duras's books in which, explicitly, the violence of desire leads to the only violence and death").

32. In French, *L'Arc* 61 (1975): 39–54 (42 n.).

33. Duras's list runs as follows: "Les grandes lectures de ma vie, celles de moi seule, c'est celles écrites par des hommes. C'est Michelet. Michelet et encore Michelet, jusqu'aux larmes. Les textes politiques aussi, mais déjà moins. C'est Saint-Just, Stendhal, et bizarrement ce n'est pas Balzac. Le Texte des textes, c'est l'Ancien Testament" (*Écrire* 43) ("The great readings of my life, those all my own, are those written by men. I read and read and read Michelet, to the point of tears. Political texts also, but already less. I liked Saint-Just and Stendhal, but oddly enough not Balzac. The Text of all texts for me is the Old Testament").

34. "[O]n ne peut plus parler d'influence, mais d'intertextualité ou, pourquoi pas? de culture. Marguerite Duras 'écrit avec,' puisque, aussi bien, nul écrivain n'avance en terrain découvert [. . .] Très loin d'elle, Balzac, tout près, Virginia Woolf ou Louise Labbé [*sic*] évoquée dans *L'Amant de la Chine du nord*" (Blot-Labarrère 233–34).

35. Anaïs Nin compared Woolf and West: Nin thought Woolf "'over-intellectual' and indistinguishable from Rebecca West: 'each write[s] like a man and I don't like it.' She thought that either woman could have written *A Room of One's Own*" (Bair 102). Nin also read Colette and "credited [Colette] with 'the most powerful descriptive style of all the women in literature'" (Bair 110, 542). Nin, according to Bair, made Colette's novels her life. She "cast herself in the role of Colette's Léa instructing whichever youth was her Chéri of the moment" (Bair 314).

36. For West's review of *Orlando*, see "High Fountain of Genius" in Bonnie Kime Scott, *The Gender of Modernism*, 592–96.

37. Another article by West on Colette appeared in *Le figaro littéraire*, January 24, 1953, 5.

38. These were not the first translations of Colette's work. *Claudine at School* was originally translated by Janet Flanner in 1930.

39. In a letter Richardson suggests that the only thing Woolf and Jane Austen share is their snobbishness (43).

40. Richardson's assessment is echoed by French writer Hélène Cixous: "'I was in the world of men almost exclusively. I worked on Shakespeare, Joyce, Kafka, on an amazing number of texts. But women? I did work on Virginia Woolf; in a sense I taught everyone, Marguerite Duras, Virginia Woolf, all the great writers. But Virginia Woolf, who is a great writer, isn't someone who satisfies me because she is slanted toward pain, which I understand very well, but I love life too much to content myself with such a morbid rapport to a form of death in women or death inflicted on women'" (unpublished notes, quoted in Penrod 11). "Woolf was cut

off from an understanding of the day-to-day life of the women whom she wished
to inspire; characteristically, she rebelled against aspects of female experience that
she had never personally known and avoided describing her own experience"
(Showalter quoted in Moi 4).

41. Kingsley Amis responded to Woolf's work in a similar way. "Of Woolf he
said he found her created world wholly contrived: when reading her he found that
he kept interpolating hostile negatives, murmuring 'Oh no she didn't' or 'Oh no
he hadn't' or 'Oh no it wasn't' after each and every authorial proposition" (Martin Amis 31).

42. The interview "Doris Lessing: Hot Dawns" by Harvey Blume was originally published in 1962 in the *Boston Book Review*. Lessing's first novel, *The Rain Is Singing*, which is set in Africa, was published in 1950, a year after she arrived in England.

43. See Woolf's essay "The Russian Point of View," in her *Common Reader*.

44. Despite Lessing's disavowal of Woolf, Brewster and other critics have speculated about Woolf's influence on Lessing. Brewster links the female friendships in Lessing's work, such as that shared by Molly and Anna in *The Golden Notebook*, to Woolf's comments in *A Room of One's Own* about Chloe and Olivia: "'When women are alone, [. . .] unlit by the capricious and coloured light of the other sex,' what are their gestures, their half-said words?" (138). Further, she asks whether Lessing and Woolf have created a true picture of man, Lessing in *The Golden Notebook* and Woolf in *Orlando* or with Mr Ramsay in *To the Lighthouse*. Attention to rooms also ties the two writers together, according to Brewster: "Doris Lessing's marked interest in rooms is not just the novelist's usual concern with background [. . .] that fascinating room of her childhood; the big living room in 'Winter in July,' with the African night outside; the cramped, shabby, suffocating little bedroom in *The Grass Is Singing* where Mary Turner slowly decays; the blitzed but cosy basement which Rose in *The Other Woman* hated to leave; *Room Nineteen*, where Susan drifts off down the dark river of her suicide; the swaying tower room of 'Dialogue'; the spacious workroom where Anna's four notebooks—black, blue, red and yellow—are spread out upon the long trestle table" (138–39). Michael Cunningham's recent novel *The Hours* makes an implicit connection between Woolf and Lessing as he blends a rewriting of Lessing's story, "To Room Nineteen," into his Woolf novel.

45. Echoing Byatt's contention that her work is in some senses a reaction against that of Woolf, one critic is adamant about Woolf's absence from the work of another British writer, Muriel Spark (1918–), author of *The Bachelors* (1960) and *The Prime of Miss Jean Brodie* (1961): "The writer who is constantly falling, because she is pushing herself off her perch, calls no place her own. That means, among other things, that every word, every page Spark ever wrote simply loathes each beautifully phrased tittle and jot in Virginia Woolf's *A Room of One's Own*. I can go even further than that. Her entire career insists that a room of one's own can never be a room with a view worth savoring. What 'One' really needs—if one is a writer—is a room of somebody else's, a room that one might rent for a while with ease, and then just as easily abandon, divorce. A room, unburdened by one's past, in which a writer can always begin again. (I point this out here, in this collection of essays, merely as a kindness. The reader who believes that all worthwhile twentieth-century fiction by women must somehow affiliate to Woolf, and to

Woolf's own room, will give this chapter a pass.) No room of one's own, and no time of one's own" (Glavin 294).

46. Byatt insists: "Of course I am a feminist. But I don't want to be required to write to a feminist programme, and I feel uneasy when this seems to be asked of me. I am a bit too old to be a naturally political animal [. . .] I held a full-time university reading post for eleven years and now feel entirely happy, for the first time in my life, at the prospect of writing full time, thinking things out from beginning to end, and reading for my own purposes. I enjoyed teaching John Donne, Robert Browning, George Eliot, Charles Dickens, Samuel Taylor Coleridge, John Keats, Wallace Stevens, Emily Dickinson, and Henry James. But now reading is even more exciting. The novelist I love most is Marcel Proust. After him Balzac, Dickens, Eliot, Thomas Mann and James, Iris Murdoch, Ford Maddox Ford, and Willa Cather. And Leo Tolstoy and Fyodor Dostoevsky" (www.asbyatt.com).

47. See also "Virginia Woolf: A Personal Debt" (*Harper's Bazaar and Queen* [September 1972], 90–91, 128). Drabble is A. S. Byatt's sister.

48. In *Nights at the Circus* Lizzie says of Walser to Fevvers, recalling Max of *La vagabonde:* "He's too *young* for you, my girl. He's living proof that travel don't broaden the mind; instead, it renders a man *banal.*" To which Fevvers responds: "'Not his mind as interests me [. . .] Not his *face* as interests me'" (172). Like Colette's Renée Néré in *La vagabonde,* and Colette herself, Fevvers is a transient stage performer with a somewhat witless male in tow. Jouve finds other evidence of Colette among the pages of Carter's stories: "In the first, the Bluebeard story that gives its name to the collection, I recognised a canny reader of Colette. It shimmered with skillfully modified bits from the *Claudine* novels, from *My Apprenticeships, My Mother's House*—and put to impertinent use a wonderfully intimate knowledge of the art and life of *fin-de-siècle* French decadence" (quoted in Jouve, "Mother Is a Figure of Speech" 144). She adds that Carter had "unnervingly and irreverently explored the alienating figures of romance, the rebellious Heathcliff-type hero (Jewel in *Heroes and Villains*), then the Wild Older Man (de Sade, Bluebeard, Mr Rochester, Colette's first husband, Willy) and disposed of them [. . .] Fear had to be conquered. Nothing sacred. Fear it is that makes predators of our wolves and tigers. 'If Little Red Riding Hood had laughed at the wolf and passed on, the wolf could never have eaten her' said Colette [. . .] 'The tiger will never lie down with the lamb; he acknowledges no pact that is not reciprocal. The lamb must learn to run with the tigers' [writes Carter in *The Bloody Chamber*]. Girls' fearlessness delivers man from his beastliness" (145). In Carter's rewriting of the Little Red Riding Hood story, "The Company of Wolves," Little Red Riding Hood indeed laughs at the Wolf, a gesture interpreted by Colette: "Note that it was Little Red Riding Hood who was the first to speak to the Wolf. If, seeing a Wolf in place of Grandmother, she had gone on her way, the Wolf would have never existed" (Colette, *Looking Backwards* 99). When Jouve sent Angela Carter her book about Colette, "she sent back a Christmas card with fat puddings on it. Inside it said: 'Read it at one gulp. Mmmm'" ("Mother Is a Figure" 150).

49. In the course of her article, Carter compares Colette and Willy to Virginia and Leonard Woolf. A loving relationship, Carter suggests, does nothing to improve a writer's output. After she met Goudeket, Carter reminds us, Colette wrote very little fiction; Leonard Woolf, she suggests, did not do "his wife a favour by mothering her . . ." (524).

50. In "Wrapped in the Stars and Stripes: Virginia Woolf in the U.S.A.," Jane
Marcus addresses the American cooption and fetishization of Virginia Woolf and
advocates that Woolf be returned home. Marcus considers that the English are
wrong, and she cites Angela Carter and Terry Eagleton (strange bedfellows, she
contends) as holding this view, to cast Woolf as a class enemy. "The reader from
outside this culture," suggests Marcus, "often has been attracted to Virginia Woolf
for precisely the expression of radical social ideas and critiques of class patriarchy
and state institutions which her novels and essays provide. It seems to me possible
to maintain views abusing Virginia Woolf as a figure of dread only if (as I also
believe is true) she is widely unread, unread certainly by those who edit the literary journals and the review columns in newspapers and probably by those who
teach Joyce, Yeats and T. S. Eliot" (21).

51. In an article entitled "Woolf by the Lake, Woolf at the Circus: Carter and
Tradition," Isobel Armstrong argues that Anita Brookner and Angela Carter have
a common precursor in Virginia Woolf: "Carter's work comes out of the possibil-
ities for bravura fantasies in *Orlando* (1928) and the surreal critique of *Between the
Acts* (1941). Brookner's work comes out of the lyric novels, *Mrs Dalloway* (1925)
and *To the Lighthouse* (1927) in particular. [. . .] It is not surprising," suggests
Armstrong, "to find out that Carter had worked on a libretto of *Orlando*" (258).
Armstrong likens Orlando to Fevvers (271). Brookner's *Hotel du lac*, suggests
Armstrong, explores desire issuing from lack, in a desiccated middle-class world. In
Hotel du lac Edith, who looks like Virginia Woolf, has a pseudonym. It is Vanessa
Wilde. In the novel Edith is given the task of coming to terms with contemporary
sexual decadence (Fullbrook 97). "Carter's *Nights at the Circus* is concerned with
the assertive desire issuing from the desire to make demands on life, and with
redefining desire itself with the farce, cunning and high spirits of Benjamin's sto-
ryteller" (Armstrong, "Woolf by the Lake" 271).

52. This volume is the last of Kristeva's three-volume work entitled *Le génie
féminin*, the first two volumes of which cover Hannah Arendt and Melanie Klein.
While Arendt and Klein offer a picture of the political and psychic climate of the
twentieth century, respectively, Colette, as Kristeva states in a 1999 interview, provides another face to the century, that of pleasure: "Tout en étant celui du totali-
tarisme thématisé par Hannah Arendt et celui de la folie traité par Melanie Klein,
notre siècle est aussi un siècle de plaisirs, de joies, de bien-être. A côté de ces deux
juives dramatiques que sont Arendt et Klein, *il me fallait une paysanne française,
charnelle, paienne et jubilante*. Colette s'est imposée." (my emphasis; "Interview")
("While being one of totalitarianism thematized by Hannah Arendt and one of
madness treated by Melanie Klein, our century is also a century of pleasures, joys,
well-being. Alongside these two dramatic Jewesses, Arendt and Klein, I needed a
French peasant, carnal, pagan, and jubilant. Colette was just what I was looking
for"). (Kristeva also asserts, "Lorsque j'écris des romans, j'aime la lire. Ses écrits
sont *une sorte de bain de langue* qui me ressource" [my emphasis; "Interview"] ["I
like to read her books while I'm writing. Her books are like a sort of bath of language that restores me"].)

53. Other contemporary British writers have acknowledged their debt to
Colette, as well as to Woolf. Novelists Emma Tennant and Sue Roe in conversation discuss their debts to Woolf and Colette: "ET: your writing has very strong
colour and sensuality, as indeed had Colette. SR: Colette was very formative, as

was Virginia Woolf, of course" (Monteith 126). Critics have noted Woolf's place in Tennant's work: "[I]n *Alice Fell* (Tennant) Virginia Woolf seems to animate the vision of the particularities of family life as set against the larger world. I was reminded of the 'Times Passes' section of *To the Lighthouse,* in which small moments and details of life in a country house [. . .] are suddenly reimagined in terms of the impinging forces of time and politics: 'What people had shed and left—a pair of shoes, a shooting cap, some faded skirts and coats in wardrobes—those alone kept the human shape and the emptiness indicated how once they were filled and animated; how once hands were busy with hooks and buttons; how once the lookingglass had held a face; had held a world hollowed out in which a figure turned, a hand flashed, the door opened, in came children rushing and tumbling, and went out again'" (Wesley 185). Writer Michèle Roberts, who is half French and half English, suggests that Colette is loved by women for her brazen disregard for patriarchy. "Colette (1873–1954) [. . .] is beloved of women, particularly, for her courage in raising two fingers to the moral and literary establishments of her time" (11). A novel based on Colette, entitled *After Colette* (1993), by a Scottish writer, Joan Lingard, further attests to the interest of English authors in their French literary foremother. The Woolfian counterparts to this novel are the Pulitzer Prize winner *The Hours* (1998) by Michael Cunningham, Robin Lippincott's novella *Mr. Dalloway* (1999), and, in French, Jacqueline Harpman's *Orlanda* (1996).

54. Winterson echoes Toril Moi. Moi criticizes Showalter for "[defining] effective feminist writing as work that offers a powerful expression of personal experience in a social framework" (4). Moi questions Showalter's criticism of Woolf for her detachment from her narrative. Further, she takes issue with Showalter's suggestion that Woolf's famous statements regarding the androgynous mind of the writer mark a "flight away from a 'troubled feminism'" (2), the elusiveness of her perspective in the text, and a failure to produce a committed feminist text. Moi cites the following passage from Showalter's *A Literature of Our Own:* "Woolf was cut off from an understanding of the day-to-day life of the women whom she wished to inspire; characteristically, she rebelled against aspects of female experience that she had never personally known and avoided describing her own experience" (quoted in Moi 4). Moi contends that Showalter is wrong to advocate a reading that does not take into account the narrative strategies of the text. Moi also dislikes the way in which Jane Marcus (who calls Woolf a "guerilla fighter in a Victorian skirt") relies on biographical information to support her assertions about Woolf's writing (Moi 17). "Implicit," Moi writes, in Showalter's and others' work is "the assumption that good feminist fiction would present truthful images of strong women with which the reader may identify" (7).

55. Sido and the narrator's mother in *Oranges Are Not the Only Fruit* have an almost exclusive relationship with their daughter; in each case the father is almost nonexistent. Winterson's characterization of herself as collector and hoarder recalls Colette's characterization of Sido in *La naissance du jour* (and elsewhere, herself) as "une thésauriseuse" (52) ("a hoarder"). "I draw on everything I can find for my work—I'm a robber and a hoarder and a pawnbroker and a collector. The trick is to merge all this stuff into my own preoccupations and make new connections and a new whole. What is important though, is that creative work influences theory and not the other way round" ("Interview"). Her presence on the Internet, available at *www.jeanettewinterson.com,* the brashness with which she has promoted

herself, and her openness with regard to her personal life might all have appealed to Colette. According to her Web site, Winterson recently reread Colette's work, rereleased by Vintage Press.

56. "Colette a trouvé un langage pour dire *une étrange osmose entre ses sensations, ses désirs et ses angoisses, ces 'plaisirs qu'on nomme, à la légère, physiques' et l'infini du monde*—éclosions de fleurs, ondoiements de bêtes, apparitions sublimes, monstres contagieux. Ce langage transcende sa présence de femme dans le siècle—vagabonde ou entravée, libre, cruelle ou compatissante. Le style épouse ses racines terriennes et son accent bourguignon, tout en les allégeant dans une alchimie qui nous demeure encore mystérieuse. Elle-même l'appelle un 'alphabet nouveau.' Quel alphabet?" (my emphasis; 13–14).

57. "Provocante, scandaleuse par l'audace de ses mœurs et de son parcours, cette femme attachante refuse de s'enfermer dans un quelconque militantisme et ne prêche aucune transgression" (17).

58. In her book on Colette, Kristeva compares Woolf and Colette: "Alors que les grandes œuvres littéraires de ses consœurs européennes excellent dans la mélancolie—d'Emilie Dickinson à Virginia Woolf en passant par Anna Akhmatova—, Colette la Française, si elle eût pu devenir 'favorite à Versailles, elle eût gouverné le roi et le royaume' (plaisante François Nourissier)" (*Le génie féminin* 24) ("While the great literary works of her European and American female compatriots excel in misery—from Emily Dickinson to Virginia Woolf, passing via Anna Akhmatova—, the French woman Colette, if she had become 'favorite at Versailles, she would have governed the king and the kingdom' (jokes François Nourissier)"). In her novel *Les samouraïs,* suggesting a tribute to Woolf, Kristeva includes a character called Edward Dalloway. "For Dalloway, eroticism was connected with sound: he transformed his perceptions into aural perceptions, traveling among resonances, losing himself in contours of sonority, drowsing under the spell of tones" (*Les samouraïs* 269). In *Des Chinoises* (*About Chinese Women*) Kristeva reflects on Woolf's suicide, comparing it to those of Russian poet Marina Tsvetayeva and American poet Sylvia Plath. "I think of Virginia Woolf, who sank wordlessly into the river, her pockets weighed down with stones. Haunted by voices, waves, lights, in love with colours—blue, green—and seized by a strange gaiety that would bring on the fits of strangled, screeching laughter recalled by Miss Brown" (quoted in *Kristeva Reader* 157). She turns to these suicides in a section entitled "I who want not to be" as part of an exploration of the double bind in which woman finds herself at the present time—defined, according to Moi, by Judeo-Christian culture as "the unconscious of the symbolic order, as a timeless, drive-related *jouissance,* which through its very marginality threatens to break the symbolic chain"—she must neither refuse her role as the unconscious truth about patriarchy, for in so doing she identifies with the father and thus supports the patriarchal order, nor must she refuse to insert herself into the symbolic order, and in so doing embrace the masculine model of femininity (*Kristeva Reader* 139).

59. Cixous notes a similar phenomenon in terms of the reception of her work: "à l'étranger par contre je suis moins menaçante, parce que je ne suis pas là; c'est toujours pareil: à l'étranger je suis lue et ma force—ce qui vient, si vous voulez, du lecteur et qui est essentiel pour moi comme écrivain—vient d'Angleterre, des Etats-Unis, du Canada etc. Je suis lue et aimée à l'abri de la distance [. . .] la France donne une image trompeuse, on pense toujours que c'est un pays éclairé,

révolutionnaire, penseur . . . et c'est vrai, c'est vrai qu'il y a la philosophie, la psy-
chanalyse etc. . . . mais la France est profondément misogyne" (Cremonese 146)
("Abroad on the other hand I am less threatening, because I am not there; it's
always the same: abroad I'm read and my force—that which comes, if you like,
from the reader, who is essential to me as a writer—comes from England, the United States, Canada, etc. I am read and liked under the shelter of distance [. . .]
France gives a false image, people always think that it's an enlightened, revolutionary, thoughtful country . . . and it's true that it has philosophy, psychoanalysis, etc. . . . but France is profoundly misogynistic").

Notes to Conclusion

1. Books on Colette and food include Henri Béraud's *Colette gastronome: Le
capitole* (cited in Chauvière). *Les recettes de Colette* consists of recipes adapted from
Colette's work in collaboration with Pauline, Colette's longtime housekeeper,
compiled by Marie Christine and Didier Clément.

2. "jambon de pays, tomates et pêches, fromages, tartes de frangipane [. . .]"
(*La naissance du jour* 138).

3. One exception is Allie Glenny's *Ravenous Identities: Eating and Eating Distress in the Lives and Works of Virginia Woolf* (1999). Glenny argues for a more
careful reading of food in Woolf's work. Starting from the perspective of her own
experience as an anorexia sufferer, Glenny addresses Woolf's difficulties with food
and then goes on to explore in great depth the centrality of food to her work. She
suggests that "dwelling on food was, as Woolf saw it, an act of female liberation.
It was part of the process both of seeing the world through our own, female, lens-
es and, more actively, of righting a skewed world which had purged the sensual and
elevated the rational [. . .] Writing was for her a pursuit that took place within the
context of domesticity, not in monastic seclusion from the activities of the
kitchen" (xii).

4. See Quentin Bell's *Virginia Woolf: A Biography* (147).

5. In 1930 Woolf imagines herself at liberty in France with Roger Fry sitting on
the pavement drinking coffee (*Diary* 3: 323). In 1929 she writes to Dorothy
Bussy, "But what I want to suggest is that we might meet in France—where I suppose you to be. I'm having windows put in a small peasants hut in a wood near
Cassis—I hope to be there off and on. Couldn't we postpone our tea till January?—and it would then be better than tea; it would be wine and ices in blazing
sun" (*Letters* 4: 86). A little later she writes to Hugh Walpole: "I have a wild desire
to rush over to France and furnish my peasants hut—I told you I had three rooms
in a wood didn't I, near Cassis?—and live on coffee and maccaroni and sit in the
sun and drink quantities of Captain Teed's cheap white wine; but I suppose I
shant" (*Letters* 4: 91).

6. "Est ce un privilège de naître un 26 janvier 1882 (*sic*), à Londres, dans une
famille bourgeoise et respectable pour qui le bœuf bouilli, les meubles de peluche,
la cérémonie du thé, la conversation sont encore des institutions; le système familial une tyrannie; le goût pour la solitude une originalité provocante interprétée
comme une preuve de rébellion? La famille est un cercle qui vous protège et qui,
si vous n'êtes pas solidement constitué, risque fort de vous détruire."

7. The possibility that Woolf was anorexic has been addressed by many critics. See Lee (175–200) and Glenny's *Ravenous Identities.*

8. In Noble's *Recollections* Louie Mayer describes how Woolf taught her to make bread: "But there was one thing in the kitchen that Mrs Woolf was very good at doing; she could make beautiful bread. The first question she asked me when I went to Monks House was if I knew how to make it. I told her that I had made some for my family, but I was no expert at it. 'I will come into the kitchen Louie' she said, 'and show you how to do it. We have always made our own bread.' I was surprised how complicated the process was and how accurately Mrs Woolf carried it out. She showed me how to make the dough with the right quantities of yeast and flour, and then how to knead it. She returned three or four times during the morning to knead it again. Finally, she made the dough into the shape of a cottage loaf and baked it at just the right temperature" (757). Woolf talks very possessively about "my bread" in a letter to Leonard Woolf (*Letters* 2: 194).

9. "Débordante de vie, d'activité, elle resplendit de joie physique, serrant sur son cœur fort tout ce qui palpite pour l'étreindre, pour l'écraser, pour en exprimer la moelle substantifique. Puis, les mains en avant, elle va, elle va vers l'univers pour saisir encore et goûter à tout. Entre temps, passive, musarde, gourmette, elle croque des pommes et éventre des éclairs au chocolat" (1).

10. "Quel ancêtre me légua, à travers des parents si frugaux, cette sorte de religion du lapin sauté, du gigot à l'ail, de l'œuf mollet au vin rouge, le tout servi entre des murs de grange nappés de draps écrus où la rose rouge de juin, épinglée, resplendit" (6).

11. "J'ai toujours aimé manger, mais qu'était mon appétit au prix de celui de Lina? Sa majesté fondait, remplacée par une expression de volupté douce et d'innocence. L'éclat des dents, des yeux, de la bouche lustrée était d'une jeune fille. Rares sont les beautés qui peuvent bâfrer sans déchoir! Quand Lina repoussait enfin son assiette, c'est qu'elle l'avait vidée quatre, cinq fois . . ." (*Œuvres* 3: 991).

12. Vivien is also discussed by Colette in her *Aventures quotidiens.* For a portrait of her lover, the American Natalie Clifford Barney, see *Mes apprentissages* (1071/128).

13. "Si je suis farouche sur le point de la littérature, et avare de paroles sauf que volontiers je m'écrie d'admiration, je rencontrai chez Renée une parfaite pudeur de métier, un silence de bonne compagnie" (89) ("I am sparing of words on that subject [literature], except for occasional exclamations of admiration, and in Renée Vivien I found the same diffidence and well-bred restraint" [81]).

14. "[L]es languettes de poisson cru roulées sur des baguettes de verre, le foie gras, les écrevisses, des salades au sucre et au poivre, un Piper-Heidsieck brut très bien choisi et des cocktails—déjà—d'une exceptionelle roideur" (91).

15. "Ce qu'on appelle la vie de bohème m'a toujours convenu aussi mal que les chapeaux emplumés ou une paire de pendants d'oreille" (1012).

16. See Bettina Knapp's short article on the *bœuf en daube* and French impressionism.

17. Mr Pepper of *The Voyage Out* thinks no private cook can cook vegetables (84). At dinner he toys with fragments of lettuce "with the gesture of a man pronging seaweed, detecting gravel, suspecting germs" (84).

18. Vanessa Bell is also seduced by the beef. On first reading *To the Lighthouse*

in 1927, she asks Virginia for the recipe: "But how do you make Boeuf en Daube? Does it have to be eaten on the moment after cooking 3 days?" (*Letters* 3: 573).

19. The sensual nature of fruit also appears in *The Years*. At Sara's house, on her way to Delia's party, Maggie looks at the fruit on the table, her description perhaps doubling as a description of her sister, Sara. "On the dinner table lay the dish of fruit; the heavy sensual apples lay side by side with the yellow spotted bananas. It was an odd combination—the round and the tapering, the rosy and the yellow [and in the dark] ghostly apples, ghostly bananas" (350).

20. In "A Feast of Words in Mrs Dalloway," Molly Hoff ties Lady Bruton's lunch to its classical predecessors, arguing that "Lady Bruton's luncheon truly merits its place among the set pieces of culinary literature like Trimalchio's hilarious yet profound feast in Petronius' Satyricon V" (91). She argues that "the vocabulary of food and literary style overlap" (95).

21. "La première chose qui saisit, en entrant chez Colette, c'est l'odeur: ça sent bon le chocolat, la cire, la pêche mûre, le pain grillé" (237).

22. "Ses textes sont comme des appels d'offre aux fantasmes de l'oralité [. . .] Il faut que les mots prennent la forme de la sensation, la bonne forme, de même que Pati-Pati ouvre une bouche ronde pour manger une fraise ronde" (46). Milner goes on to describe Colette's response to her friend Marguerite Moreno's efforts to describe a "charming and delicate" dinner. Colette reproaches Moreno for not only not making anything visual, but also not making anything taste of anything (45).

23. "En les achetant mûres et les laissant pourrir un petit peu, les bananes, c'est le bon Dieu en culotte de velours liberty!" (33).

24. "[L]es bananes trop avancées et des grogs froids avec des gâteaux salés" (130).

25. "Je mange une petite timbale aux truffes qui consolerait une veuve de la veille" (53).

26. "[U]ne admirable glace à la mandarine [qui] me détache d'ailleurs de toute autre préoccupation" (54).

27. "Mon cousin l'Oncle [. . .] me demande du thé, exige de la crème, plus que ça, deux sucres, un sandwich, pas celui du dessus parce qu'il a dû sécher, et quoi encore? *Mais nos deux gourmandises se comprennent* et je ne m'impatiente pas" (my emphasis; 87).

28. "[D]es bonbons, des pâtisseries, des petits oiseaux à manger. Et mieux que ça, du champagne à dîner" (160).

29. "Gigi [. . .] est si gourmande! Si elle avait la tête aussi active que les mâchoires!" (17).

30. "Les ortolans, coupe-les en deux, d'un coup de couteau bien assuré qui ne fasse pas grincer la lame sur l'assiette. Croque chaque moitié" (37).

31. "Elle savait sa leçon, rompait délicatement son pain, mangeait la bouche close, se gardait, en découpant sa viande, d'avancer l'index sur le dos de lame" (36).

32. "[Elle] déjeuna dans une solitude joyeuse, souriant au Vouvray sec et aux fraises de juin servies avec leurs queues sur un plat de Rubelles, vert comme une rainette mouillée" (17–18).

33. "[D]es bonnes fraises, de la crème fraîche, des tartes, des petits poulets grillés" (34).

34. "'Prends le pain le plus cuit . . . Ne mange pas tant de mie fraîche . . . Tu n'as jamais su choisir un fruit'" while, "maussade" in secret, she rebuked herself: "elle se gourmandait" (63).

35. "Un poids invisible tirait en bas le menton et les joues, attristait les coins tremblants de la bouche. Dans ce naufrage de la beauté, Chéri retrouvait, intacts, le joli nez dominateur, les prunelles d'un bleu de fleur bleue . . ." (185).

36. "Elle se souvint qu'elle déjeunait seule, et n'eut envie d'aucun restaurant. [. . .] elle acheta sur sa route des fenouils frais, une boîte de thon, des œufs à la coque, du fromage blanc et un quart de champagne. Mais la faim impérieuse qui la mordait au creux de l'estomac compromit sa dînette. Pendant qu'un œuf dansait dans l'eau bouillante, Alice mangeait le thon sans pain, le fromage poudré de poivre, et elle croquait les fenouils en guise de dessert lorsqu'elle s'avisa qu'elle n'avait pas débouché la petite bouteille de champagne. Elle la rangea dans 'le padirac-deux,' qui était le placard de la cuisine. Sur l'évier, une paire de bas de soie trempait dans une cuvette émaillée" (150).

37. "Un second couvert . . . Cela tient peu de place, maintenant: une assiette verte, un gros verre ancien, un peu trouble. Si je fais signe qu'on l'enlève à jamais, aucun souffle pernicieux, accouru soudain de l'horizon, ne lèvera mes cheveux droits et ne fera tourner—cela s'est vu—ma vie dans un autre sens. Ce couvert ôté de ma table, je mangerai pourtant avec appétit. Il n'y a plus de mystère, plus de serpent lové sous la serviette que pince et marque pour la distinguer de la mienne, la lyre de cuivre qui maintenait, au dessus d'un vieil ophicléide du siècle dernier, les pages désertes d'une partition où l'on ne lisait que des 'temps forts,' semés à intervalles égaux comme des larmes . . . Ce couvert est celui de l'ami qui vient et s'en va, ce n'est plus d'un maître du logis qui foule, aux heures nocturnes, le sonore plancher d'une chambre là-haut . . . Les jours où l'assiette, le verre, la lyre manquent en face de moi, je suis simplement seule, et non délaissée" (25–26).

38. "'Il n'est vendange que d'automne . . . ' Peut-être qu'en amour aussi" (49).

39. "N'importe quel amour, si on se fie à lui, tend à s'organiser à la manière d'un tube digestif" (49).

40. "[U]n déjeuner méridional, salades, rascasse farcie et beignets d'aubergines, ordinaire que je corsais de quelque oiseau rôti" (55).

41. "[Q]uatre petits poulets fendus par moitié, frappés du plat de la hachette, salés, poivrés, bénis d'huile pure, administrée avec un goupillon de *pebreda* dont les folioles et le goût restent sur la chair grillée" (55–56).

42. "Ce n'est pas aujourd'hui, mais c'est bientôt, je pense, que je renoncerai à la chair des bêtes" (56).

43. "Quand certain cannibalisme meurt, tous les autres déménagent d'eux-mêmes, commes les puces d'un hérisson mort" (56).

44. "Il pencha son torse nu, lustré de soleil et de sel, dont la peau mire le jour. Selon qu'il bougeait, il était vert autour des reins, bleu sur les épaules, à l'image des teinturiers de Fez. Quand je commandai 'stop,' il coupa le fil d'huile dorée, se redressa, et je reposai ma main un moment sur son poitrail, comme sur un cheval, flatteusement. Il regarda ma main, qui annonce mon âge,—à la vérité, elle porte quelques années de plus—mais je ne retirai pas ma main" (56–57).

Works Cited

Primary Sources

COLETTE'S WORKS

Fiction, Essays, Memoirs

Claudine à l'école. Paris: Livre de poche, 1976. (1900)
Claudine à Paris. Paris: Livre de poche, 1962. (1901)
Claudine en ménage. Paris: Mercure de France, 1902. (1902)
Claudine s'en va. Paris: Livre de poche, 1965. (1903)
The Complete Claudines. Trans. Antonia White. New York: The Noonday Press, 1976.
Retreat from Love. Trans. and introduction by Margaret Crosland. Indianapolis: The Bobbs-Merrill Company, 1974. (1907)
La vagabonde. Paris: Albin Michel, 1926. (1911)
Chéri. Paris: Fayard, 1920. (1920)
Chéri and the Last of Chéri. Trans. Roger Senhouse. New York: Noonday, 1951.
La maison de Claudine. Paris: Hachette, 1960. (1921)
My Mother's House and The Vagabond. Trans. Una Vincenzo Troubridge and Enid McLeod. New York: Doubleday Anchor, 1955.
La naissance du jour. Paris: Flammarion, 1984. (1928).
The Break of Day. Trans. Enid McLeod. New York: Farrar, Straus and Cudahy, 1961.
Sido suivi de Les vrilles de la vigne. Paris: Hachette, 1961. (1908, 1929)
Le pur et l'impur. Paris: Hachette, 1971. (1932 as *Ces Plaisirs,* 1941 under current title)
The Pure and the Impure. Trans. Herma Briffault. New York: Farrar, Straus and Giroux, 1967.
Duo suivi de Le toutounier. Paris: Hachette, 1960. (1934, 1939)
Duo and Le toutounier. Trans. Margaret Crosland. London: Peter Owen, 1999.
Mes apprentissages. Œuvres. Vol. III. Ed. Claude Pichois. Paris: Gallimard, 1991. (1936)
My Apprenticeships. Trans. Helen Beauclerk. New York: Farrar, Straus and Giroux, 1957.

The Tender Shoot and Other Stories. (*Bella Vista,* 1937). Trans. Antonia White. Paris: Farrar, Straus and Giroux, 1958.
Journal à rebours. Œuvres complètes 9. Paris: Flammarion, 1973. (1941)
Looking Backwards. Trans. David Le Vay. Bloomington: Indiana University Press, 1975.
Le Képi. Œuvres complètes 9. Paris. Flammarion, 1973. (1943)
Gigi. Paris: Hachette, 1960. (1944)
Gigi, Julie de Carheilhan, Chance Acquaintances. Trans. Roger Senhouse and Patrick Leigh Fermor. New York: Farrar, Straus and Giroux, 1952.

Articles, Interviews, Addresses

"Discours de réception à l'Académie Royale belge." In *Mélanges. Œuvres complètes 14.* Paris: Flammarion, 1973.
"Mes idées sur le roman" (originally appeared in *Le Figaro,* 1937). *Œuvres complètes 3.* Paris: Flammarion, 1973.

Collected Works

Œuvres complètes de Colette (16 volumes). Paris: Flammarion, 1973–76.
Colette. Œuvres. Vols. 1–3. Ed. Claude Pichois. Paris: Gallimard, 1984, 1986, 1991.

Letters, Diaries

Lettres de la vagabonde. Œuvres complètes 15. Paris: Flammarion, 1973.
Lettres à Marguerite Moreno. Œuvres complètes 14. Paris: Flammarion, 1973.
Lettres à ses pairs. Paris: Flammarion, 1973.
Lettres à Annie de Pène et Germaine Beaumont. Paris: Flammarion, 1995.
Letters from Colette. Selected and translated by Robert Phelps. New York: Farrar Straus Giroux, 1980.

VIRGINIA WOOLF'S WORKS

Fiction, Essays, Memoirs

The Voyage Out. London: Penguin Twentieth Century Classics, 1992. (1915)
Jacob's Room. New York: Harcourt Brace Jovanovich, 1950. (1922)
The Common Reader. New York: Harvest, 1953. (1925)
Mrs Dalloway. San Diego: Harvest/Harcourt Brace Jovanovich, 1981. (1925)
To the Lighthouse. San Diego: Harvest/Harcourt Brace Jovanovich, 1927. (1927)
Orlando. San Diego: Harvest/Harcourt Brace Jovanovich, 1928. (1928)
A Room of One's Own. San Diego: Harvest/Harcourt Brace Jovanovich, 1929. (1929)
The Waves. London: Panther, 1979. (1931)
The Years. San Diego: Harvest/Harcourt Brace Jovanovich, 1965. (1937)
Between the Acts. London: Penguin Twentieth Century Classics, 1992. (1941)
Moments of Being. San Diego: Harvest/Harcourt Brace & Company, 1985. (1976)

Articles, Interviews

"Men and Women." In *Women and Writing.* Ed. and introduction by Michèle

Barrett. San Diego: Harvest/Harcourt Brace Jovanovich, 1979. (1920)
"On Not Knowing French." *The New Republic,* February 13, 1929.
"Professions for Women." In *Women and Writing.* Ed. and introduction by
Michèle Barrett. San Diego: Harvest/Harcourt Brace Jovanovich, 1979.
(1931)

Letters, Diaries

Congenial Spirits: The Selected Letters of Virginia Woolf. Ed. Joanne Trautmann
Banks. London: Hogarth Press, 1989.
The Diary of Virginia Woolf. Ed. Anne Olivier Bell and Andrew McNeillie. San
Diego: Harcourt Brace Jovanovich, 1978. 5 volumes.
Woolf, Virginia. *The Letters of Virginia Woolf.* Eds. Nigel Nicolson and Joanne
Trautmann. New York: Harcourt Brace Jovanovich, 1975–80. 6 volumes.
Virginia Woolf and Lytton Strachey: Letters. Eds. Leonard Woolf and James Stra-
chey. London: Hogarth Press, 1956.
A Writer's Diary. Ed. Leonard Woolf. San Diego: Harcourt, Brace & Company,
1953.

Secondary Sources

Abastado, Claude. *Les "Claudine" extraits.* Paris: Bordas, 1969.
Abel, Elizabeth. "Spatial Relations: Lily Briscoe's Painting." In *Virginia Woolf
and the Fictions of Psychoanalysis.* Chicago: University of Chicago Press, 1989.
Amis, Martin. *Experience.* London: Vintage, 2001.
Armstrong, Isobel. *New Feminist Discourses: Critical Essays on Theories and Texts.*
London: Routledge, 1992.
———. "Woolf by the Lake, Woolf at the Circus: Carter and Tradition" in *Flesh
and the Mirror: Essays on the Art of Angela Carter.* Ed. Lorna Sage. London:
Virago, 1994.
Bair, Dierdre. *Anaïs Nin.* New York: Penguin, 1995.
Baker, Michael. *Our Three Selves: The Life of Radclyffe Hall.* London: Hamish
Hamilton, 1985.
Bal, Mieke. *La complexité d'un roman populaire: Ambiguité dans "La chatte."*
Paris: La pensée universelle, 1974.
Barbour, Sarah. *Nathalie Sarraute and the Feminist Reader.* Lewisburg, Penn.:
Bucknell University Press, 1993.
Beach, Sylvia. *Shakespeare and Company.* London: Plantin, 1987 (1956).
Beaton, Cecil. *The Book of Beauty.* London: Duckworth, 1930.
Beer, Gillian. "Introduction." *Between the Acts.* London: Penguin Twentieth Cen-
tury Classics, 1992.
Bell, Quentin. *Virginia Woolf: A Biography.* New York: Harcourt Brace Jovano-
vich, 1972.
Benstock, Shari. *Textualizing the Feminine: On the Limits of Genre.* Norman: Uni-
versity of Oklahoma Press, 1991.
———. *Women of the Left Bank: Paris, 1900–1940.* Austin: University of Texas
Press, 1986.
Bernikow, Louise. *Among Women.* New York: Harper & Row, 1980.

Berthu-Courtivron, Marie-Françoise. *Espace, demeure, écriture: La maison natale dans l'œuvre de Colette.* Paris: Libr. A.-G. Nizet, 1992.

———. *Mère et fille: L'enjeu du pouvoir: Essai sur les écrits autobiographiques de Colette.* Amsterdam: Droz, 1993.

Blanche, Jacques-Emile. "Entretiens avec Virginia Woolf." Article on *To the Lighthouse* and translation of "Kew Gardens." *Les nouvelles littéraires,* August 13, 1927.

———. *More Sketches of the Past.* Trans. Walter Clement. London: J. M. Dent & Sons, 1939.

———. *Portraits of a Lifetime.* Trans. Walter Clement. New York: Coward-McCann, Inc., 1938.

———. "Un nouveau roman de V. Woolf." Article on *Orlando. Les nouvelles littéraires,* February 16, 1929.

———. *La pêche aux souvenirs.* Paris: Flammarion, 1949.

Bloom, Harold. *The Anxiety of Influence: A Theory of Poetry.* 2nd ed. New York: Oxford University Press, 1997.

Blot-Labarèrre, Christiane. *Marguerite Duras.* Paris: Éditions du Seuil, 1992.

Blume, Harvey. "Doris Lessing: Hot Dawns." Originally published in the Boston Book Review, Feb. 7, 1998.

Bonne, Rena Barbara. "The Female Presence in the Novels of Virginia Woolf and Colette." Ph.D. dissertation, Case Western Reserve University, 1978.

Booth, Valerie Ann. "Our Late Flowers Are Rare and Splendid: Middle Aged Women in the Novels of Virginia Woolf and Colette." Ph.D. dissertation, Emory University, 1996.

Bowlby, Rachel (Ed.). *Virginia Woolf.* New York: Longman, 1992.

———. *Virginia Woolf: Feminist Destinations.* Oxford: Basil Blackwell, 1988.

Bradbury, Malcolm, and James McFarlane (Eds.) *Modernism: A Guide to European Literature.* London: Penguin, 1991.

Brée, Germaine. "Interview with Two French Novelists: Natalie Sauraute and Célia Bertir." *Contemporary Literature,* Spring 1973, Volume 14, No. 2.

Brewster, Dorothy. *Doris Lessing.* New York: Twayne, 1965.

Brittain, Vera. *Radclyffe Hall: A Case of Obscenity?* London: Femina, 1968.

Carter, Angela. *The Bloody Chamber.* New York: Penguin, 1981 (1971).

———. *Nights at the Circus.* New York: Penguin, 1986 (1984).

———. *Shaking a Leg: Collected Writings.* New York: Penguin, 1998 (1997).

Caws, Mary Ann, and Nicola Luckhurst (Eds.). *The Reception of Virginia Woolf in Europe.* London: Continuum, 2002.

Caws, Mary Ann, and Sarah Bird Wright. *Bloomsbury and France: Art and Friends.* Oxford: Oxford University Press, 2000.

Chalon, Jean. *L'éternelle apprentie.* Paris: Flammarion, 1998.

Chauvière, Claude. *Colette.* Paris: Librairie de Paris (Firmin-Didot et Cie), 1931.

Cixous, Hélène. *La jeune née.* Paris: Union Générale d'Édition, 1975.

———. "Le rire de la méduse." *L'Arc* 61, 1975.

———. *Readings: The Poetics of Blanchot, Joyce, Kafka, Kleist, Lispector and Tsvetayeva.* Ed. and trans. Verena Andermatt Conley. Minneapolis: University of Minnesota Press, 1991.

Clément, Marie-Christine, and Didier Clément. *Les Recettes de Colette.* Paris: Albin Michel, 1997.

Cliche, Elène. "La réécriture du texte Woolfien, *The Waves* (1931), dans la traduction (1937) de Marguerite Yourcenar." In *Marguerite Yourcenar: Ecriture, réécriture, traduction.* Tours: Société Internationale d'Etudes Yourcenar-
riennes, 2000.

Cline, Sally. *Radclyffe Hall: A Woman Called John.* London: John Murray, 1997.

Cocteau, Jean. *Colette: Discours de réception à l'Académie Royale de Langue et de
Littérature Françaises.* Paris: Grasset, 1955.

———. *My Contemporaries.* Ed. Margaret Crosland. London: Peter Owen, 1967.

Collet, Georges Paul. "Jacques-Emile Blanche and Virginia Woolf." *Comparative
Literature* 17, 1965.

Collis, Louise. *Impetuous Heart: The Story of Ethel Smyth.* London: William Kim-
ber, 1984.

Corbin, Laurie. *The Mother Mirror: Self-representation and the Mother-Daughter
Relation in Colette, Simone de Beauvoir and Marguerite Duras.* New York:
Peter Lang, 1996.

Cremonese, Laura. *Dialectique du masculin et du féminin dans l'œuvre d'Hélène
Cixous.* Paris: Didier Erudition, 1997.

Crosland, Margaret. *Colette: A Provincial in Paris.* London: Peter Owen, 1954.

———. *Women of Iron and Velvet: French Women Writers After George Sand.* New
York: Taplinger, 1976.

———. *Beyond the Lighthouse.* New York: Taplinger, 1981.

Cunningham, Michael. *The Hours.* New York: Picador, 1998.

Daiches, David. *Virginia Woolf.* New York: New Directions, 1963.

de Beauvoir, Simone. *Le deuxième sexe I.* Paris: Gallimard, 1949.

———. *The Second Sex.* Trans H. M. Parshley. New York: Vintage, 1974 (1949).

———. *La force des choses.* Paris: Gallimard, 1963.

———. *The Coming of Age.* Trans. Patrick O'Brien. New York: Warner, 1973.

———. "La femme et la création." In *Les écrits de Simone de Beauvoir: La vie,
l'écriture, avec en appendice, textes inédits ou retrouvés.* Ed. Claude Francis and
Fernande Gontier. Paris: Gallimard, 1979.

———. *Letters to Sartre.* Trans. and ed. Quintin Hoare. New York: Arcade,
1992.

———. *A Transatlantic Love Affair: Letters to Nelson Algren.* New York: The
New Press: 1998.

de Cossart, Michael. *The Food of Love: Princesse Edmond de Polignac (1865–1943)
and Her Salon.* London: Hamish Hamilton, 1978.

Defromont, Françoise. *Virginia Woolf: Vers la maison de lumière.* Paris: des
femmes, 1985.

Del Castillo, Michel. *Colette: Une certaine France.* Paris: Stock, 1999.

de Noailles, Anna. *Le livre de ma vie.* Paris: Mercure de France, 1976.

DeSalvo, Louise. *Virginia Woolf: The Impact of Sexual Abuse on Her Life and
Work.* London: The Women's Press, 1991.

D'Hollander, Paul. *Colette, ses apprentissages.* Montréal: Presse de l'Université de
Montréal, 1978.

Doan, Laura, and Jay Prosser (Eds.). *Palatable Poison: Critical Perspectives on* The
Well of Loneliness. New York: Columbia University Press, 2001.

Dowling, David. *Bloomsbury Aesthetics and the Novels of Forster and Woolf.* London: Macmillan, 1985.

Drabble, Margaret. "How Not to Be Afraid of Virginia Woolf." *Ms. Magazine*, November 1972.

Duncan, J. An. "The Early Novels of Paul Adam." *Modern Language Review* 69, 1974.

Dunn, Jane. *Antonia White*. London: Jonathan Cape, 1998.

Dupont, Jacques. *Colette*. Paris: Hachette, 1995.

Duras, Marguerite. *Écrire*. Paris: Gallimard, 1993.

———. *Emily L.* Trans. Barbara Bray. New York: Pantheon Books, 1989.

Dusinberre, Juliet. *Virginia Woolf's Renaissance: Woman Reader or Common Reader*. Iowa City: University of Iowa Press, 1997.

Eisinger, Erica Mendelson and Mari Ward McCarty (Eds.). *Colette: The Woman, The Writer*. University Park: The Pennsylvania State University Press, 1981

Evans, Martha Noel. *Masks of Tradition: Women and the Politics of Writing in Twentieth Century France*. Ithaca, N.Y.: Cornell University Press, 1987.

Field, Andrew. *Djuna: The Life and Times of Djuna Barnes*. New York: Putnam, 1983.

Fitch, Noel Riley. *Sylvia Beach and the Lost Generation: A History of Literary Paris in the Twenties and Thirties*. New York: W. W. Norton, 1983.

Flanner, Janet. *Paris Was Yesterday: 1925–1939*. Ed. Irving Drutman. San Diego: Harvest/Harcourt Brace Jovanovich, 1972.

Flieger, Jerry Aline. *Colette and the Fantom Subject of Autobiography*. Ithaca, N.Y.: Cornell University Press, 1992.

———. "Colette and the Captain: Daughters as Ghost Writers." In *Refiguring the Father: New Feminist Readings of Patriarchy*. Eds. Patricia Yaeger and Beth Kowaleski-Wallace. Carbondale: Southern Illinois University Press, 1989.

Francis, Claude, and Fernande Gontier. *Colette*. Paris: Perrin, 1997.

———. *Simone de Beauvoir: A Life . . . A Love Story*. Trans. Lisa Nesselson. New York: St. Martin's Press, 1987.

Franks (Southworth), Helen. "Rhododendrons in the Strand; Mammoths in Piccadilly: Reconsidering Space in the Works of Virginia Woolf and Colette." Ph.D. dissertation, University of Southern California, 1999.

Freund, Gisèle. *Gisèle Freund, Photographer*. Trans. John Shepley. New York: Harry N. Abrams, 1985.

———. *Three Days with Joyce*. Trans. Peter St. John Ginna. New York: Perseus Books, 1985.

———. *The World and My Camera*. Trans. June Guicharnaud. New York: The Dial Press, 1974.

Galey, Matthieu. *With Open Eyes: Conversations with Matthieu Galey/Marguerite Yourcenar*. Trans. Arthur Goldhammer. Boston: Beacon Press, 1984.

Fulbrook, Kate. "Anita Brookner: On Reaching for the Sun." In *British Women Writing Fiction*. Ed. Abby Werlock. Tuscaloosa: Alabama University Press, 2000.

Gide, André. "Hommage à Colette." *Colette. Le Point: Revue Artistique et Littéraire*, 39, May 1951.

Gilbert, Sandra, and Susan Gubar. *The Madwoman in the Attic: The Woman Writer and the Nineteenth-Century Literary Imagination*. New Haven, Conn.: Yale University Press, 2000 (1979).

Glasgow, Joanne (Ed.). *Your John: The Love Letters of Radclyffe Hall.* New York: New York University Press, 1997.

Glavin, John. "Muriel Spark: Beginning Again." In *British Women Writing Fiction.* Ed. Abby Werlock. Tuscaloosa: University of Alabama Press, 2000.

Glendinning, Victoria. *Rebecca West: A Life.* London: Weidenfeld and Nicolson, 1987.

Glenny, Allie. *Ravenous Identities: Eating and Eating Distress in the Lives and Works of Virginia Woolf.* New York: St. Martin's Press, 1999.

Gordon, Mary. *Chase of the Wild Goose.* New York: Arno, 1975 (1936).

Goudeket, Maurice. *Près de Colette.* Paris: Flammarion, 1956.

Guiguet, Jean. *Virginia Woolf et son œuvre: L'art et la quête du réel.* Paris: Didier, 1962.

Hall, Radclyffe. *The Well of Loneliness.* Garden City, N.Y.: Blue Ribbon Books, 1936.

The Hamwood Papers of the Ladies of Llangollen and Caroline Hamilton. London: Macmillan, 1930.

Hill, Katherine C. "Virginia Woolf and Leslie Stephen: History and Literary Revolution." *PMLA* 96, no. 3, May 1981.

Hite, Molly. "Virginia Woolf's Two Bodies." *Genders* 31, 2000.

Hoff, Molly. "A Feast of Words in Mrs Dalloway." *Woolf Studies Annual* 1, 1995.

Hollier, Denis (Ed.). *New History of French Literature.* Cambridge, Mass.: Harvard University Press, 1989.

Holroyd, Michael. *Lytton Strachey: The New Biography.* New York: Farrar, Straus and Giroux, 1995.

Holtby, Winifred. *Virginia Woolf: A Critical Memoir.* Chicago: Cassandra Editions, 1978 (1932/33).

Houssa, Nicole. *Balzac et Colette. Extrait de la revue d'histoire littéraire de la France* 1, Janvier–Mars 1960.

———. "Citations, références et allusions littéraires chez Colette." *Marche romane: Cahiers de l'Association des Romanistes de l'Université de Liège,* January-July 1958.

Hussey, Mark. *Virginia Woolf A to Z.* New York: Facts on File, 1995.

Jardin, Claudine. *Virginia Woolf.* Paris: Hachette Littéraire, 1973.

Jones, Danell. "The Chase of the Wild Goose: The Ladies of Llangollen and Orlando." In *Virginia Woolf: Themes and Variations.* Ed. Vara Neverow-Turk and Mark Hussey. New York: Pace University Press, 1993.

Jong, Erica. "Introduction." *Colette's* The Other Woman. New York: Meridian Classic, 1975.

Jordan, Elaine. "The Dangerous Edge." In *Flesh and the Mirror: Essays on the Art of Angela Carter.* Ed. Lorna Sage. London: Virago, 1994.

Jouve, Nicole Ward. *Colette.* Bloomington: Indiana University Press, 1987.

———. "Mother Is a Figure of Speech." In *Flesh and the Mirror: The Art of Angela Carter.* Ed. Lorna Sage. London: Virago, 1994.

———. "Oranges et sources: Colette et Hélène Cixous." In *Hélène Cixous, chemins d'une écriture.* Ed. Françoise van Rossum-Guyon and Myriam Díaz-Diocaretz. Amsterdam: Rodopi, 1990.

Jullian, Philippe, and John Phillips. *The Other Woman: A Life of Violet Trefusis.* Boston: Houghton Mifflin, 1976.

Kamuf, Peggy. "Penelope at Work: Interruptions in *A Room of One's Own*." In *Feminism and Foucault: Reflections on Resistance*. Ed. Irene Diamond and Lee Quinby. Boston: Northeastern University Press, 1988.

Kelly, Kathleen Koyne. *A. S. Byatt*. New York: Twayne, 1996.

Kirkpatrick, J., and Stuart N. Clark. *A Bibliography of Virginia Woolf*. New York: Oxford University Press, 1997.

Knapp, Bettina. "Virginia Woolf's 'Boeuf en Daube.'" In *Literary Gastronomy*. Ed. David Bevan. Amsterdam: Rodopi, 1988.

Kowaleski-Wallace, Elizabeth. *Their Father's Daughters: Hannah More, Maria Edgeworth, and Patriarchal Complicity*. New York: Oxford University Press, 1991.

Kristeva, Julia. "About Chinese Women." In *The Kristeva Reader*. Ed. Toril Moi. New York: Columbia University Press, 1986.

———. "Colette ou la chair du monde." *Conférences Roland Barthes*, February 2001.

———. *Le génie féminin. Volume 3: Les Mots, Colette ou la chair du monde*. Paris: Fayard, 2002.

———. "Interview with Julia Kristeva by Ariane Poulantzas." *Lire*, June 1999.

———. *Les samouraïs: Roman*. Paris: Fayard, 1990.

Ladimer, Bethany. *Colette, Beauvoir, and Duras: Age and Women Writers*. Gainesville: University Press of Florida, 1999.

———. "Colette: Rewriting the Script for the Aging Woman." In *Aging and Gender in Literature: Studies in Creativity*. Ed. Anne M. Wyatt-Brown and Janice Rossen. Charlottesville: University Press of Virginia, 1993.

Larnac, Jean. *Colette: Sa vie, son œuvre*. Paris: Simon Krâ, 1927.

Lee, Hermione. *Virginia Woolf*. New York: Alfred A. Knopf, 1997.

Lingard, Joan. *After Colette*. London: Sinclair-Stevenson, 1993.

Lippincott, Robin. *Mr Dalloway*. Louisville, KY: Sarabande, 1999.

Louÿs, Pierre. *Aphrodite*. Trans. Lewis Galantière. New York: Modern Library, 1960.

Low, Lisa. "'Listen and Save': Woolf's Allusions to *Comus* in Her First Revolutionary Novel." In *Virginia Woolf Reading the Renaissance*. Ed. Sally Greene. Athens: Ohio University Press, 1999.

Luckhurst, Nicola. "Photoportraits: Gisèle Freund and Virginia Woolf." In *Virginia Woolf Out of Bounds: Selected Papers from the Tenth Annual Conference*. Ed. Jessica Berman and Jane Goldman. New York: Pace University Press, 2000.

Mallet-Joris, Françoise. "A Womanly Vocation." In *Colette: The Woman, The Writer*. Ed. Erica Eisinger and Mari McCarty. University Park: The Pennsylvania State University Press, 1981.

Marcus, Jane. *Art and Anger*. Columbus: The Ohio State University Press, 1988.

———. *New Feminist Essays on Virginia Woolf*. Lincoln: University of Nebraska Press, 1981.

———. *Virginia Woolf and the Languages of Patriarchy*. Bloomington: Indiana University Press, 1987.

———. "Wrapped in the Stars and Stripes: Virginia Woolf in the U.S.A." *South Carolina Review* 29, no. 1, Fall 1996.

Marks, Elaine. *Colette*. New Brunswick, N.J.: Rutgers University Press, 1960.

———. "Foreword: Celebrating Colette." *Colette: The Woman, The Writer.* University Park: The Pennsylvania State University Press, 1981.

Marks, Elaine, and Isabelle de Courtivron (Eds.). *New French Feminisms.* Brighton, Eng.: Harvester, 1980.

Marsden, Peter V., and Noah E. Friedkin. "Network Studies of Social Influence." In *Advances in Social Network Analysis.* Thousand Oaks, Calif.: Sage, 1994.

Mavor, Elizabeth. *The Ladies of Llangollen: A Study in Romantic Friendship.* London: Penguin, 1973.

Mayoux, J. J. *Vivants piliers.* Paris: Julliard, 1960.

Meyer, Doris. *Victoria Ocampo: Against the Wind and the Tide.* Austin: University of Texas Press, 1979.

Miller, Nancy K. "Woman of Letters: The Return to Writing in Colette's 'The Vagabond.'" In *Subject to Change.* New York: Colombia University Press, 1988.

———. "The Anamnesis of a Female 'I'": In the Margins of Self-Portrayal." In *Colette: The Woman, The Writer.* Eds. Erica Mendelson Eisinger and Mari Ward McCarty. University Park: The Pennsylvania State University Press, 1981.

Milner, Christiane. "L'oralité de Colette: Une image inversée de l'anorexie." In *Colette: Nouvelles approches critiques.* Ed. Bernard Bray. Paris: Nizet, 1996.

Minogue, Valerie. *Nathalie Sarraute and the War of Words.* Edinburgh: Edinburgh University Press, 1981.

Mitchell, Yvonne. *Colette: A Taste for Life.* New York: Harcourt Brace Jovanovich, 1975.

Moers, Ellen. *Literary Women.* New York: Oxford University Press, 1985.

Moi, Toril. *Sexual/Textual Politics: Feminist Literary Theory.* London: Routledge, 1986.

Monnier, Adrienne. *The Very Rich Hours of Adrienne Monnier.* Trans. and introduction by Richard McDougall. New York: Charles Scribner's Sons, 1976.

Monteith, Moira. *Women's Writing.* Sussex, Eng.: Harvester, 1996.

Nathan, Monique. *Virginia Woolf.* London: Evergreen, 1961.

———. *Virginia Woolf par lui-même.* Paris: Editions du Seuil, 1956.

Nicolson, Nigel. *Portrait of a Marriage.* London: PBS, 1973.

Noble, Joan Russel. *Recollections of Virginia Woolf by Her Contemporaries.* New York: William Morrow and Company, 1972.

Novak, Jane. *The Razor Edge of Balance: A Study of Virginia Woolf.* Coral Gables, Fla.: University of Miami Press, 1975.

Oates, Joyce Carol. "Review of Carolyn Heilbrun and Nancy Topping Bazin, *Virginia Woolf and the Androgynous Vision.*" New York Times Book Review (April 15, 1973).

Ormrod, Richard. *Una Troubridge: The Friend of Radclyffe Hall.* London: Jonathan Cape, 1984.

Ottavi, Anne. "La mère chez Colette et V. Woolf." In *Etudes et recherches de littérature générale et comparée.* Monaco: Les Belles Lettres, Annales de la Faculté des Lettres et Sciences Humaines de Nice, 1974.

Ozouf, Mona. "Gabrielle ou la gourmandise." In *Les mots de femmes: Essai sur la singularité française.* Paris: Fayard, 1995.

Peach, Linden. *Virginia Woolf.* New York: St. Martin's Press, 2000.

Penrod, Lynn. *Hélène Cixoux.* New York: Twayne, 1996.

Phelps, Robert. *Earthly Paradise: Colette's Autobiography, Drawn from the Writings of Her Lifetime.* Trans. Herma Briffault, Derek Coltman, and others. New York: Farrar, Strauss and Giroux, 1966.

Pichois, Claude, and Alain Brunet. *Colette.* Paris: Editions de Fallois, 1999.

Poole, Roger. *The Unknown Virginia Woolf.* Cambridge: Cambridge University Press, 1978.

Prokosch, Frederic. *Voices: A Memoir.* New York: Farrar, Strauss and Giroux, 1983.

Renaudin, Christine, and Suzanne Toczyski. "(Im)possible Translations of *The Waves.*" *Virginia Woolf Bulletin* 11, September 2002.

Resch, Yannick. *Corps féminin, corps textuel: Essai sur le personnage féminin dans l'œuvre de Colette.* Paris: Librairie Klincksieck, 1973.

Richardson, Dorothy. *Windows on Modernism: Selected Letters of Dorothy Richardson.* Ed. Gloria G. Fromm. Athens: University of Georgia Press, 1995.

Roberts, Michèle. "The Empress of the Senses." *The Independent: The Weekend Review,* October 23, 1999.

Rogers, Juliette. "Colette and Her Culture of Readers." Ph.D. dissertation, Duke University, 1990.

Rose, Phyllis. *Woman of Letters: A Life of Virginia Woolf.* New York: Oxford University Press, 1978.

———. *Writing of Women: Essays in a Renaissance.* Middletown, Conn.: Wesleyan University Press, 1985.

Roy, Claude. "Classique Colette." *Colette. Le Point: Revue Artistique et Littéraire* 39, May 1951.

Ruotolo, Lucio P. *The Interrupted Moment: A View of Virginia Woolf's Novels.* Stanford, Calif.: Stanford University Press, 1986.

Rykner, Arnaud. *Nathalie Sarraute.* Paris: Editions du Seuil, 1991.

Sackville-West, Vita. *Challenge.* London: Collins, 1974.

———. *Pepita.* London: Arrow Books, 1961.

———. *The Letters of Vita Sackville-West to Virginia Woolf.* Eds. Louise DeSalvo and Mitchell A. Leaska. New York: William Morrow and Company, Inc., 1985.

Sage, Lorna (Ed.). *Flesh and the Mirror: Essays on the Art of Angela Carter.* London: Virago, 1994.

Saint, Nigel. *Marguerite Yourcenar: Reading the Visual.* Oxford: Legenda, 2000.

Sarde, Michèle. *Colette: Libre et entravée.* Paris: Stock, 1978.

Sarraute, Nathalie. *L'usage de la parole.* Paris: Gallimard, 1980.

———. *L'ère du soupçon.* Paris: Gallimard, 1956.

———. *Œuvres complètes.* Paris: Gallimard, 1996.

Savigneau, Josyanne. *Marguerite Yourcenar: Inventing a Life.* Trans. Joan E. Howard. Chicago: University of Chicago Press, 1993.

Schlack, Beverley Ann. *Continuing Presences: Virginia Woolf's Use of Literary Allusion.* University Park: The Pennsylvania State University Press, 1979.

———. "Fathers in General: The Patriarchy in Virginia Woolf's Fiction." In *Virginia Woolf: A Feminist Slant.* Ed. Jane Marcus. Lincoln: University of Nebraska Press, 1983.

Scott, Bonnie Kime. *The Gender of Modernism.* Bloomington: Indiana University Press, 1990.

————. *Refiguring Modernism. Volume 1: The Women of 1928.* Bloomington: Indiana University Press, 1995.

Shakespeare, William. *The Tempest.* London: Penguin, 1996.

————. *The Merchant of Venice.* London: Penguin, 1967.

Shields, Kathleen. "Marguerite Yourcenar: Traductrice de Virginia Woolf." In *Marguerite Yourcenar: Ecriture, réécriture, traduction.* Eds. Rémy Poignault et Jean-Pierre Castellani. Tours: Société Internationale d'Etudes Yourcenari-ennes, 2000.

Showalter, Elaine. *A Literature of Their Own: British Novelists from the Brontës to Lessing* (Expanded Edition). Princeton, N.J.: Princeton University Press, 1999.

Silver, Brenda. *Virginia Woolf Icon.* Chicago: Chicago University Press, 1999.

Smith, Leonora. "Spaces, Places, Houses, Rooms: A Feminist Perspective." In *Virginia Woolf's Themes and Variations: Selected Papers from the Second Conference on Virginia Woolf.* Ed. Vara Neverow-Turk and Mark Hussey. New York: Pace University Press, 1993.

Solomon, Julie Robin. "Staking Ground: The Politics of Space in Virginia Woolf's *A Room of One's Own* and *Three Guineas.*" *Women's Studies* 16, 1989.

Souhami, Diana. *The Trials of Radclyffe Hall.* London: Weidenfeld and Nicolson, 1998.

Southworth, Helen. "Correspondence in Two Cultures: Tracing the Social Ties That Link Colette and Virginia Woolf." *Journal of Modern Literature,* Winter 2003.

————. "Rooms of Their Own: How Colette Uses Physical and Textual Space to Question a Gendered Literary Tradition." *Tulsa Studies in Women's Literature,* Fall 2001.

Stephen, Leslie. *Borrow: Selections. With Essays by Richard Ford, Leslie Stephen, and George Saintsbury.* Oxford: Clarendon Press, 1924.

Stewart, Joan Hinde. *Colette.* Boston: Twayne Publishers, 1983.

St John, Christopher, with V. Sackville-West, Edward Sackville-West, and Kathleen Dale. *Ethel Smyth: A Biography.* London: Longmans, 1959.

Thurman, Judith. *Colette: Secrets of the Flesh.* New York: Alfred A. Knopf, 1999.

Trefusis, Violet. *Broderie anglaise.* Introduction by Victoria Glendinning. Orlando, Fla.: Harcourt Brace Jovanovich, 1985.

————. *Don't Look Round.* London: Hutchinson, 1952.

————. *Tandem.* London: W. Heinemann, 1933.

Tremper, Ellen. "In Her Father's House: *To the Lighthouse* as a Record of Virginia Woolf's Literary Patrimony." *Texas Studies in Literature and Language* 34, no. 1, Spring 1992.

Trombley, Stephen. *All That Summer She Was Mad: Virginia Woolf, Female Victim of Male Medicine.* New York: Continuum, 1982.

Troubridge, Una. *The Life and Death of Radclyffe Hall.* London: Hammond, Hammond and Co., 1961.

Tucker, Louise. "A Happy Marriage? The Missing (R)elation in the Novels of Virginia Woolf and Colette." Ph.D. dissertation. Centre for Critical and Cultural Theory, University of Wales, 1995.

Tyler, Lisa. "'Nameless Atrocities' and the Name of the Father: Literary Allusion and Incest in Virginia Woolf's *The Voyage Out.*" *Woolf Studies Annual* 1, 1995.

Updike, John. *Hugging the Shore*. New York: Vintage, 1983.

Villeneuve, Pierre-Eric. "Virginia Woolf Among Writers and Critics: The French Intellectual Scene." In *The Reception of Virginia Woolf in Europe*. London: Continuum, 2002.

———. "Virginia Woolf and the French Reader: An Overview." *South Carolina Review* 29, no. 1, Fall 1996.

Violet to Vita: The Letters of Violet Trefusis to Vita Sackville-West. Ed. Mitchell A. Leaska and John Phillips. London: Methuen, 1989.

Vita and Harold: The Letters of Vita Sackville-West and Harold Nicolson. Ed. Nigel Nicolson. London: Putnam, 1992.

Wajsbrot, Cécile. (Trans.). *Les Vagnes (Virginia Woolf's the Waves)*. Paris: Calmann-Lévy, 1993.

Werlock, Abby (Ed.). *British Women Writing Fiction*. Tuscaloosa: University of Alabama Press, 2000.

Wesley, Marilyn. "Emma Tennant: The Secret Lives of Girls." In *British Women Writing Fiction*. Ed. Abby Werlock. Tuscaloosa: University of Alabama Press, 2000.

West, Rebecca. *Ending in Earnest: A Literary Log*. New York: Doubleday, Doran and Company, 1931.

———. *The Strange Necessity: Essays and Reviews*. London: Virago, 1987 (1928).

Wharton, Edith. *French Ways and Their Meaning*. Lee, Mass.: Berkshire House, 1997.

White, Antonia. *Diaries, 1926–1957*. Ed. Susan Chitty. London: Constable, 1991.

White, Edmund. *The Flâneur: A Stroll Through the Paradoxes of Paris*. New York: Bloomsbury, 2001.

Wickes, George. *The Amazon of Letters: The Life and Loves of Natalie Barney*. New York: G. P. Putnam's Sons, 1976.

Willis, J. H. *Leonard and Virginia Woolf As Publishers: The Hogarth Press, 1917–41*. Charlottesville: University Press of Virginia, 1992.

Winterson, Jeanette. *Art [Objects]: Essays on Ecstasy and Effrontery*. New York: Alfred A. Knopf, 1996.

———. "Interview." *The Guardian,* September 7, 2000.

Women Writers at Work: The Paris Review Interviews. Ed. George Plimpton. New York: The Modern Library, 1989, 1998 (rev. ed.).

Woolf, Leonard. *Downhill All the Way: An Autobiography of the Years 1919 to 1939*. London: Hogarth Press, 1967.

———. *The Journey Not the Arrival Matters: An Autobiography of the Years 1939 to 1969*. London: Hogarth Press, 1970.

———. *Letters of Leonard Woolf*. Ed. Frederic Spotts. San Diego: Harcourt Brace and Company, 1985.

Yourcenar, Marguerite. Introduction to *Les vagues* (trans. Yourcenar). Paris: Stock, 1937.

Zwerdling, Alex. *Virginia Woolf and the Real World*. Berkeley: University of California Press, 1986.

Index

her contemporaries, 180n6; and
Mansfield, 180n6; and Joyce,
180n6; and Ocampo, 181n13,
184n39; and disengagement,
202n1; and Nin, 207n35; and
Cixous, 207n40; and Kristeva,
212n58. *See also individual works
by title*
work: and love in *La vagabonde,* 85
World War I, 44
World War II, 14–15
Wuthering Heights (Brontë), 59

Years, The (Woolf), 6, 29, 35, 107,
137, 151, 158, 185n3, 197n15,
202n1, 215n19
Yourcenar, Marguerite, 119, 126, 132,
136, 145; and Woolf, 120–23; and
her translation of *The Waves,*
120–21, 122–23; and Colette,
123–24, 203n8

Zola, Émile, 178n13, 201nn39–40